LEADERSHIP
for *21st* CENTURY
LEARNING

I wish I had had this book years ago. For any fool can learn from his own mistakes and hopefully I did: the wise soul learns from those who have made the journey of leadership and lived to tell the tale. Leadership is at once the highest of the arts and the most perilous: the highest because it is so creative in its outcomes, the most perilous because it is achieved through people. Nowhere is it more difficult than when disturbing the established order of things. A book like this, founded on experience, makes the journey of leadership in educational innovation less hazardous and the more certain of success.

Lord Dearing
Former Chancellor of Nottingham University, past chairman of the
Higher Education Funding Council for England and author of the
Dearing Report, *Higher Education in the Learning Society*

One of the most significant developments of the latter part of the 20th century was the changed relationship between higher education and society. Alan Greenspan called it 'the conceptual economy'. Other have referred to it as 'the information era' or 'the knowledge age'. Whatever the characterization, the value and demand for learning has escalated. Education is now a major public policy concern. For individuals, the need is for access to quality education, for life. The implications are global. Traditional colleges and universities are changing. New learning providers are emerging. New approaches, applying new technologies, are reaching new learners. Each day learning systems become more diverse, open, and accessible. I am especially pleased that Colin Latchem, Donald Hanna and their colleagues have chosen to focus on the issue of leadership. Ultimately it will be the leaders of the 21st century who will craft a response to the new era. From around the globe, the authors offer new perspectives and fresh thinking and a sense of excitement in the opportunities and challenges that lie ahead.

Dr Stanley O Ikenberry
President of the American Council on Education, and formerly
President of the University of Illinois, USA

Make no mistake, higher education worldwide is undergoing a fundamental realignment which is being driven, in large measure, by new forms of educational communications and technology. New opportunities abound for educational institutions that position themselves creatively and aggressively. The authors and contributors explore key concepts of leadership, the changing nature of opportunities and challenges for institutions, and the personal dynamics, qualities, and characteristics they have found important in their own leadership experiences.

They reflect very personally on the risks and rewards of leadership for change. All educators, governmental leaders, and policy-makers who are concerned about the future should read this book.

Dr James C Votruba
President of Northern Kentucky University, USA

This book should be on the shelf of every university president, senior institutional administrator, dean and department chair, board member, and mid-manager and faculty member who has responsibilities for leading open and flexible learning organizations. Moreover, it should be part of every graduate program in open and flexible learning because of its synthesis of scholarship, practice, and vision for the field.

Dr Don Olcott, Jr
Vice President for Higher Education, VCampus Corporation, Tucson, USA

Leading a contemporary educational organization requires complex skills and qualities. It is no good just managing; organizations need leadership. Leaders have to sniff the winds of policy, markets and community aspirations and then pick the right directions for their organizations. *Leadership for 21st Century Learning* provides valuable insights into how leaders from around the world have set the course for their organizations and why. These global perspectives bring these attributes together in a stimulating collection.

Professor Terry Evans
Director of Research, Faculty of Education, Deaking University, Australia

Colin Latchem, Donald Hanna and the other contributors provide the necessary knowledge foundation for creating cohesive strategic plans for open and flexible learning environments and new directions for education and training using advanced digital technology. This book of international perspectives should be in the libraries of universities worldwide and read by all leaders of open and flexible learning.

Professor Insung Jung
Director, Multimedia Education Institute,
Ewha Woman's University, Seoul, Korea

open &
distance
learning
series

LEADERSHIP
for *21st CENTURY*
LEARNING

Global Perspectives from Educational Innovators

**edited by
colin latchem &
donald e hanna**

KOGAN
PAGE

First published in 2001

Kogan Page Limited
120 Pentonville Road
London
N1 9JN
UK

Stylus Publishing Inc.
22883 Quicksilver Drive
Sterling
VA 20166-2012
USA

British Library Cataloguing in Publication Data

A CIP record for this book is available from the British Library.

Paperback: ISBN 0 7494 3204 7
Hardback: ISBN 0 7494 3205 5

Typeset by JS Typesetting, Wellingborough, Northants
Printed and bound by Biddles Ltd, Guildford and King's Lynn

Contents

List of contributors

Professor Dominique Abrioux, President, Athabasca University, Canada

Robert C Albrecht, Former Vice-President for Academic Affairs and Chancellor Emeritus, Western Governors University, USA

Professor Denise Bradley, Vice-Chancellor, University of South Australia

Professor Rajesh Chandra, Deputy Vice-Chancellor, University of the South Pacific

Professor Betty Collis, Faculty of Educational Science and Technology and Centre for Telematics and Information Technologies, University of Twente, The Netherlands

Sir John Daniel, Assistant Director General for Education, UNESCO; formerly Vice-Chancellor, Open University, UK

Professor Dato' Gajaraj Dhanarajan, President and CEO of the Commonwealth of Learning

Professor Donald E Hanna, Professor of Educational Communications, University of Wisconsin-Extension, USA

Glenn R Jones, Founder and CEO, Jones International University™: The University of the Web™ and JonesKnowledge.com™, USA

Professor Abdul Khan, Assistant Director General for Communication and Information, UNESCO; formerly Vice-Chancellor of Indira Gandhi National Open University (IGNOU) and Chairperson, Distance Education Council (DEC), India

Roger Lewis, Regional Consultant with the UK Higher Education Funding Council

Professor Marmar Mukhopadhyay, National Institute of Educational Planning and Administration, India

Dr Muriel Oaks, Associate Vice-President for Extended University Services, Washington State University, USA

Janet Poley, President, American Distance Education Consortium, USA

Sister Joel Read, President, Alverno College, USA

Bernadette Robinson, Special Professor of Comparative Education, School of Continuing Education, University of Nottingham, UK

Barbara Spronk, Executive Director, International Extension College, UK

Dr Brian Talbott, National Executive Director, Association of Educational Service Agencies, USA

Series editor's foreword

Upon reading this book I discovered that the US brokerage house Merrill-Lynch estimated the global expenditure on education and training in 2000 to be about US$2 trillion with 50 per cent being spent in Europe, 33 per cent in the United States and 15 per cent in developing countries. I also discovered that the global number of learners is set to more than double from an estimated 70 million today to 160 million by 2025. It is clear that the challenge facing us, in generating the wealth needed to spend these sums on education and training, to provide increased access to quality materials and at a realistic cost is formidable. What is more, this global expenditure and growth in the number of learners is occurring in the midst of a revolution in learning and teaching and in the use of the new technology.

In his book *Learning and Teaching in Distance Education* (Kogan Page, 1998), Professor Otto Peters examined the pedagogy that has evolved in different countries and how the shift from expository to constructivist teaching is gaining momentum. Others, such as Professor Marc Eisenstadt and Professor Tom Vincent in their book *The Knowledge Web* (Kogan Page, 1998), have argued and illustrated how the knowledge media are influencing our teaching and learning. What emerges from these and similar books is that open, distance and distributed learning can make a significant contribution to teaching and training. However, the extent to which we are able to do this, and meet the broader challenge, is directly related to the leadership provided within each and every institution.

In this book, *Leadership for 21st Century Learning,* the authors explore those issues associated with leadership within educational and training institutions. They consider the process of formulating and sharing a vision, of managing change such as responding to the shift from supply-driven to demand-driven systems, of investing in staff via academic and professional development programmes and of fostering an entrepreneurial culture. The arguments they provide are eloquent and the framework invaluable – whether we aspire to be leaders in education or to better understand the pressures such people face. The series of case studies provided from acknowledged leaders in open and distance learning not only reads like a global who's who but serves to reinforce the analysis that Colin and Don offer. For me the challenge facing us is summarized by Janet Poley in her chapter when she says, 'It takes great vision and leadership and team management and passion and hard work to achieve anything of the magnitude we are attempting – not to mention quite a bit of luck.'

I am sure that after reading this book no one will be complacent regarding the challenge facing us. I am also sure that Colin Latchem and Don Hanna will have stimulated many to respond. I wish you every success in facing the challenge ahead of us – and also a bit of luck.

Fred Lockwood

Preface

The imperatives for change in education and training are relentless, never-ending and worldwide. Education is itself contributing to changes in expectations and practices but change is not something that necessarily comes easily to this sector. A former board member of a major public US university (Weinstein, 1993) describes changing the system as akin to 'moving a battleship with your bare hands', a South African vice-chancellor observes 'the plane has to be serviced in mid flight' (Randell and Bitzer, 1998) and a voice from history warns:

> there is nothing more difficult to plan or more uncertain of success than an attempt to introduce new institutions, because the introducer has as his enemies all those who profit from the old institutions, and has as lukewarm defenders all those who will profit from the new institutions. . . thus lukewarm subjects and innovating prince are both in danger. (Machiavelli, 1963: 26)

Such observations will surely strike a chord with many working in education. Educational institutions have to face the ramifications of globalization, the explosion in digital communications and the shift from a 'supply-driven' to a 'demand-driven' market. Worldwide, educators and trainers are confronted with demands for greater accessibility, flexibility, cost-effectiveness, quality and relevance and lifelong provision. They are also grappling with the implications of the new educational and information technologies. Both in developed and developing countries, educators and trainers are expected to achieve more with less as a consequence of budgetary pressures on governments and inter-sectoral competition for funding.

One response to the imperatives to increase access and equity and achieve economies of scale has been to establish dedicated distance teaching institutions, open to all and using new approaches and technology to achieve greater access at lower costs. Another has been for conventional face-to-face institutions to transform themselves into dual-mode providers, offering some mix of distance and classroom teaching. Another has been to form consortia, partnerships and alliances, in some cases involving international or cross-sectoral collaboration. Yet another has been to create corporate and 'virtual' institutions, heavily reliant upon online delivery. Not all of these are funded through public provision and there is a growing tendency to adopt the principle of 'the beneficiaries should pay' and to see the commercial potential of open and flexible learning.

In 1999, the UK Open University's International Centre for Distance Learning database listed over 31,000 distance learning programmes, and over 1,000 institutions teaching at a distance. It has been estimated that well over 4 million students study through open and flexible learning around the globe. These numbers may well seriously underestimate the extent to which open and flexible learning is being introduced into education and training because of the rapid developments in applying computer-based and online learning and the blurring of any distinction between on-campus and off-campus teaching and learning.

There are both wonderful opportunities and dangerous pitfalls in introducing open and flexible learning. The challenges confronting its adopters are complex, requiring multiple specialists to collaboratively develop appropriate management, development, delivery and support systems. Such a destabilized and uncharted environment calls for leaders of change at all levels to energize and empower others to share their vision of what can be accomplished through open learning, to change work cultures and to create systems that are built to last but constantly adaptable.

We cannot predict with any certainty the course of the changes in education and training, but we can be confident of two things: that the economic landscape of communications and technology will be radically different, and that this change will have revolutionary implications for education and training. Currently, the information and communication technology infrastructure makes it difficult to deliver education and training over 'the last mile' into many remote and disadvantaged regions. However, one has only to see the speed at which satellite, wireless and other networks are going into hitherto poorly served communities to realize that now is the time to plan for the educational and technological opportunities that will be realizable within a very short timeframe.

There is a great hunger and need for learning in developed and developing countries alike. There is a need to reach out and to serve new student groups and provide lifelong learning through the exciting variety of learning environments and technologies at our disposal. Open and distance education is also becoming a commercial and globally competitive environment, wherein stakes are very high. There is strong pressure for education to be more accountable and 'business like' in dealing with its customers. We therefore make no apology for stressing the need to import and apply some concepts and approaches from the world of business into open and flexible learning but ultimately, change must be driven by educational rather than economic or technological imperatives.

Our aim in writing this book is to give the reader some insights into what we have come to see as the major issue in open and flexible learning – the need for forward looking transformational leadership that is concerned with change, innovation and entrepreneurship. We scan the global developments in open education and training and the challenges confronting its application in developed and developing countries. We examine the issues that leaders must be sensitive and responsive to in open learning. We look at change and the barriers to change in education and training. We examine the theory and practice of leadership and seek to apply these to open and distance learning. We also share and draw heavily upon the experiences and insights of some of the world's most experienced leaders in open learning who are working in a variety of organizational and cultural settings.

We hope that our book will help to inspire and guide those who are keen to lead, manage and improve education and training in response to the needs of the 21st century.

Colin Latchem
Donald E Hanna

Chapter 1

Open and flexible learning: an environmental scan

Colin Latchem and Donald E Hanna

Introduction

Distance education has always been quick to exploit new delivery systems and service providers. As correspondence education, pioneered in the United Kingdom in the 1840s by Sir Isaac Pitman to teach office workers his new Stenographic Soundhand system, it capitalized on the improved surface mail (Rumble, 1997). Throughout the 20th century, as external studies or distance education, it extended its basic print/correspondence methodology by incorporating radio, television, audioconferencing, videoconferencing (particularly in the United States), the computer and the Internet/Web. Today's open and flexible learning (commonly known as 'distributed learning' in North America) uses a mixture of presentational and constructivist (guided inquiry, collaborative learning and mentoring) pedagogies and enables learners and teachers to interact synchronously or asynchronously across classrooms, workplaces and other settings, increasingly, but not exclusively, by means of information and communications technology (Dede, 2000).

Educationally, open and flexible learning is adopted in pursuit of access, equity and lifelong learning and to provide learning environments wherein learners can create their own understanding and teachers play a guiding rather than a dominant role. Strategically, it is used in response to changing student demographics, the shifting balance of power caused by information and communications technology and learners' access to alternative sources of knowledge, reduced public funding, globalization and commercial imperatives. In developing countries, it is used to help overcome the critical problems of numbers, resources and quality in providing primary and secondary schooling, 'second chance' adult learning, teacher training, and support for social and economic development (Perraton, 2000). Seventy-six developing countries – 34 in Africa, 2 in the Middle East, 19 in Asia, 3 in Oceania, 6 in the Caribbean, and 12 in Latin America – have adopted distance and open learning (Hawkridge, 1999), sometimes with the support of such agencies as UNESCO, the UN Food and Agriculture Organization, International Development Bank, World Bank, Africa Development Bank, Asia Development Bank, Consortium Francophone de Formation à Distance and the Commonwealth of Learning.

This chapter provides an environmental scan of what governmental, institutional and community leaders have achieved in open and flexible learning and the challenges that lie ahead.

Open schooling

Open schooling provides for isolated primary-age pupils in small, remote populations, children unable to attend school because of illness, disability, or migratory lifestyle, indigenous students in traditional communities, and secondary-age pupils in small country schools or 'second chance' adult learners unable to access particular courses by conventional means. It reduces teacher recruitment, travel and accommodation costs, eliminates or defers the need for attendance at boarding school, and transforms isolated and disadvantaged schools from 'small' to 'large' in terms of students enrolled and from 'closed' to 'open' in terms of curriculum and teacher expertise.

When first introduced into countries such as Australia and New Zealand, open schooling was restricted to correspondence, talkback radio and on-site teaching by parents or peripatetic teachers. Many countries have used schools broadcasting modelled on the BBC approach and interactive radio instruction first developed in Nicaragua. Today, open learning networks such as the Australian Distance Education Centres and Schools of the Air, New Zealand Correspondence School, US Star Schools, Contact North/Contact Nord in northern Ontario, Open School of British Columbia, and Chilean Schools Learning Network use the latest information and communications technologies and 'virtual' online high schools have been developed in the United States.

Open schooling is also helping developing countries to overcome their acute difficulties in providing sufficient classrooms, teachers and teaching resources. The world's largest open schooling system, India's National Open School, offers bridging programmes and alternative secondary, senior-secondary courses for those who cannot attend schools and vocational programmes. In 1998–1999, the NOU had more than 500,000 students on its rolls and an annual enrolment of over 130,000, of which 35 per cent were female and 25 per cent from scheduled castes and tribes and handicapped groups. The Bangladesh Open School operates as an integral part of the Bangladesh Open University, providing school equivalency and non-formal education programmes. Indonesia's Open School, SMP Terbuka, teaches 200,000 students through a mix of print, broadcasts and teachers' aides and a network of study centres linked to junior secondary schools. Malawi's College of Distance Education provides for 150,000 primary and secondary students through a network of 564 community-managed distance education centres and night-time classes in secondary schools. Mexico uses radio and television to supplement the classroom teaching of 12–15-year-old pupils in *telesecundaria,* small rural and remote secondary schools with fewer than 100 pupils, and to meet the special needs of young working men and women wishing to complete middle school education.

The UN Convention on the Rights of the Child declares that every child has the right to education without discrimination and in 1990, the UN organizations, the World Bank and other bilateral and multilateral donor agencies committed themselves at the Jomtien conference to achieving universal elementary education. The developed nations have repeatedly fallen short on their pledges and this goal has been shifted to 2015, which on present projections, seems equally unachievable. Globally, more than 125 million children, predominately girls, are currently denied schooling. Without some means of dramatically increasing enrolments, this number is predicted to soar to 165 million by 2015. In India alone, 30 million 6–10-year olds and 33 million 11–14-year olds lack schooling. In many sub-Saharan and South Asian countries, children can only expect four to seven years of education compared with the 15 to 17 years taken for granted in wealthier nations. Only nine African countries have achieved secondary participation rates of 50 per cent. Most have failed even to achieve the 20 per cent considered essential for socio-political and economic development. As Director of UNESCO's International Institute for Capacity Building in Africa, Fay Chung (1999) observes, it is small wonder that uneducated, unemployed youths and child soldiers are drawn into destroying their own countries in places like Sierra Leone, Rwanda and Mozambique.

Graca Machel (1999), South Africa's former first lady and President of the Foundation for Community Development, stresses that this failure to provide universal education is not attributable to any lack of resources – an additional US$8 billion or four days' global arms expenditure would fund basic education for all the world's children – but to a lack of political will. Fay Chung (1999) emphasizes that such developments can only take root when governmental leadership, commitment, and resources combine with community and parental commitment, participation and responsibility. UNESCO's Richard Siaciwena (1999) notes that while open schooling may be part of the answer, many administrators and teachers unfamiliar with the philosophies inherent in its operations resist it.

Non-formal adult and community education

Spronk (1999) describes non-formal adult and community education as the most elusive and ill-defined sector of open and flexible learning, and Dodds (1996) notes that work in this area is poorly and uncritically documented. However, Perraton (2000) suggests that the scale and achievements of non-formal education linked to applications of mass media may be more significant than the printed record suggests. In developed countries, the focus is typically on lifestyle or work enhancement for the already well educated. In developing countries, it is concerned with literacy and numeracy, primary healthcare, occupation skills, community or social development and political awareness among marginalized communities, refugees and nomads (Yates and Bradley, 2000).

Print is the traditional and most favoured medium for this work but has limited application in a world where almost one billion people, two-thirds of them female, are illiterate. Where affordable, audiovisual media are used to attract and teach adult learners lacking the necessary reading skills. Villages in developing countries may not have electricity or running water, but the chances are that they will have radio-cassette players, and so radio-led education is found to be very useful for such initiatives as the *Escuelas Radiofónicas* of Latin America and Canary Islands, and the Canadian, Ghanaian, Zambian and Indian 'listen-act-discuss' radio farm forums and audiocassettes are used extensively by such providers as Pakistan's Allama Iqbal Open University and the Sudan Open Learning Organization. Television and videocassettes are used by *Telecurso 2000* in Brazil, Centre de Service de Production Audiovisuelle in francophone Africa, and the Indira Gandhi National Open University in India. Indian adult educators have also shown how video cameras and videoconferencing can be used to enable non-literate rural people to express their needs and viewpoints to the outside world and support self-development and self-government in rural areas (Dighe and Reddy, 1996).

Unfortunately, such applications are all too often restricted by a lack of funds, technology access and technical skills, but one way of bringing telephony and computer-based services into disadvantaged communities is to create public-access centres, variously called telecentres, telecottages, infocentros, espaces numérisés, telestugen, phone shops, cabinas públicas and so on. Many international development agencies are now supporting the establishment of such centres in countries ranging from Ecuadorian Amazonia to Bhutan, and from rural Ireland to the Australian outback, providing previously undreamed-off opportunities for info-exchange tailored to local requirements, teleeducation, teletraining, telemedicine, teletrading, telecommerce, and telework (Latchem and Walker, 2001).

The 1990 'Education for All' UNESCO Jomtien conference declared that such basic learning needs demanded an 'expanded vision' surpassing present resource levels, institutional structures, curricula and conventional delivery systems. Initiatives such as UNESCO's 'Learning Without Frontiers' and by agencies such as the International Telecommunications Union and the Commonwealth of Learning are encouraging the collaborative development of 'open learning communities'. However, as Dodds (1996) observes, open learning is rarely applied to this sector in a sustained, systematic, and concerted way. It is often accorded low status and low priority and is typically reliant upon non-government agencies and small groups of devotees. There are serious gaps in provision and most programmes are under-resourced, vulnerable beyond the pilot phase and questionable in long-term impact. Yates (2000) suggests that open and distance education appear to hold great promise in training the thousands of basic education teachers, literacy workers and support cadres needed to provide both adult basic education and open schooling. But the harnessing of open non-formal learning for national regeneration demands political commitment to meeting the needs of the poor and oppressed, partnerships between governments and public and private providers, and far greater recognition of local values, knowledge systems, experiences and resources that can be drawn upon within the communities.

Vocational education and training

Changes in the world of work are impacting dramatically on vocational education and training. And in a world where it is predicted that future employees will need higher levels of skill than those they replace, re-training at least five times during their working lives, and for nearly half the new jobs created, the equivalent of 17 years' full-time education, such change is only likely to increase. Many governments now argue that vocational education and training benefits not only the state, but also the employer and the individual, and so an increasing share of the costs has to be borne by the latter two. The colleges are required to compete in the open market and operate on a 'user pays' basis. A recent Australian National Training Authority report concluded that the employers felt that this more competitive and rigorous market had improved the employers–providers relationship and the providers' performance, while the training providers felt that this approach and a national quality assurance framework had been incentives for change and service improvement (Rowe, 1999).

Faced with the need for economy in upgrading the knowledge and skills of large numbers of employees, sometimes over great distances and with high employee turnover, and to ensure uniformity of content and delivery, many providers are adopting online or some mix of Web-based and instructor-led training strategies.

Such is the demand for vocational educational and training that in Europe, 70 per cent of the open learning market is estimated to be in this sector, which has become a key industry in its own right, attracting many new private providers. In the United Kingdom, it is estimated that there are about 4,000 private providers as against about 350 colleges (Calder and McCollum, 1998). Major organizations such as the Ford Motor Company, J C Penney, British Aerospace, Qantas and South Africa Telkom have also developed corporate training networks to meet their internal needs. New alliances are being forged. For example, in the United Kingdom, the government has established a new public–private partnership – the University for Industry (http://www.ufiltd.co.uk), to deliver flexible training programmes to boost the competitiveness of business and industry and the performance and employability of individuals through a national Learndirect network linked to 250 Learning Centres and smaller Access Centres in workplaces and educational and community settings (http://www.learndirect.com.uk/).

Horsfield (1999) notes that corporate training programmes are primarily concerned with developing specific operational, supervisory, management and leadership skills matched to organizational strategic priorities and to national or international benchmarks. Rowntree (1992) observes that such programmes may be 'distant', catering for employees who are off-site, and 'flexible', accommodating those for example, on shiftwork, but not 'open', being closely tailored to company objectives, proprietary content, specific personnel development requirements or technical infrastructure.

The shift from 'supply-driven' to 'demand-driven' challenges the values and practices of the traditional providers, the colleges. The sector has had to become more entrepreneurial, accustomed to new world-of-work quality standards and prepared to cater to a wider student cohort. Many businesses and industries have decided to work only with those institutions that offer quality, flexibility and value for money. Some colleges have 're-branded' themselves as businesses, drawing their governing bodies largely from industry, and mandating their CEOs to increase productivity and the national and international customer base.

Reviewing open learning in this sector, Calder and McCollum (1998) suggest that leaders and managers need to inculcate a new work-learning ethic, become more aware of what open learning can achieve, increase the employees' sense of ownership in work-based learning, and address the lifelong learning needs of basic grade staff and the unemployed as well as the high- and middle-grade staff.

Universities

Dual-mode or extended traditional universities

Dual-mode universities extend their traditional role by providing their on-campus courses to a non-traditional constituency of off-campus, part-time, working adults. They had their origins in the correspondence course pioneers of the late 19th and early 20th centuries: such institutions as the University of South Africa, the University of Chicago and the US land-grant universities, the University of London, the University of Queensland and the University of Western Australia. The last two decades have seen exponential growth worldwide in university-level dual-mode provision.

Distance learning may start as a marginal activity in universities, embraced by a few but perceived by many as diverting scarce resources, lowering quality, diminishing status and threatening time-honoured roles and practices. But with the growing demand for access, convenience and flexibility and the increasing realization of the commercial potential of distance education, there is often commensurate growth in its influence and status, especially where there is institutional commitment to long-term change. The new forms of course development and delivery influence the curriculum, the new technologies permeate the offices and classrooms, and distinctions blur between the different on- and off-campus methodologies, types of student and funding bases and ultimately lead to a re-framing of missions and operations.

Some universities provide open learning through a non-profit arm. One of Australia's leading distance-teaching universities, Deakin University, has over 40,000 enrolments in its corporate programmes, as opposed to 28,000 in its mainstream courses.

Single-mode open universities

The past 30 years have also seen the rise of a number of single-mode open universities, typically modelled upon the UK Open University. Some have enrolments exceeding 100,000 in their degree-level courses – the UK Open University, France's Centre National d'Enseignement à Distance, Spain's Universidad Nacional de Educación, Iran's Payame Noor University, Turkey's Anadolu University, The University of South Africa, India's Indira Gandhi National Open University, Indonesia's Universitas Terbuka, Thailand's Sukhothai Thammathirat Open University, China's Radio and Television Universities and the Korea National Open University. Daniel (1996) observes that by increasing university capacity dramatically while lowering costs sharply, these 'mega-universities' represent a rare discontinuity in the evolution of higher education.

Other open universities include Canada's Athabasca University, British Columbia's Open University/Open College, Télé-université du Québec, the Empire State College and Thomas Edison State College in the United States, Venezuela's Universidad Nacional Abierta, Costa Rica's Universidad Estatal de Educación a Distancia, Germany's Fern Universität, Open Universitëit Nederland, Pakistan's Allama Iqbal Open University, Bangladesh Open University, Sri Lanka Open University, Myanmar University of Distance Education, Open University of Hong Kong, Asian International Open University in Macao, Open University of the University of the Philippines, University of the Air of Japan, Open University of Tanzania and Zimbabwe Open University.

The open universities have achieved notable gains in access and equity for the geographically and socially disadvantaged and older and female students. Daniel (1996) sets the cost per enrolled student in the mega-universities at 10–50 per cent of that in conventional universities in the same countries (although the cost per graduate may be higher in some of these institutions because of higher dropout rates than in comparable institutions). Some open universities enjoy parity of esteem with the conventional institutions and some have gained high national and international reputations. For example, India's Indira Gandhi National Open University received the 1994 Commonwealth of Learning Centre of Excellence Award and Sukhothai Thammathirat Open University, the 1995 Commonwealth of Learning/International Council for Distance Education Award for Institutional Excellence; the latter has been designated by UNESCO as the lead institution for distance education in the Asia-Pacific. The UK Open University has been particularly successful in ensuring status and quality, gaining a maximum score of 24/24 in the national teaching assessment scheme and attracting 180,000 students worldwide to its degree-credit programmes and a further 100,000 to its continuing professional development courses.

However, open learning is not universally accepted. There are still professional bodies and others, especially traditional academics, who regard the graduates of such institutions as 'second chance' and 'second best'. Such perceptions derive in part from inherent elitism and conservatism and in part from recollections of some earlier correspondence courses designed for financial gain or political expediency rather than educational excellence.

Ramanujam (1997) warns of the problem of introducing western models of open learning into developing countries where they may be neither fully understood nor in accord with the traditional values and practices of the educators or society at large. Koul (1998) observes that some politicians and planners have been carried away by success stories of open learning overseas, and have totally underestimated the problems of thrusting self-directed learning upon staff, let alone learners conditioned by the traditional classroom, lacking the necessary reading and study skills and without any privacy and study facilities in their homes.

For-profit universities

US brokerage house Merrill-Lynch estimates global expenditure on education and training to be US$2 trillion, 50 per cent of which is in Europe, 33 per cent in the United States and 15 per cent in developing countries. The US Department of Commerce ranks higher education as the nation's fifth largest service sector export and in Australia, higher education export ranks eighth behind coal, tourism, transport, gold, iron ore, wheat and aluminium. The World Bank predicts that the number of students seeking university education will rise from 70 million to 160 million by 2025.

This burgeoning global market is attracting new for-profit universities that are substantially different from their traditional non-profit public counterparts. Their revenue base is tuition fees and they need to maximize dividends to their shareholders. They serve niche markets, offering a narrow range of career-oriented courses in profitable fields such as business and information technology. They also minimize investment in physical plant and student services, and they rarely commit resources to social or community activities. Those staff who teach do not necessarily research, and curriculum development, delivery and assessment may be carried out by different people, in-house or outsourced.

Such institutions present formidable competition to the traditional universities. Their courses are specifically designed to attract large numbers of students, focus on fields offering plentiful and lucrative career prospects, are offered in multiple locations, and may be completed in less time through year-round part-time study, thus minimizing loss of earnings by the students.

For-profit universities are currently mainly an American phenomenon and the largest, best known, and most successful of these is the University of Phoenix (UoP). In less than 25 years, UoP's undergraduate and graduate enrolments in the United States, Puerto Rico and elsewhere have reached 75,000. About 19 per cent of these students are enrolled in UoP Online Division programmes and off-campus enrolments are increasing by 45 per cent per annum. UoP is also expanding into the corporate sector and internationally through partnerships with institutions in countries such as Brazil, China, India and Mexico. UoP develops its own courses and recruits well-credentialed teaching staff on a part-time basis. Its 'virtual classrooms' offer a teaching ratio of 1:10–15 and its modularized programmes and weekly assignments require online 'attendance' at least five days a week. Service protocols are strictly monitored and end-of-course surveys reveal high levels of 'customer' satisfaction.

Other US for-profit institutions include Strayer Education Inc, DeVry Inc and Sylvan Learning Systems Inc, all of which are publicly traded on the New York

Stock Exchange. White (1999) suggests that these institutions 'have the advantage of being able to hire and fire managers and teachers and offer them a share of the "profits" and that Wall Street analysts eye the US$635 billion education sector as ripe for investment because it is seen as a low-tech industry managed by amateurs'.

Corporate universities

During the 1980s, some US corporations such as American Express, Apple, Disney, First Bank of America, Intel, MasterCard, Motorola, Xerox and McDonald's established human resource development organizations that they called 'universities' but rarely offered degrees. These did not develop to the extent predicted and it now seems that most corporations will focus on their core business and offer certification and degree options for their employees through outsourcing and strategic alliances with universities and colleges. But the concept of the corporate university is not entirely dead. In New Zealand, the government's qualifications authority has indicated that it will license companies to award their own degrees if a certain percentage of their staff have PhDs and a certain percentage of their budget is spent on research.

Consortia and strategic alliances

A growing number of institutions are forming consortia or strategic alliances to capture the members' primary strengths and compete against potential rivals or interlopers. The US-based National Technological University (NTU) was conceived in 1984 as a non-profit university catering primarily for engineers in IBM, Motorola and other large corporations. NTU harnesses expertise in 50 affiliate universities and delivers competitive and profitable certificate, baccalaureate-degree and graduate-level programmes by satellite television and online within North America and overseas. Earlier expectations were unrealized and NTU's for-profit arm, NTU Corp, has now merged with the Business Channel (the commercial arm of the Public Broadcasting Service) to provide video and Internet non-credit courses for learners at home rather than at corporate sites.

Many of the consortia have a brokering role. The US National Universities Degree Consortium sponsors degree and sub-degree programmes on behalf of its nine accredited member institutions and the American Distance Education Consortium provides similar services for its 58 affiliates. Open Learning Australia acts as a private educational broker, enabling eight shareholding universities and affiliate universities and colleges to collaboratively provide non-matriculation entry to fee-for-service degree and non-degree programmes studied through institutions and modes of the students' choice. Engineering Education Australia, a subsidiary of the Institution of Engineers Australia, brokers off-campus doctoral, masters, bachelors and diploma programmes in management, engineering and technology for engineering personnel in Australia and overseas. The UK OU on the other hand, forms international alliances to overcome hurdles of language, culture, accreditation, articulation and student support in 'exporting' its own range of courses.

University–industry partnerships

The growing market for professional degrees and short courses is leading to new collaborative open learning ventures between universities, publishers and multimedia companies. The universities provide the 'brand names', intellectual property, pedagogy, credentials and credibility. The companies offer the business and marketing expertise, technology, and opportunities for the universities to profit from their endeavours. Examples of this include:

- A global consortium of 12 universities in Australia, Canada, Holland, New Zealand, the United Kingdom and the United States partnered with the Hong Kong-based educational and training infrastructure company NextEd targeting the Asia higher education market.
- The Scottish Knowledge consortium comprising the 14 Scottish universities and colleges and commercial and industrial providers in which News International plc has a 25 per cent equity, selling distance education postgraduate programmes to the United States, United Arab Emirates and Malaysia.
- UK management consultants Ernst & Young partnering with Henley Management College to create a 'virtual business school' and offer their staff worldwide opportunities to study and research business and leadership programmes leading to MBAs and PhDs. Ernst & Young saw this as a means of accumulating intellectual capital, encouraging staff to stay with or join the company, and achieving competitive advantage. Henley's staff saw themselves gaining from first-hand involvement with the issues currently confronting the business world (White, 1999).
- Illinois-based UNEXT.com partnering with Columbia University, Stanford University, University of Chicago, the London School of Economics and Political Science and other high-profile universities to sell business-oriented online courses to multinational and overseas corporations. The collaborating universities receive royalties and if UNEXT.com goes public, the right to convert these royalties into stock (Blumenstyk, 1999).
- US publishers Macmillan partnering with Sylvan Learning Systems Inc to provide training for information technology professionals with Macmillan providing the courseware and instructors and Sylvan its Caliber Learning Network.
- Universitas21, a consortium of 18 universities in 10 countries and education publisher and provider Thomson Learning, in which the member universities would be responsible for the badging and quality assurance, Thomson and the universities for the content and intellectual property, and Thomson for the course material, assessment, student database management and translation (Illing, 2001).
- i-Global, a joint venture between the University of California-Berkely, University of Waterloo in Ontario, University of Manchester Institute of Science and Technology, and University of Technology Sydney, marketing electronically-supported skills-based modules and postgraduate programmes in business, IT

and communications to corporations, peak professional associations and government bodies in Australia, the Asia–Pacific and South America (Foreshaw, 2001).

Universitas21 was the brainchild of University of Melbourne Vice-Chancellor Alan Gilbert, who recognized that Melbourne would never be a global brand name on its own. U21 will buy courses from various providers, not necessarily universities, add its own brand and quality stamp, and sell them online and via satellite and cable television. Gilbert says: 'First into this market wins. . . Waiting six months in this kind of endeavour can mean missing out forever'. In this he follows the entrepreneurial strategy of aiming at permanent leadership and market dominance, which Drucker (1985) describes as 'the Fustest with the Mostest', which was how a famous Confederate general claimed he won all his battles. According to Drucker, this is a highly risky strategy. If it goes wrong, it opens the way for 'creative imitation' by other newcomers, but if it succeeds, the rewards can be great. U21 will make its own awards with testamurs bordered by the logos of the consortium members. Its contribution to the joint venture will be in the form of intellectual property for which members will receive an income stream, although trading equity for royalty or equity investment is a possibility in the future. The main challenges in this initiative are seen to be the possibility of cultural conflicts between academia and industry, the development of a worldwide quality assurance structure and the certifying of the various degrees conferred (Richardson, 2000).

University-industry partnerships provide excellent opportunities for tapping into the major growth areas in higher education: corporate training, continuing and distance education and the international market. But to build long-term relationships, each side must learn a lot about the others' objectives, values, methods, and standards. Cunningham *et al* (1997) note that there can be cultural conflict in such inter-sector partnerships, with the various parties ending up perplexed if not contemptuous of each other. When film-maker Lord Puttnam sought to establish World Learning Network, an educational export initiative involving UK universities, broadcasters and media producers, one of the problems he encountered was the mutual mistrust of the ultimate aims and ambitions of the academic and the business communities (Puttnam, 1996).

There is strong debate in the universities about the deployment of academic resources and reputations for financial gain and the tacit endorsing of commercial organizations and products. However, David Brady, associate dean at the Stanford Business School reasons that universities have traditionally claimed rights to staff's inventions and made money from patents but not from their textbooks. He further notes that distance education provides a whole new means of institutions profiting from intellectual property (Blumenstyk, 1999).

Online and virtual universities

Many universities are capitalizing on the capacity of the Internet to support collaborative but asynchronous learning. The United Kingdom, Canada and Australia are significant players in online delivery, but the US presence is large and overwhelming. America's first fully accredited for-profit online university is Jones International University™, established in 1995 and offering undergraduate and graduate degrees in business communications. Enrolments are as yet small, but affiliation with other Jones companies in the United States and Europe is seen as offering a substantial base for marketing, programme delivery and enrolment growth.

The leaders of such institutions need to be risk-takers, as evidenced by the experiences of distance learning consortium Western Governors' University that aimed to offer competency-based programmes, but initially attracted significantly lower enrolments than envisaged, arguably because of a lack of track record and recognizable 'brand name'. However, the very establishment of WGU mobilized the more traditional US universities to become more inclusive and outward looking.

A number of US states have established so-called 'virtual universities', but these are currently limited to brokering and providing online course information and delivery, library services and student support on behalf of the member institutions rather than granting their own degrees, and to date are enjoying mixed success. Other online US organizations bearing the title 'university' are the California Virtual University, Southern California University of Professional Studies, American Coastline University, Athena University, Commonwealth Open University, Coast University, Cyber State University, Greenleaf University, Kennedy Western University, International University, Magellan University, Virtual Online University, and a virtual university in which textbook publisher Harcourt has invested US$25 million.

Private online universities are also being developed in some developing nations. Universiti Telekom (Multimedia University) and Universiti Tun Abdul Rasak are part of the Malaysian government's Silicon Valley-type location, the Kuala Lumpur Multimedia Super Corridor. The Korean government, with the support of hi-tech industries such as Hyundai and Samsung, has encouraged the establishment of the Korean Virtual University Consortium (Jung, 1999). The World Bank has sponsored a pilot African Virtual University using information and communications technology to share expensive resources and specialized staff across 14 anglophone and 8 francophone sub-Saharan universities and provide fee-for-service computing and engineering degree programmes and professional development.

The cost of establishing such ventures, without any requirement to maintain campuses or research infrastructure, can be relatively low. Turoff (1997) estimated that for US$15 million, or less than the cost of a single major building, a virtual university could be established to serve 2,000–4,000 students paying fees of US$7,500–15,000 per year and could hire instructors at US$150,000 a year to teach online classes of 25–50. Such reasoning leads Daniel (1999a) to warn of the 'imperial fantasies' of alternative providers and the threat of their skimming off the cream of undergraduate and professional programmes, leaving only the less lucrative courses to the public institutions. However, Cunningham *et al* (1997) conclude that there is currently more rhetoric than reality in the concept of the virtual university and Farrell (1999) observes that while the term 'virtual university' is used widely and indiscriminately, there are few examples of university teaching and learning mediated entirely through new technology. Institutions are finding the development and support costs to be higher than estimated and most have encountered technological problems and student resistance in their online trials (*ODLAA Times,* 1999). The former dean of New York University's online programme admits, 'Online is a big, important field in higher education, but it does not have a business model that works. The dirty little secret is that nobody's making any money' (Arenson, 1998). Despite this, many governments and institutional managers, like gold prospectors searching for the mother lode, believe that ICT can bring cost savings to education, just as they have to banking. Unfortunately, as shown in the fraudulent 'Columbia State University', closed by the Louisiana courts in 1998, questionable operators will also seek to exploit this market and Cunningham *et al* (2000) suggest that vigilance, care and tight regulatory frameworks will be needed to deal with these.

The future

Various predictions are made for the future of higher education. It seems inevitable that universities will become 'clicks and mortar' institutions, structured more like 'virtual universities', expanding their market reach and operating more like businesses. Some 'brand name' universities, like the US Ivy League campuses, believe they can go it alone in the global e-education market. Others see a need to form alliances or focus on niche markets.

Poole (2000) reports that the Association of Commonwealth Universities envisages four possible scenarios:

1. The invaders triumph. Higher education becomes a global big business dominated by a few players.
2. The Trojan horse. Universities seek outside and international partners, offering services such as international degrees.
3. Community champions. A wide range of educational services is widely available through community hubs.
4. Explorers international. Educational service providers are a university/business hybrid.

Dhanarajan (1998) predicts the emergence of a number of pan-global open learning systems, not necessarily funded from the public purse, but led by entrepreneurs with a vision of global developments, a desire to help reduce unhealthy disparities among people and nations and a willingness to strive for mutual respect, trust and benefit.

Chipman (1999) predicts that within 20 years all universities will be universal or nearly so, entered and re-entered at multiple points in people's lives, international in focus and delivery, and robust in their quality standards. None will receive anything like the current levels of taxpayer support. Some will be high-cost, high-price, high-status providers. Some will deliver a few unique or particularly outstanding programmes globally. Others will organize their programmes to meet rising student expectations of convenience-focused delivery and reduce input costs per graduate to be price-competitive. Yet others will develop strategic partnerships to shore up weaknesses in their programmes and services. All will need to shed time-honoured assumptions and practices. None will be able to ignore the external imperatives, not even those currently at the top of the pyramid.

Chapter 2

Changes, challenges and choices

Colin Latchem and Donald E Hanna

Imperatives for change

Today's uncertain, fast-paced and competitive environment is forcing change upon, and some believe, threatening our educational institutions. Peter Drucker believes that the continually rising costs of the US universities without any appreciable improvement in quality make them untenable and envisages that within 30 years, their large campuses will be relics (Lenzner and Johnson, 1997). Bates (1995) argues that our existing institutions were designed for societies and economies that are fast disappearing and that new organizational systems are needed to support flexible lifelong learning and exploit technology. He sees a need for change right across the system. He notes that the open universities, designed to meet unserved mass markets, are not good at customizing, preferring homogeneous products, while conventional universities find it hard to move beyond 'lone ranger' projects and to be fast to market (Bates, 1999). Laurillard (1993: 223) argues that 'The academic system has to learn, has to be able to respond to its environment, which is a hostile one in most countries now, and respond to its internal changes, which again in most countries, are radical ones', suggesting that what is needed is a 'more robustly adaptive mechanism'. It is predicted that if traditional institutions fail to heed the imperatives for change, they may leave the field open to new 'borderless' providers, for as Hanna (2000) points out, whenever there is rapid change and uncertainty in the external environment and the existing institutions are unprepared to respond quickly and effectively, new organizations will emerge to seize advantage. Conversely, Daniel (1999b) observes that there is a danger in everyone clambering onto the self-directed, technology-mediated bandwagon and inventing new terms to try to give distinctiveness to their activities. Economic and political pressures, the lure of new technology and the hype of the new millennium can easily lead to such quick-fix solutions as the wholesale conversion of courses to digital form and can expose students to unethical marketing practices, questionable private providers and inferior courses and qualifications.

Change can shape or make, as well as break, an organization. The Chinese symbol for crisis combines the two symbols, one signifying danger, the other opportunity. The demand by learners to be able to plug into study at any level and proceed as far as they desire, wherever they are, 365 days a year and 24 hours a day, and for globally relevant and portable qualifications, combined with the techno- logical revolution, has brought about what Morgan and Hawkridge (1999) describe as one of the most dramatic phenomena in recent educational history – an exponential increase in open and flexible learning applications, providers and students. Dhanarajan (1998) reports that globally, 10–20 per cent of post-secondary students now study through open and distance learning. Moran and Myringer (1999) observe that what is occurring is not simply the addition of some distance education here and some online learning there, but a convergence of distance and face-to-face teaching to fundamentally transform the learning environment.

In embracing change, we need to uphold the core educational values of our institutions and ensure that neither public nor private funding contaminates or subverts their standards. At the same time, we need to challenge many of the beliefs and practices held so dear in many of our institutions and establish a new, strong rationale and framework for organizational change, one which is founded upon:

- the relationship of education to social purposes and goals;
- the concept of education as an open system, powerfully influenced by external factors;
- seeking alternative means of achieving similar or improved processes and outcomes;
- a readiness to address multiple points of resistance to system-wide change;
- fostering innovation;
- collaboration as a vehicle of change;
- technology as a lever for transformation.

Such a vision needs to be matched by a strong sense of customer focus, a concern for quality, branding, cost, well-developed applications of technology and a desire to change the educational system or institution as a whole.

Customer focus

There is need for educational institutions to radically overhaul the way that they relate to their customers. Until recently, the need for customer focus was not obvious to many of our institutions. They enjoyed geographic monopolies, carefully selected their students from local markets, and only benchmarked themselves, if they did this at all, against their local competitors. This culture of complacency is now being seriously challenged by governments, employers and the wider community, and all institutions have to be vigilant about being 'blind-sided', not only by their traditional rivals but also by new and even international competitors. The education 'market' is growing exponentially and, as Alan Gilbert, Vice- Chancellor of the University of Melbourne, observes, 'What causes industry revolutions is demand. If supply outstrips demand, you just get a collapse of the supply side. But if demand vastly outstrips supply, the industry structure crumbles as the new entrants come in to break up the old monopolies' (Gluyas, 1999: 38).

Many of today's students are fee-paying. They are more knowledgeable, more discerning, more assertive and more market-oriented. They expect quick outcomes, quality, currency and applicability in their learning, not hype. Recent cases in the United Kingdom and New Zealand show that they are quite prepared to sue for breach of contract where they judge courses to be misleadingly advertised, substandard, leading to worthless qualifications, or not advancing their career prospects. The students may be technologically literate but they don't expect all the 'bells and whistles' that technology can provide. Nor do they automatically respect authority, admire self-absorbed academic work or tolerate bureaucracy. They expect good 'customer relationship management' and some require 'customer intimacy', for example, through Web-based customization.

It is imperative that all educational and training providers see their central mission and purpose as satisfying the customers' needs. As Viljoen (1994) observes, organizations have many cost centres, but usually only one revenue centre – their customers. So the first crucial question to ask is: 'Who are our customers?' Educational or training institutions have external customers, for example the governments or other agencies who provide their funding, the students, and the employers of the graduates. They also have internal customers for, as McIlroy and Walker (1996) observe, everyone within an organization is the customer of someone else within that organization. It is vitally important to correctly identify all of these external and internal customers (sometimes known as 'clients' or 'stake-holders').

The second crucial question to ask is: 'Where are our customers?', the answers to which will raise important considerations about equity, access, distribution, technology reach and costs.

The third important question is: 'What do our customers value?' and the fourth, 'Are we meeting our customers' expectations?' In asking and considering the responses to these two last questions, we must avoid making any assumptions about our customers' needs and expectations and seek the answers directly from them. As Drucker (1974) observes, what each customer sees, thinks, believes and wants at any given time is partly situational and partly subjective, but we must treat all of their feedback as objective fact if we are to reinforce the positives and excise the negatives.

Chattell (1995) suggests that there is a danger that the commercialization of open learning and pressures to recruit more students will lead to the customer, despite all the rhetoric, being simply seen as an economic target to be captured and held. All of our students have highly differentiated needs and preferences, and as Farrell (1999) observes, the educational market is fragmenting into niche markets. Internet marketing experts stress the importance of viewing the Internet, not as a market of 100 million, but as 100 million markets. The new, successful e-commerce providers capture business from long-standing providers by placing the customer at the centre of their marketing strategies. They not only provide online catalogues of their products or services but show where these rank in sales, provide customers' reviews and apply sophisticated 'data mining' systems to gauge what their individual customers will or will not accept, based upon what they order, and then, one-to-one, offer further products and services that might meet their needs. They work on the basis that the happy customer is the one who says: 'It wasn't what I asked for. It was more!'

Open and distance education must be seen as far more than serving mass markets with generic, pre-packaged courseware. Such an approach will simply perpetuate institutional dependency or narrow self-interest in the students. What is needed is 'mass customization', meeting the volatile individual needs of large numbers of students while achieving the economies of mass production. Open learning must co-create learning, provoke debate and inquiry and help establish patterns and networks of learning. Many studies show that open and flexible learning is better suited to mature-aged, self-motivated learners with the capacity to manage their own learning. It cannot be suddenly thrust upon inexperienced learners more accustomed to the transmission methods of the traditional classroom. This is especially true for beginning students who are anxious about their performance and how to juggle learning, work, family and other commitments. It is important to remember too that many students in developing countries enrol in distance education, not through choice but through necessity. Studies in developed and developing countries alike show that tuition, counselling and performance feedback are major factors in retention and performance, whether through on-campus sessions, networked study centres, online learning, or some mix of these.

Student services such as admissions, advising, registration and placement must also be designed to accommodate the needs of individuals, wherever they may be. Our students and those who contract with us to provide programmes and services expect timely delivery of materials, feedback and replies to queries or concerns. They will simply not tolerate those who work to their own timelines and priorities or put unnecessarily complex or time-consuming procedures in their way.

A strong customer focus means also that content and pedagogy must respect linguistic and cultural diversity. In an environment of globalized markets and communications, it is important to ensure that open learning does not de-emphasize, devalue, or disenfranchise non-western or minority cultures. We also need to be sensitive to the fact that while over 90 per cent of all Web content is in English (Wice, 1997) and over 60 per cent of all sites and commonly-used browsers and search engines are American (Boshier *et al*, 1999), English is the first language or frequently used second language of only 20 per cent of the world's population.

Quality

In the 1970s and 1980s, open learning was primarily driven by a commitment to access and equity. Today, it is often driven by the profit motive and politics of economic liberalism. It is vitally important that open learning providers do not become party to the creation of two systems, one enjoying high status and providing quality programmes, the other offering inferior services and qualifications to the already disadvantaged. It is also important to ensure that open learning is seen as something that adds value to the community and not as a market commodity or cash cow.

Daniel (1999b) refers to the challenge of reconfiguring the eternal triangle of cost-access-quality. We need to ask critical questions about the courses, teaching, administration, and support services:

- Do they lower the costs?
- Do they expand access?
- Do they achieve the highest standards of social utility and intellectual development?
- Do they provide what the customers want?
- Do they represent the best value for the learners, workforce and economy?

And, if delivered internationally:

- Are they culturally relevant?
- What is the quality of the local partnerships and support systems?
- How are the graduates and their qualifications regarded in the host country?

No institution can afford to ignore such questions. There is a need for continuous performance improvement and a rooting out of all poor practices and ways of doing things that have outlived their usefulness. All products and services are ultimately called to account by the customers. No success lasts forever. In the commercial world, brands that once seemed unassailable are now losing market share and facing a backlash from consumers and shareholders. Precisely the same could happen in the education sector.

Open learning has come a long way in achieving parity of esteem but there is still scepticism in some countries about its legitimacy (Harry and Perraton, 1999). It has not entirely lived down the poor reputation of some of the early correspondence courses that were run largely as businesses, collected up-front fees and profited from high non-completion rates. Some still look upon this form of education as second best, suspect and even a 'rip off' (Boshier and Pratt, 1997). The Bruneian Minister of Education warns, 'Until and unless we can be assured of the quality. . . it would be misleading, if not wasteful, for prospective candidates to undertake distance learning programmes, under the impression that these would be automatically recognized. . . The proliferation of (programmes) of dubious quality, as a result of the commercialization of higher education, is a worrying trend' (Umar, 1999). Despite Malaysian Prime Minister Mahathir Mohamad's emphasis on democratizing education and expanding distance learning to meet the targets for graduates set in the government's plan, Vision 2020, the engineering, legal and medical professional associations still do not recognize, or alternatively, impose additional requirements on, part-time, mature-aged, distance education graduates whom they regard as inherently inferior to full-time school leavers graduating through on-campus study (Moreira, 1998).

Daniel (1996), Ramanujam (1997) and others observe that it is often difficult to obtain reliable data on completion rates from some distance teaching institutions in developing countries. When they do publish the results of opening their doors to non-traditional and under-prepared students, they are castigated for their poor graduation rates and there is anecdotal evidence that some discourage the gathering and publishing of these data, or urge a lowering of standards, for fear of revealing shortcomings and 'losing face'. However, ignoring or 'putting a spin' on such problems may prove costly in the long term. The authorities, employers and wider community must be assured of the value and achievements of open learning and persuaded that education is not simply something confined to the classroom or the younger generation. In an era of competition and external standards setting and auditing, success will go to those who most fully internalize the new quality paradigm and engage in continuous performance improvement in all of their operations.

Managers, teachers and everyone else throughout the institution must analyse and reflect upon all actions and outcomes, and the conditions under which these occur. There is need to:

● Assess the quality of the teaching, assessment and support services, the appropriateness of the workloads and the role and benefits of technology.
● Monitor the students' motivations, perceptions of open learning, learning styles and conditions of learning.
● Inquire into course grade distributions and dropout/repetition rates and the factors contributing to these.
● Follow up on graduates' contributions to the world of work and the wider community.
● Gather evidence on the recruitment, retention and achievements of students from disadvantaged backgrounds.
● Develop 'adjusted sector benchmarks' to allow for different missions, entry systems, student mixes and study patterns in making inter-institutional comparisons.
● Evaluate how well all internal customers' needs are being met.

In short, just as airline pilots use radio beacons to navigate the skies, we need to ask, year-on-year, 'How far have we come?' and, 'How far have we yet to go?' – even at the risk of revealing things that senior management and staff may not wish to know.

Branding

Marketing experts hold that wherever products or services are of much the same quality and price, the customer must be appealed to through 'branding', giving a product or service a meaning that customers will want to buy into because it appeals to their sense of identity or inchoate aspiration to belong to some subgroup or subculture. Sir John Daniel observes in his chapter that 'branding' is becoming an important issue in higher education. Some universities are already 'high brands' – for example, Harvard, Stanford, Oxford and Cambridge, or in the world of open learning, the UK Open University – and taken as benchmarks for national and international comparison.

Cost

Open and flexible learning requires major up-front expenditure on staff, infrastructure, and course materials and delivery systems development. There is usually an expectation that it will reduce costs by delivering more programmes to larger numbers of students. And governments, institutions and their customers clearly need assurance of returns on their investments. Cost analysis is therefore critically important in reconfiguring processes, resources and roles for open and flexible learning.

Determining the current costs (cost–efficiency), expected costs (cost–utility), quality and quantity of outcomes (cost–effectiveness) and returns on investment (cost–benefit) of open learning and comparing these with the costs of conventional education is bedevilled by problems of definition, data collection and interpretation. Cost analysis in education is often pragmatic, designed to address particular tasks in hand, regarded as 'someone else's problem', or treated as privileged information, particularly where there are commercial or competitive ramifications. Rumble (1999a) notes the problems of accounting for all the variations in course design and renewal, services provided for different kinds of students, and applications of technologies. Tinkler *et al* (1994) and Jevons and Northcott (1994) found great difficulty in differentiating between the capital, staff and recurrent costs of the overlapping activities of on- and off-campus teaching in Australian universities. They could find no reliable measures of costs in traditional teaching for comparative purposes because each institution calculated and apportioned the accommodation, overheads and service costs in quite different ways and sometimes 'absorbed' them. Bates (1995) describes the complexities of determining the fixed and variable costs of various combinations of media and technology and notes that quantifiable additional resources are often justified by claims of qualitative improvements in learning. The costs and benefits of staff knowledge, commitment and energies are intangibles, as are the costs and benefits of open learning initiatives over the longer term in environments lacking consistency.

All of these factors lead to considerable subjectivity in costing and judging educational innovations. Nevertheless, despite all these difficulties, it is important for managers and practitioners to try to establish the long-term costs and resource implications of open and flexible learning and whether these are justified by the outcomes. For example, it may be necessary to justify an open learning initiative by comparing its costs with those of establishing a new campus or programme, or the cost of not responding to a particular set of needs and circumstances. It is also important to identify the level at which such judgements and decisions will be made and present the findings in forms that will guide the policy-makers.

To ensure equity, it is also important to factor in the study costs for the students, including any loss of income. A growing number of institutions are having to be largely or wholly self-funded and in many poorer countries, students from low-income groups may actually be required to bear a higher proportion of their teaching costs than their more privileged counterparts in conventional institutions (Latchem *et al,* 1999).

Rumble and Oliveira (1992), Rumble (1987; 1999a), Dhanarajan *et al* (1994), Daniel (1996) and others show that distance education can be cheaper *per student* than comparable conventional education. However, Daniel (1996) and others observe that dropout and repetition rates can be high in some of the mega- and open universities, so the *cost per graduate* may turn out to be far less impressive, and in saying that distance education can be cheaper, Rumble (1999a) adds the important proviso, *under the right circumstances.* Rowntree (1992) shows that this point is reached when the higher *fixed cost* of developing an open learning programme and providing the technology infrastructure is spread over such large numbers of learners that the cost per student is lower than that of a conventional programme with its steeper *variable cost* of additional teachers and classrooms as student numbers increase. 'Mega-universities', 'virtual universities' and the utilization of new technology are largely driven by such considerations of cost and scale. Rumble (1999a) agrees that large-scale multimedia-based distance teaching systems can be cost-efficient relative to *un-reformed* traditional systems, but questions whether they are necessarily so compared with *reformed* systems. He argues that significant cost savings can be made by universities developing flexible learning programmes for their on-campus students and then using these with their off-campus students, and that if he were a minister of education, he would not be advocating a revolution based on mass higher education outside the campus-based system. However, Karelis (1999) records that while US universities find greater educational benefit in using 'distributed learning' than traditional lectures, they find it difficult to achieve similar returns on investment, let alone savings. He concludes that such returns would only be achievable if enrolments were to exceed significantly what was both possible and conducive to quality learning. He suggests that such funding gaps can only be bridged by direct state, institutional or grant funding, by introducing some form of cost recovery, through strategic alliances and partnerships with other public or private sector agencies, or by hiring low-cost instructors to handle the content delivery and interaction and only using the higher-paid academics to provide the content and overall guidance.

Technology

It is all too easy to link the new millennium with ICT, hail the new platforms, portals and technology, take the Web as a metaphor for the long-heralded global village and make heady predictions of seismic change in education. The commodification and computerization of education and training is a marketers' dream and, unfortunately, some technophiles are like the proverbial carpenter who only has a hammer and perceives every problem to be a nail. Paul (1998: 20) observes:

> Even though it is obvious that technology is only a means to an end that must not be allowed to become an end in itself, this supposed axiom is frequently belied in educational practice. Instead of starting with the learning needs of the students and then trying to find the best combination of learning strategies to meet them, so many 'innovative' programmes start with the technological toys.

Technology is becoming ever more central to teaching, providing access, administering programmes and opening up horizons of possibility across institutional, sectoral and international boundaries. It is inevitable that technology will re-shape institutional plans and resource allocations but it still warrants close and sceptical examination. It is important to avoid 'technological determinism' and ill-considered 'do it yourself' approaches. Many staff venturing into work with the multimedia or the Internet seem reluctant to utilize the expertise of those long involved in distance education (Evans *et al,* 1997; Moran, 1997). Jakupec (1998) found that Australian universities with a tradition of open and distance education recognized the need for a learner focus and a variety of modes and technologies, and adopted policies and practices that were 'market' oriented, coherent and strategically focused. Those universities recently converted to open and flexible learning focused more on the 'product' and digital technology, making the spurious assumption that somehow, these would take care of the 'market'. Significantly, his findings suggest a relationship between these orientations and the perceptions and ambitions of the institutional leaders.

There is a need for great caution in making assumptions about the cost advantages or profitability of converting traditional courses to digital form. In theory, a teacher who teaches 100 students could reach 10,000 over the Internet. But open and flexible learning involves much more than packaging and delivering teacher-led content. It calls for learners to interact with their teachers and with other students, for problem-based and collaborative learning and inquiry using a variety of resources. Mason (1998; 1999) argues that while there will undoubtedly be a massive increase in technology-mediated distance education, it has been oversold as a 'cost saviour'. She points out that new technology may promise wider student reach and reduced unit costs, but in reality is often an added cost because it parallels or enhances, rather than replaces, existing systems. Misapplied, technology can be a drain on institutional resources. The constant cycling through generations of hardware and software can be extremely costly and it is estimated that for every dollar spent on technology, three dollars are needed for the ongoing costs.

Mason also notes that more preparation time is needed for technology-mediated teaching than for equivalent face-to-face teaching. Attempting to minimize online development costs by relying more heavily upon subsequent interaction and knowledge-building by the learners invariably results in staff being deluged with online queries, particularly from fee-paying students expecting value for money. Rumble (1999b) reports that UK Open University tutors are spending more time supporting learners online than they used to through correspondence and telephone contact, to the point that the University is considering protocols to curb student demands on their tutors.

Technology enables educational and training providers to market their programmes globally. The downside of this is that other providers can do the same, and that students can shop around for the best courses at the best prices. Michael Bloomberg (1999), CEO of Bloomberg Inc, argues that ease of access in fact represents the greatest problem for organizations using the Internet. Citing the case of the early PC manufacturers, he suggests that being first to market is no assurance of long-term survival and he predicts that with growing online competition, marketing costs will soar, impacting negatively on profitability. He also warns that only those who offer something unique and non-copyable will survive, contrasting the growing number of online providers of what everyone else can supply with the handful of companies such as Reuter and Bloomberg who provide unique and indispensable services to the business world. He repeats Adam Smith's theory that selling at a profit depends upon small supply and high demand.

There is much debate over the relative merits of the 'new' and 'old' media. The Web provides free or inexpensive, rapidly updatable and customized information that can be manipulated according to the learner's needs. Technological development is accelerating, hardware and access costs are falling and print and postal services are becoming increasingly uncompetitive. However, print is still used extensively in open and flexible education all around the globe. It is well tested, universally accessible, reliable and portable. Many providers are concerned about placing large chunks of content on the Web and transferring costs of printing onto the student. Until we have the promised foldable electronic books with reloadable chips, we will probably still have to use print. And it may be that the 'feel of paper' will withstand even sophisticated challenges from 'electronic print'. Many studies show that no single technology is inherently superior in all situations and that some learning situations call for multiple technologies. The critical questions to ask are: what forms of learning and which students are best served by which technology and do the learners have appropriate access, training and capacity to utilize the technologies? An inviolable principle of good management is that before considering new facilities, those already existing should be fully utilized, especially where resources are scarce.

Technology-based learning is only as good as the instructional content and design provided by the teachers. It is certainly re-energizing many teachers and promoting some exciting collaborative developmental work. However, many still see such work as conflicting with their teaching philosophy, threatening their status, devaluing their teaching and adding to their workload. Progress is being made but hearts and minds have to be won and workloads and reward systems well managed if technology is to be valued and value-added.

'Cutting edge' technology allows people to enter virtual learning communities. It can bring enormous benefits to developing countries, or at least to their more economically advanced regions, but it can also leave the poorer nations and communities floundering in the wake of change, dependent upon western expertise and unable to control their information flow. There is an enormous gap between the technological 'haves' and 'have-nots'. There are more computers in the United States than the rest of the world and a computer represents a month's salary for the average American as opposed to eight years' income for the average Bangladeshi. There are as many telephones in Tokyo as the whole of Africa. About 90 per cent of people in the Third World have never used a telephone and 40 per cent are still without electricity. There is also the issue of the many millions of illiterate, technically illiterate and disabled persons. The G8 leaders at the 2000 Okinawa summit and the UN at its 2000 Millennium summit have set up task forces to address the issue of technology transfer to aid development and reduce poverty. However, it is yet to be shown whether the world's wealthier nations are truly prepared to provide global solidarity, ongoing funding and support for sustainable technology provision and development strategies.

Paul (1990: 120) observes:

> Of all the challenges facing the modern manager, the integration and management of new technology may be the greatest. Technology can offer tremendous opportunities for competitive advantage through cost savings and exciting innovations, or a nightmare of escalating needs and costs, and an institution out of control.

The Gartner Group (Roberts, 1999) reports that more than 50 per cent of all ICT projects in the corporate sector fail to deliver the expected benefits and that many end up late and over budget. Laurillard (Illing, 1999: 36) says, 'Wherever you see IT, you see waste and inefficiency because it's so difficult to do.' Tapsall and Ryan (1999) note the costly problems in introducing ICT into Australian universities, with the collapse of the contract with a systems supplier losing one university consortium $100 million plus litigation costs. Many institutions are experiencing problems with ICT support systems that could cope with the few 'early adopters' but find it hard to gear up to the demands of the majority at a time of shrinking budgets.

Most of these failures are management- rather than technology-related. Farrell (1999) found that, despite the obvious linkage, strategic planning for the development of ICT often proceeded with little consideration for the educational applications. Like Laurillard (Illing, 1999: 36), he stresses the need for national and institutional strategies and coordination in using ICT for teaching. Schein (1992) suggests that many of the problems in introducing ICT into organizations derive from differences in the management and information technology subcultures which embody potentially conflicting assumptions about the nature of information, people, learning, management, organizations and technology. He concludes that senior managers must examine the assumptions of these different organizational subcultures, make their own assumptions explicit, and work through these intercultural issues early in the planning process.

Organizational structure

As shown in Chapter 1, the changing environment is leading to many new types of institution, ranging from India's National Open School, publicly-funded and providing basic education to the disadvantaged, to new private, 'virtual' institutions and consortia that look beyond local markets to exploit the potentially lucrative corporate and international markets. Alan Gilbert, Vice-Chancellor of the University of Melbourne, creator of the Universitas21 initiative, observes: 'The real risk is not failure. It's missing the wave altogether' (Gluyas, 1999: 38). At the other end of the scale, there are some who opt to work outside their institutions, individually or collaboratively developing and presenting their programmes on the Web, a trend that Rumble (1999b) sees as analogous to the scholars of the Middle Ages living off the fees from their students and forming themselves into what subsequently became today's colleges and universities.

The old organizational forms, bureaucratic, hierarchical and command-controlled, no longer apply. Hague (1991) observes that society has problems whereas universities have departments. Chattell (1995) suggests that tomorrow's organizations will be characterized by a lack of pre-determined form and the dynamics of possibility-creating instability. Hecksher (1994: 24) suggests that we are witnessing the emergence of post-bureaucratic organizations in which 'everyone takes responsibility for the whole' and relationships 'are determined by problems rather than pre-determined by structures'. Champy and Nohria (1996) suggest that today's dynamic internal and external environments call for adaptive and agile networks of cross-functional project teams, some permanent, others formed as needed. Those who lead and manage such networks and teams of 'front-line' experts need to understand and achieve an accommodation between the various subcultures, knowledge, skills and assumptions, and so 'ride' and manage the boundaries as to expand the horizons. Drucker (1996) likens such organizations to symphony orchestras wherein the leaders work with teams of specialists and everyone knows the score – in both senses of the term.

As institutions realign their goals in open and flexible learning they may need to review the boundaries and operations of such discrete territories as library and information services, computing, media, distance education and staff development. However, nothing will be achieved by adopting a 'Rubik's Cube' approach, continuously reconfiguring elements in the pious hope of achieving a correct alignment. University of Canberra Vice-Chancellor Don Aitkin (1998) argues that placing great emphasis on changing structures is, on the whole, erroneous, and he suggests that any organizational form can be made to work well if all of those who work inside it know what they are doing, why it is important, and that they are valued for playing their part. He suggests that structural change should come at the very end, rather than the beginning of any review and planning process because it consumes enormous amounts of time and effort, usually without much profit.

Chapter 3

Developing an entrepreneurial culture

Colin Latchem and Donald E Hanna

The consumer and technological revolution is forcing change upon almost every aspect of work, communications and learning. We cannot tell where the 'dotedu/dotcom' revolution will take our educational and training institutions – the new technology-driven market forces have yet to fully evolve – but it seems inevitable that there will be winners and losers. Those institutions that succeed will not simply throw technology into the current mix of operations but will have developed:

- A fresh vision of learning that transcends current boundaries and practices and allows unprecedented access and learner-provider interaction.
- A map of the opportunities and challenges they face.
- The organizational means of achieving this vision and surmounting the challenges.
- An entrepreneurial culture, driven by 'idea-push' (creating new markets) as well as 'market-pull' (responsiveness to needs).

New contexts of learning

Drucker (1999) argues that new technologies not only provide greater communication and access to more information than ever before, but a radically new platform for a new economy, based upon 'e-commerce'. Comparing the potential of e-commerce with the earlier railroad systems, he argues that while the latter overcame distance to aid development, the new technology and e-commerce totally eliminate distance: 'The effect of this is that every business must become globally competitive, *even if it manufactures or sells only within a local or regional market*. The competition is not local anymore – in fact, it knows no boundaries' (Drucker, 1999: 51; emphasis added). This idea is equally applicable to educational and training organizations.

However, we still need to be sensitive to the fact that, as Evans (1995) reminds us so graphically, globalization is anything but global in shape. The world has not shrunk uniformly. Modern communications mean that London and New York and Melbourne and Tokyo have drawn much closer, but many lesser regions, particularly in the resource-poor nations, have become comparatively further removed in time and space from each other and more significantly, the places of power and influence. Evans also notes that this new distorted form is not fixed but fluid as political, economic and natural events constantly open up or close off lines of communication. There are still many educational have-nots in the world, but distance learning and technology are both drawing upon, and contributing to, the process of globalization as they permeate the furthermost regions of Asia, Oceania, Eastern Europe, Africa and South America. For many, the financial barriers are falling as the costs of knowledge acquisition, application and dissemination drop dramatically.

Internet users are currently concentrated in rich developed countries, but for those unable to afford individual access, such communal access systems as phone shops, telekiosks and telecentres are being established by international aid agencies, national governments, educational institutions, local entrepreneurs and community groups. In countries such as Mauritius, Bangladesh and India, largely illiterate rural communities are able to access essential Web-based weather and market reports and agricultural information through technology installed in village community centres and even rural markets. In Sri Lanka, 'infomediaries' on local community radio read out useful information from the Web. The G8 Okinawa Charter on Global Information Society declares that no one should be excluded from the benefits of the global information society. A networked world and improved information systems may not of themselves guarantee greater knowledge or understanding, but the ever-increasing currency of, and access to, broader sources of information are core requirements for education and training.

The new economy depends upon 'knowledge workers', initiators and drivers of human resource and social development, economic growth and reform and the free flow of information and knowledge. To create these, educational and training institutions must not only accommodate change but also must reinvent themselves and lead change. It is this latter expectation that provokes so much consternation and debate and challenges so many of the traditional assumptions and practices, particularly in those countries where policy-making rests with one dominant political group or conservative coalition, and is not only bureaucratic, but for deep-seated cultural reasons, consensual rather than adversarial.

Barriers and boundaries in institutional change

Hague (1991: 14) suggests that:

> For universities, permeability is the key. The more the universities are permeable and the more the knowledge industries and all citizens who embrace intellectual pursuits and causes come within them, the more successful they will be. . . The aim must be to create a republic of the intellect open to all.

It often appears that educational institutions are inherently resistant to change and self-absorbed in their own affairs. Thus the stereotypical image of the university as an 'ivory tower' or what has even been described as a 'tower of babble'.

The Carnegie Council on Policy Studies in Higher Education (1980: 9) observes:

> Universities in the past have been remarkable for their historic continuity, and we may expect this same characteristic in the future. They have experienced wars, revolutions, depressions, and industrial transformations, and have come out less changed than almost any other segment of their societies.

Cohen and March (1974) go so far as to describe the typical academic structure within universities as an 'organized anarchy' in which almost any idea can be justified and attacked, thwarting internal change. Such justifications are typically voiced in terms of faculty self-governance, academic autonomy and independence of thought. In practice, such arguments may often ring hollow, because many universities are subject to political, economic, managerial, or external influence and even control, and it is not at all unusual for nonconforming academics to be marginalized or muzzled when their views run counter to the prevailing values.

Bergquist (1992) points out that all organizations possess a mission or purpose and a set of boundaries, and that the traditional university has a diffused mission but clear, well-established and fixed boundaries, particularly in terms of membership. By contrast, the missions of the more recently established institutions – for example, the community colleges or open universities – are quite clear, but the boundaries are more permeable, with much greater flexibility and fluidity in their prior learning requisites, registration, attendance and completion policies, programme and study schedules, location, credit or non-credit offerings and expectations of their students.

Levine (1980) suggests that organizations protect their character or personality against potential forces both within and external to the organization by establishing clear boundaries that circumscribe or stipulate the character of the organization. Stinchcombe (1965) suggests that organizations will be 'imprinted' with the social, cultural and technical features that were common in the environment at the time of their founding and that it is difficult to adapt these characteristics to change. Analysing the challenges of change for universities in the United States, Seymour (1996) suggests that these institutions:

- Are highly specialized in the horizontal dimension (academic departments).
- Provide significant autonomy for professionals (faculty members).
- Employ professionals who are at the core of the organization and who are protected by administrators whose job it is to 'buffer' them from external pressures.

He observes (1996: 20), 'As long as the environment remains stable, the professional bureaucracy encounters few problems. The autonomous nature of the organizational structure allows the professionals to perfect their skills, free of interference. Problems arise, however, when conditions change.' This may occur, for example, when there is a rising tide of discontent over the cost of education or the perceived quality of teaching and learning. If new expectations and innovative practices are to enter the educational environment, the institutions' boundaries must become more permeable.

Kimberly and Rottman (1987) and Kimberly (1988) suggest that when an organization is established, key decisions are made in regard to *domain, governance, core values* and *organizational design*. These decisions, made within the particular set of circumstances prevailing at the time, determine the kinds of programmes that will be offered, the particular markets that will be served, the types of people who will be recruited and served, and the structure, functioning and accountability of the organization. In prescribing the organization's character, they also determine its future, for as Hericlitus noted more than 2,500 years ago, 'character is destiny'. Locking into a modus operandi can have very positive outcomes. Collins and Porras (1997), in their ground-breaking six-year research project into exceptionally successful, sustainable and forward looking companies, found that the one thing these all had in common was 'a core ideology – core values and sense of purpose beyond just making money'. On the other hand, markets can be very fickle and circumstances can change dramatically and, as Machiavelli (1963: 91) observes:

> If, for one whose policy is caution and patience, times and affairs circle about in such a way that his policy is good, he continues to succeed; if times and affairs change, he falls, because he does not change his way of proceeding. Nor is any man living so prudent that he knows how to accommodate himself to this condition, both because he cannot deviate from that to which nature disposes him, and also because, always having prospered while walking in one road, he cannot be induced to leave it. Therefore the cautious man, when it is time to adopt impetuosity, does not know how.

Hannan and Freeman (1989) indicate that organizations founded to accomplish particular purposes within a stable and conducive environment develop formalized roles, rules, structures and procedures and consume substantial time and resources in maintaining these, as may be seen in the internally focused governance process in many of the more well-established institutions.

Given these circumstances and, at least until fairly recently, the relative stability of the external environment, it is not surprising that so many of our educational institutions have significant staying power and are so resistant to organizational transformation. Hall *et al* (1996), in identifying barriers to organizational change in higher education, suggest that the following have implications for the distance education community:

● priorities determined by political expediency and the need to balance budgets rather than educational considerations;
● impenetrable bureaucracies that are slow to react to change;
● structural inequalities and varying educational standards;
● institutions focusing on organizing how they teach, not learning how to teach better or differently;

- institutions' connections with working life being weak or non-existent;
- resistance to new learning theory and practice;
- rigidity of organizational structures;
- tyranny of time.
- persistence of traditional faculty roles and rewards;
- assumptions about learning content;
- constraints of regulatory and accrediting practices;
- traditional funding formulas.

The Australian National Council for Open and Distance Education (1996) suggests that innovation in resource-based learning is impeded by:

- ingrained conservatism amongst many staff and students;
- academics' insecurities about their tenure;
- a distaste for standardized learning packages and/or fear of technology;
- students' difficulties in taking responsibility for their own learning;
- fears that open learning will be imposed in the simplistic belief that it is a cheap solution to large-scale delivery;
- tyranny of time.

Kimberly (1988: 168) suggests that 'Those who have become a part of the culture and the identity of the organization are those least able to precipitate major changes' and argues that the energy and perspective needed to fundamentally transform an organization must come from outside its own culture. Baldridge *et al* (1983) also hold that the external environment is by far the most powerful source of internal change. Toffler (1985: 14) emphasizes that organizations only change significantly when three conditions are met: 'First, there must be enormous external pressures. Second, there must be people inside who are strongly dissatisfied with the existing order. And third, there must be a coherent alternative embodied in a plan, a model, or a vision.'

The external pressures are certainly apparent, particularly in the postsecondary sector:

- Institutions are receiving less money from governments and are challenged to derive a greater percentage of their revenue from student tuition, grants and auxiliary revenue.
- The percentage of teaching staff with lifetime or career tenure is dropping.
- The costs of study are being transferred from the state to the individual and students, employers and other stakeholders have a far greater concern for quality and relevance in teaching and learning.
- Institutions are required to document their performance on the basis of student and employer feedback.
- Institutions that traditionally eschewed entrepreneurial activities are becoming more aggressive in targeting and developing new markets.
- There are more for-profit institutions and for-profit agencies within institutions.

The second condition for change, insider dissatisfaction with the existing order, comes about as a consequence of external changes (for example, in government or community support, levels and sources of funding, student demographics and market opportunities) and internal factors (for example, the availability of new technology, new generations of students demanding new patterns of teaching and learning, and new generations of teaching staff challenging existing organizational assumptions and practices).

The third condition for change, a coherent model or plan for change, calls for a thorough examination and analysis of compelling visions, strategies and procedures for responding to this volatile environment. Leaders of forward-looking institutions articulate approaches that will make sense in future environments. As ice hockey superstar, Wayne Gretzky, puts it, the challenge is 'to skate to where you think the puck will be'. Instilling such values, promoting continual innovation and putting in place systems with staying power requires a much more entrepreneurial culture than is common in most higher education institutions.

The entrepreneurial culture

Having their origins in periods of relatively slow change and tranquillity, Bergquist (1992) suggests that our universities and colleges typically have four predominant cultures:

1. The *managerial* culture, which finds meaning in the organization of work, and which conceives the institution's enterprise as the inculcation of specific knowledge, skills and attitudes in its students who will become successful and responsible citizens.
2. The *developmental* culture, which finds meaning in furthering the personal and professional growth of all members of the collegiate community, primarily defined as within the campus environment.
3. The *negotiating* culture which is concerned with, and responsible for, establishing and executing equitable and egalitarian policies and procedures for the distribution of resources and benefits in the institution, and in which the focus is on developing or maintaining systems that create negotiated and reasoned compromises in matters of personnel, reimbursement and other distribution of rewards.
4. The *collegial* culture, that is the core of any institution, sustained primarily by faculty members, and finding meaning in academic disciplines, valuing faculty research, scholarship and governance, and holding sway over the institution's most important assets – its curriculum and its faculty.

Bergquist suggests that these four cultures are present in all institutions to some degree, although the mix may vary according to institutional type, context and culture in the degree of prominence of any one of these four cultures. However, as new educational and training institutions organized in accord with entrepreneurial values and characteristics emerge, existing institutions, public and private, are challenged to adopt and support a fifth culture, a culture which we can see in new institutions and institutions transforming themselves:

5. *The entrepreneurial* culture, a culture which values proactivity and capacity to change and to change quickly, to be opportunistic and responsive to market forces, to connect with and generate support from external constituencies, and to introduce new ideas, programmes, delivery mechanisms, goals and purposes. Such a culture takes as given the necessity of change and greater self-sufficiency and sets out to seize the opportunities that come from building linkages across institutional boundaries, disciplines, constituencies and regions (Hanna, 2000: 85).

Entrepreneurship is by no means unknown in the university world. Drucker (1993) shows that the modern university owes much to the invention of the university as change agent by German diplomat and civil servant, Wilhelm von Humboldt, who in 1809 conceived and founded the University of Berlin. This concept was further extended during the last decades of the 19th century with the establishment of the American research and land-grant universities. After World War II, American academic entrepreneurs designed new 'private' and 'metropolitan universities' for a new and different market, people in mid-career. Open learning owes everything to such educational entrepreneurs as Ernest Boyer, founding Empire State College in the 1970s to offer degree programmes to adults without full academic credentials, and Walter Perry (now Lord Perry of Walton), the founding vice-chancellor of the UK Open University. Nobel Laureate Bengali poet, Rabindranath Tagore, had a similar vision for open education for India in the early years of the 20th century, unrealized in his lifetime because the traditional universities refused to collaborate in such an unconventional scheme (Mukherjee, 1997), but now manifest in India's Indira Gandhi National Open University, state open universities and many conventional universities providing distance education. The English social entrepreneur, Leonard Elmhirst, once worked as secretary to Tagore, and was strongly influenced by his thinking. Years later, in the UK, he tried to give substance to a vision of the abundant life, in which the values of learning, community, worthwhile jobs and sound business practice might be balanced and combined, by founding Dartington Hall. One of Dartington's pupils who grew up with these ideas was Michael Young (now Lord Young of Dartington), who in 1962 proposed the establishment of an open university in the United Kingdom and, a year later, established the National Extension College as a pilot for such an initiative (Perraton, 1999). The work of significant innovators challenges others to follow their course and many have responded to the challenge to introduce open and flexible learning around the globe.

Today, there is a heightened expectation of entrepreneurial behaviour in education and training. The entrepreneurial culture is not simply evident in the open universities and commercial enterprises interested in online education. It is seen in all those who are responding imaginatively to market shifts in the conventional institutions or initiating and leading open and distance education in Third World settings. Such undertakings require an adventurous spirit, boldness and energy. They also involve considerable risk. The entrepreneurial leader needs to generate an entrepreneurial spirit throughout the management group and organization. This often generates political ill will internally; the entrepreneurial culture is not particularly compatible with the other cultures and is very much at odds with the dominant collegial culture prevailing in many institutions.

Table 3.1 suggests some key differences between the collegial culture of traditional institutions and the entrepreneurial culture of new and reformed institutions.

Table 3.1 *Traditional and collegial institutional cultures and new and reformed institutions and entrepreneurial cultures*

Traditional institutions and the collegial culture	New and reformed institutions and the entrepreneurial culture
Leaders and staff abide by time-honoured rules, policies, procedures and protocols	Leaders and staff draw on their knowledge and experience but take risks because they often lack a methodology
Formal academic programmes drive the decision-making and are responsive to the needs of the institution	Learners' needs drive the decision-making and academic programmes are responsive to the needs of the individual learner
Teaching staff are pre-eminent academic decision-makers	Teaching staff share academic decision-making with key customers/stakeholders
Emphasis is on developing administrative structures that support the delivery of programmes and courses	Emphasis is on developing academic support structures tailored to the needs of the learner
People who can work within given structures are the most important. The message is, 'Don't rock the boat'	People who can anticipate the market are the most important. The message is. 'Seize the day'
Communication strategies are: – internal – vertical – formal	Communication strategies are: – external and internal – horizontal – informal
Emphasis is on systems and resources 'in hand'	Emphasis is on systems and resources 'in waiting'
Strategic partnerships go unrecognized and untapped	Strategic alliances and partnerships are sought out and implemented
Segmented, specialized organizational structures are prevalent	Integrated, cross-functional organizational structures are reinforced

Table 3.1 *Traditional and collegial institutional cultures and new and reformed institutions and entrepreneurial cultures (continued)*

Traditional institutions and the collegial culture	New and reformed institutions and the entrepreneurial culture
Budgets are stable and committed to existing programmes; deficit financing is avoided	Budgets are fluid and opportunity seeking; deficit financing is common
New programmes complement existing programmes	New programmes create openings for new markets
New programmes must fit with existing structures	The best structure is determined for each new programme
Actions tend to be evolutionary	Actions tend to be revolutionary
Risk-adverse behaviour seeks to minimize competition with others through regulation	Risk-seeking behaviour seeks to exploit competitive advantage over others
Stewardship and preservation are the critical elements of leadership	Vision and strategy are the critical elements of leadership
Stewardship and preservation focus on the impact of new activities upon existing undertakings	Strategies gravitate toward new market 'niches'
Change efforts focus upon improving programmes and activities deemed valid by competitors	Change efforts focus upon being first to develop a new programme or activity
Staff tend to work to their own agendas and act independently of their colleagues	Staff often collaborate with each other and across disciplines in pursuit of organizational goals
Appraisal, reward and recognition are based primarily on individual, scholarly performance	Appraisal, reward and recognition are based on individual and group scholarly and entrepreneurial performance
Organizational recognition comes from interaction with, and recognition by, peers in other institutions and in terms of contribution to the discipline	Organizational recognition may also come from interaction with, and recognition by, immediate colleagues and in terms of contribution to the organization
The culture rewards individual productivity and therefore staff become highly competitive	The culture rewards collaboration and therefore staff become more open and collaborative

'Time-to-market' is particularly problematic for the traditional academic culture. Historically, success was often a question of 'big over small'. Today it is more likely to be the triumph of the 'quick over the slow'. The future won't wait. Netscape founder Jim Clark (1999) in his book, *Netscape Time*, details the transition of Netscape Corporation in just a few months from an innovative concept incubated at the University of Illinois at Urbana-Champaign to a privatized product that changed the world. He argues forcefully that universities must compete in a new world of entrepreneurial enterprise, and that to successfully grasp this new world, they must change their cultures, their processes and their programmes.

Levine (1980) indicates that organizations that continually neglect to respond to environmental imperatives are candidates for extinction. Problems in meeting expectations and goals can only be tolerated for so long before there is a call to account from those who 'pay the piper'. Jack Welch, the former CEO of General Electric, puts the issue quite simply: 'When the rate of change outside the organization exceeds the rate of change inside, the end is in sight' (Davis and Botkin, 1994: 109).

To compete in the future, educational and training providers must be capable of moving more quickly, streamlining their decision-making and improving their responsiveness. In an entrepreneurial society wherein customers have many choices, all of the customers' needs, and every aspect of each learner's experience, must be given primary focus. No longer protected by governments, institutions, academics and administrators can no longer dictate how many students will be admitted, on what basis and into what subjects, or how, when and where they will learn. Those organizations that fail to recognize that they are in an entrepreneurial business will see their customers go elsewhere.

Leading entrepreneurial change

Entrepreneurial leaders introducing change into existing institutions characterized by the four traditional cultures need to be aware of the degree to which the transformations shown in Figure 4.1 and the greater use of technology challenge existing core values and assumptions, especially at a time of declining resources and staff morale and confidence. As Hannan and Freeman (1989: 5) observe, 'Organizations develop lives of their own, with action at least partly disconnected from organizational goals, from the demands of relevant environments, and often from the intentions of organizational leaders.'

The entrepreneur by definition innovates, providing a new form of business, a new form of product or a new form of service. Seymour (1996: 80) suggests that there can be four possible outcomes for innovations within an institution:

1. *Diffusion*, in which the innovation's characteristics are allowed to spread throughout the host institution.
2. *Enclaving,* in which the innovation assumes an isolated position within the institution.

3. *Resocialization,* in which the innovative unit is made to renounce its past deviance and institute the acceptable norms and practices.
4. *Termination,* in which the innovation is eliminated.

All of these outcomes will be experienced in institutions in which innovations such as open, flexible and technology-based delivery are attempted. The outcomes of enclaving, resocialization, and termination may be all too familiar to some reformers and proponents of change in education and training. The reasons are not hard to fathom. Many staff see such change as highly threatening to the status quo and would side with Noble (1998) who, writing from the US perspective, observes that education is being commercialized and instruction reduced to an automated commodity, and predicts that teaching staff will no longer be needed:

> Because education, again, is not what all this is about; it's about making money. In short, the new technology of education, like the automation of other industries, robs faculty of their knowledge and skills, their control over their working lives, the product of their labor, and, ultimately, their means of livelihood.

He suggests that change is being driven by a combination of technology businesses, university administrators, and 'technozealots':

> With the avid encouragement of their private sector and university patrons, they [the technozealots] forge ahead, without support for their pedagogical claims about the alleged enhancement of education, without any real evidence of productivity improvement, and without any effective demand from either students or teachers.

Consider too the recent predictions of prominent University of Miami School of Law professor, A Michael Froomkin. Assuming the role of devil's advocate at a conference, he was surprised to find that most of his colleagues agreed with him when he predicted that the growth of online legal education would throw many law professors out of work, and that the real losers would be the second- and third-tier institutions which lacked name recognition and concomitant prestige and so would either have to become discount law schools or go online, thus eliminating any need for a physical entity or expensive law library (Leibowitz, 2000: 45).

Those who advocate and lead change must take heed of such concerns. They must also recognize and be sympathetic to the phenomenon of change-weariness, which can lead to the staff passing through a denial phase. There is also a need to address the disillusionment and demoralization that characterize too many institutions. These are all realities that 'come with the territory'. But the message needs to be clear – the radically different and more complex external environment will impact significantly on the curriculum, work patterns and working conditions, staff–student ratios and interactions, organization, infrastructure and funding and will require new forms of response. Many educational and training providers have recognized that such changes are irreversible and inexorable and are already busily conducting environmental scans, engaging in strategic change and quality improvement and bringing about the necessary cultural changes to deliver superior value to customers through innovation. Political realities as well as educational ideologies are ensuring that this happens.

Our first chapter demonstrates the extent to which new organizational models are being developed throughout the world because the missions, cultures and boundaries of traditional education are no longer working or satisfying demand. We see open schooling systems being established, using technology or making use of classrooms or community halls in out-of-school hours. We see non-formal and adult education being delivered via ICTs directly into rural and remote communities by government, nongovernmental and community agencies seeking to improve women's rights, literacy, health, social welfare, farming and fishing methods, local government, etc. We see the traditional universities and colleges extending their operations, the open universities striving for new ways of reaching the disadvantaged and new markets, and the new for-profit institutions exploring online delivery and providing new global competition. We are also seeing strategic alliances between institutions, between public and private providers, and across national boundaries. These models exploit new forms of teaching and learning, new learning technologies and new infrastructures for learner support. These developments inevitably change the institutional cultures and show how much more entrepreneurial many of our institutions have become since Bergquist's (1992) portrayal of them less than a decade ago.

The emerging models, with special reference to the postsecondary sector in the US, are outlined in Table 3.2. The traditional 'Carnegie structure' distinguishes between institutions by their missions, structures, strategies and programmes. Duderstadt (2000), suggesting possible developmental paths for the institutions of the future, describes these by the use of metaphors. Hanna (1998) categorizes the universities of the future by strategy. Some institutions may choose one path and concentrate on shaping themselves and their programmes to support that path; others may choose to mix and match these models. However, what is clear from Duderstadt's and Hanna's representations is the rapid diversification of models for future universities and the specialization of mission within each model, as shown in Table 3.2.

Altering the institutional landscape

The challenge for educational and training institutions is to:

- Develop linkages and boundary-spanning strategies that enable innovations to enter the institution and the institution to take innovation out into the wider community.
- Correctly identify innovations and changes that the internal environment will support and sustain.

Table 3.2 *Higher education models–structures, metaphors and strategies*

Carnegie structures and missions	Duderstadt conceptual metaphors	Hanna organizational strategies
Research I and II universities	World universities	Traditional campus-centred universities
Doctoral I and II universities	Diverse universities	Extended universities
Comprehensive I and II universities	Creative universities	Distance education/ technology-based universities
Liberal arts colleges I and II	Division-less universities	For-profit universities
Community and technical colleges	Adult universities	Competency-based universities
Professional and specialized schools	Cyberspace universities	Corporate universities
	Lifelong universities	Strategic alliance universities
	Ubiquitous universities	Global universities
	Laboratory universities	

- Focus the institution in clear directions that will allow it to take advantage of its natural competitive strengths.
- Place a premium on risk-taking and entrepreneurial and collaborative behaviour.
- Facilitate the diffusion of innovation across the institution.
- Prevent the enclaving or isolation of change into self-contained and invisible sub-units.
- Protect important innovations, and their leaders, from premature termination.

Such goals are simply stated, yet extremely difficult to achieve. The process of transformation is not merely a question of developing a new vision, important as this is, but involves careful development and nurturing of new outlooks, systems and activities which, when fully mature, will radically alter the institutional landscape. And the initiators of this transformation are most often the institutional or organizational leaders who both in intention and execution, commit themselves to change and innovation, court the unexpected, and show the business of knowledge-based innovation to be an intellectual as well as an entrepreneurial activity.

If those who oppose the new paradigm succeed in isolating or enclaving open and flexible learning within the institution, staffs' fears about the future diminution of public postsecondary education are even more likely to become a reality, given the current frenzy of social, technological and economic reconstruction in the external environment.

Chapter 4

Processes of organizational change

Colin Latchem and Donald E Hanna

Systemic change

Unless all of the resources and capabilities of the educational or training system or institution are enabled to work as one, any attempts to introduce open learning into new contexts or from small-scale trials to ongoing applications will flounder and fail. Change processes have to address multiple points of inertia and resistance and have to be systemic rather than piecemeal. They call for clearly articulated and commonly accepted learner–centred teaching goals and values, and a matching of these to policies, procedures and resources.

An enthusiastic and capable group of staff in one particular university successfully applied for internal and external development grants to develop some innovative and pilot multimedia applications that proved successful in terms of learning outcomes and popular with their students. They then managed to convert their department head to this new approach and persuade him to purchase some new workstations. After a successful extended trial proving that the programme was viable and educationally effective, the department decided to mainstream multimedia–based learning for all of its students, a course of action that called for a major upgrading of the workstations and online connections. At this point, the university's senior management suddenly decided to change the institutional budgetary policy of centralized funding for ICT infrastructure and devolved all responsibility for such funding to the individual academic departments. With the sudden withdrawal of central support, and with other funding priorities to deal with, the academic department found this valuable teaching innovation now well beyond its means. Its expectations of institutional funding were dashed and most of the earlier investment in the project had been wasted by the lack of institutional prioritization, consistency, coordination and support.

This example shows why innovation in open and flexible learning must be seen to reside in the whole and not in the part, and why it depends so heavily upon the broad perspectives and consistent engagement of the senior managers who control the resources. Bates (2000) suggests the institution as a whole must have a clearly defined academic strategy or plans aggregated across the institution to identify the academic priorities for the use of technology and technology investment. Geer (1997: 25) goes further, arguing that 'to respond to the new challenges, changing teaching and delivery models is not enough. Development policies must include deeper, structural issues that will transform the system. . . re-configuring knowledge, presenting knowledge, re-examining disciplines and their boundaries (and providing) flexibility of programming'. Whether creating open schooling systems in developing countries or virtual or for-profit universities for global markets, it is necessary to break with outdated rules and assumptions about learners, access, management and work processes and respond to the driving forces of competition, change and customer focus.

Re-engineering

Unfortunately, some institutions seem to think it is possible to achieve 'innovation without change'. One distance educator was invited to develop a vision and strategic plan for a major traditional university. He involved a wide range of senior and influential staff in defining the external factors, opportunities, critical success factors, vision, and proposals for open, flexible and global delivery. When the final plan was presented to senior management, despite its having been commissioned by them and developed through institution-wide consultation, it was seen by the CEO and his team as too radical and set quietly to one side. Such inaction was attributable more to institutional inertia and senior staff being too concerned with more immediate matters than any conscious decision or testing of the academic mood on the vision and changes proposed.

To challenge underlying organizational assumptions, it may be necessary to engage in what Hammer and Stanton (1995) describe as 're-engineering', a radical re-thinking and re-development of goals, plans and procedures that holistically address end-to-end processes. The goal of this assessment and redirection is to bring about dramatic improvements in processes and outcomes.

Re-engineering has major leadership, managerial, resource and logistical implications. In the open and flexible learning context, it demands a strong nexus between strategic planning, human resource management and staff development focused on education, entrepreneurism and technology (Latchem and Lockwood, 1998). Without such a radical and system-wide overhaul, all that will be achieved is what Fullan (1993: 14) describes as a 'continual stream of fragmented surface, ephemeral innovations'.

Hammer and Stanton (1995) claim that re-engineering can never proceed bottom-up and that where there is no top-down leadership, or where the leadership is nominal rather than serious and not prepared to give the fullest commitment to change or innovation, failure may not occur straight away – but will be inevitable. They conclude (1995: 36): 'In our experience, the quality of an organization's leadership is an absolute predictor of its re-engineering success' and they advise that the leaders of re-engineering must create an environment in which people not only feel that it is safe to have breakthrough ideas but required. Lewis (1998) observes, 'the major challenge to institutional managers is. . . to bring about change in an environment currently characterized by low trust and low energy. . . Mandated change cannot create a new learning environment. Staff energies and imagination will only be released if they are working towards a future to which they too aspire'.

The leader is essential for conceiving the vision, creating the environment for success, providing the resources, and setting the standards. Senior managers also need to be continuously involved in the change processes, sharing 'the pain' as well as 'the gain'. But re-engineering can never be a one-person show. Middlehurst (1995) indicates that there is a need for 'learning leadership', a reciprocity of influence between leaders and colleagues that emphasizes mutual responsibilities.

Hammer and Stanton (1995) suggest that it is important to re-engineer quickly and plan for visible short-term wins within the first year in order to prove that the new ideas and approaches will work in the real world. They stress the importance of avoiding 'scope creep', broadening and augmenting the process definition and activities and that where necessary, it is better to narrow the scope of the change to get quick results.

Daniel (1999b) concludes that if institutions want to provide open learning that is intellectually powerful and competitively cost-effective they must get right those working practices that underpin today's modern industrial and service economy: division of labour, specialization, teamwork and project management. He argues for interdisciplinary course teams, dialogue and iterative processes rather than simply repackaging the current orthodoxy of individualistic scholarship. He cites the recently developed Open University course, 'Understanding Cities', as a good example of this. In the process of developing this multidisciplinary course about the mega-cities that will dominate the world in future decades, the course team found it necessary to revise radically the standard thinking about cities. The Open University's courses and materials are open to scrutiny, nationally and internationally, and the books and other courseware are read by many others than the formally enrolled students. As a consequence, this programme like many other programmes pioneered by the Open University will resonate across the international academic community and not simply with the students taking the course. Such collaboration calls for good project management and Daniel insists that this is something that the organization must plan and take responsibility for.

Strategic planning

Directing organizational activities towards the overall attainment of medium- to long-term strategic objectives needs some form of institutional planning. At the outset of this process, working groups need to engage with current and potential customers or stakeholders – students, staff, employers and representatives of the wider community – in order to identify or anticipate external expectations, opportunities and threats, and match these to internal capabilities and weaknesses. The next stage of planning involves identifying the lead problems or opportunities – those that will have the greatest impact or exert the most leverage. The third stage entails a critical sharing of views on the organization's strategic options and how to implement and assure quality in the necessary policies and procedures. The final plan comprises an analysis of the operating environment, the institutional mission, vision and values statements, the strategic goals, key strategies and targets, and the accountability and quality assurance mechanisms. Throughout this process, there is a constant need to conduct 'reality checks'. As Gilbert (1996: 14) observes, 'The discovery of widespread convergence of answers to these questions can unleash and sustain energy for achieving the goals that emerge from them. Understanding any underlying differences can be the first step toward achieving the working consensus needed to move forward.'

Strategic plans must avoid hyperbole, misrepresentations or unrealistic expectations (Mintzberg, 1994). They must focus, not on what ought to be done, but how it will be done (Paul, 1990). They should aim to achieve what is known in the business world as 'zero latency', avoidance of delays in specific responses from subsets within the organization. Viljoen (1994) suggests that where strategic planning fails, this is typically attributable to inadequate analysis, weak leadership, exclusive use of strategic planning experts or external consultants, a lack of employee ownership of the plan, plans being too radical and intimidating, and changes in circumstances between strategy formulation and implementation. He argues that multilevel, multifunctional working parties are needed to address specific strategic issues but that the absolutely essential requirement is top management support for the process. It is critically important for the leaders and senior managers to have a clear strategic vision and work down through the process, familiarizing themselves with the strengths and vulnerability of the organizational systems, staff, technology and all the other factors that will affect the outcomes.

Anderson *et al* (1999) found that all Australian universities currently have 5–10 year strategic plans and that the institutions believed that these were critical to changing or reaffirming direction, managing change and indeed, their very survival. The researchers noted that there was a trend to separate strategic and operational plans, with some institutions developing more detailed management plans for teaching and learning, research, community service and internationalization. They saw merit in such open and transparent planning, but noted that it also presented problems of confidentiality and competitive advantage. They found that many universities had solved this problem by having *public plans,* setting out the mission, values, broad goals and some level of detail regarding implementation; *confidential plans* containing sensitive financial and operational information, for example, regarding commercial ventures and strategic alliances; and *plans uncommitted to paper* but carried around in the heads of the senior managers. However, the authors also found considerable although not universal scepticism in the sector about the value of strategic planning.

Paul (1990) stresses that it is one thing to have a plan, and quite another to persuade others to implement the plan and commit the necessary resources. Bates (2000) observes that strategic planning has its critics, being seen as too structured for a fast-moving world, insensitive to human factors and unsuitable for organizations such as universities and colleges where, traditionally, teaching staff have enjoyed independence of action. Illing (1999: 34) suggests that 'Senior managers recognize that without good planning, the institution may go to the wall. Academics however, are strongly oriented to their international disciplinary reference groups and impatient with anything that appears to interfere with that focus.' As we saw in the previous chapter, Cohen and March (1974) suggest that universities are 'organized anarchies' and essentially incapable of being 'planned'. Olcott and Schmidt (2000) suggest that the academic subculture known as the school, faculty or department is the first level of peer acceptance for most members of teaching staff. Some of the more senior tenured staff may feel free to venture out and be innovative but the more junior and non-tenured staff must adhere to the traditional departmental norms. Deviating from these, challenging the status quo of past practices or engaging in activities requiring new resources or release time subjects these staff to peer scrutiny rather than acceptance. Further evidence of universities operating as a series of academic sub-communities rather than corporate wholes was provided by an Australian review of higher education (Hoare, 1996) which showed that strategic plans for individual departments were not necessarily derived from, or integrated with, the overall institutional strategic plan.

In shaping a coherent institutional plan for open and flexible learning, it is important to focus on the overall picture, to bring together understandings of trends and advances and ensure that there is adequate discussion and agreement on the mission, objectives and priorities for teaching and learning, learner target groups, applications of technology and budget and resource allocations. Each of these key elements must complement and support the others.

The over-riding message is to think strategically and act immediately. Established organizations need constantly to review their mission to avoid being overtaken or outflanked by younger, nimbler competitors who may better understand which way the market is headed. Mention has often been made of the founder of IBM, Thomas Watson, predicting that there would be a world market for about five computers. A more recent example is Microsoft's failure to recognize that the Internet market will grow six-fold and that the most pervasive method of access to the Internet will be mobile phones while the PC market will shrink by the same factor. Until 1999, Microsoft's mission was still to put a PC on every desk and in every home. The lesson is that early movers need to continue to innovate at a rate that will leave others behind.

It is also vital for all parts of an organization to respond to events as soon as they become known to any part of that organization or its suppliers or partners. This requires commitment and changes in mindset from the CEO down to line management and across all sectors. For example, not only must teachers understand how technology can change delivery but also ICT staff must acquire a similar working knowledge of the educational enterprise.

Institutions that wish to re-engineer or re-invent themselves will also have to combat the disillusionment and demoralization that currently characterize too many of our institutions. Many university and college teaching staff are concerned about the dwindling levels of governmental and public support, and what they see as a lowering of status for teaching, attacks on their tenure, increasing teaching loads, and the 'commodification' and 'dumbing down' of the curriculum. They also complain of the corrupting influence of managerialism, commerce and the calls for greater efficiency and to serve the national interest. In Chapter 5, we look at some of the leadership styles and actions that can be used to help steer the staff towards change and new longer-term goals.

Another factor that institutional planners must come to terms with is the sheer speed and unpredictability of changing circumstances. Sometimes, decision times and timelines for action have to be short. Arguably, this will be easier where the strategic focus is clear and where contingencies have been allowed for. One way of doing this is through 'scenario planning'.

Scenario planning

Some leaders advocate scenario planning as an adjunct to strategic planning. Pioneered by such organizations as Motorola, General Electric and Shell, scenario planning entails identifying major trends and possible continuities and discontinuities in order to anticipate and deal with major shocks or opportunities. Such an approach is particularly useful where there is volatility in the external environment and the standard trends and issues analysis cannot adequately serve the strategic planning process (Schoemaker, 1992). Scenario planning focuses on two questions: 'Are all our assumptions valid?' and, 'If the unexpected happens, what shall we do?' Those against such analysis argue that one of the very few laws of history is that everything that everybody thinks is going to happen always turns out to be wrong!

Implementing the plan

Developing a vision or a plan does not in itself guarantee success in taking the institution forward in a clear direction, capitalizing on its intellectual and competitive strengths and achieving innovation and change sustained by the internal environment. It is important to choose and build innovation into strategically important projects, proving to the staff that these add value to the organization, and as we showed in the previous chapter, to develop linkages and boundary spanning strategies that enable innovations to permeate the institution. Lessons learnt from these initiatives can then shape and inform further planning and practice. Failure in innovation is invariably due to one, or a combination, of the following causes:

● Poor planning and costing.
● A lack of support from management.
● Lack of staff recognition or reward.
● Organizational context, such as values, culture, structure, and inertia.
● An inability to integrate the innovation with the institution's 'legacy systems'.

- Insufficient or inadequate staff and resources.
- A lack of 'buy-in' from the key customers or stakeholders.

Developing staff capacities

Open and flexible learning depends in large part upon being able to count upon staff who, whether in a single location or dispersed across various campuses or institutions, are committed to the new principles and methods, prepared to engage with a diversity of learners and learning needs and able to perform the tasks necessary to the new organization-wide initiatives. However, as Paul (1990) observes, most of the teaching and support staff involved with open and flexible learning and many of those dominating institutional governance are recruited from conventional institutions. The majority of teachers who apply for jobs in institutions involved with open and distance education do so for reasons of employment or personal advancement rather than any commitment to revolution-alizing education. Many lecturers in higher education are appointed for their research rather than their teaching expertise. There may be some degree of self-selection in appointments to positions involved with open and flexible learning, but this really depends upon how well the institutions' recruitment programmes advertise a coherent vision and strategic plan for open and flexible learning and specify the attributes required in the teaching and support staff and to be developed in the students – something which is all too rarely the case.

All institutions will have some teaching staff whose interests and skills coincide with the aims and practice of open learning, who are innovative, and who are prepared to give time to mastering course development, instructional design and technology. But there will always be a number of staff who are recalcitrant in the face of change, whether due to personal security, lack of information, resistance to authority and procedural specifications or other reasons. Speaking from his considerable experience as a senior manager in major American universities and at that time as Chancellor of California State University, Barry Munitz (1997) observed:

> faculty by and large are brilliant and creative people who are dramatically liberal about everything but their own work, in which case they become almost instant reactionaries. . .They are very happy travelling around the world committing everyone else to change and extra resistant to anyone who suggests they might also be changing.

And the Deputy Vice-Chancellor of the University of South Pacific, Rajesh Chandra (1997), observes:

> Academia has a poor record of change and innovation. Academics by and large do not see the need for monitoring their work. They are also intelligent and articulate, and marshal a whole array of arguments, albeit not all as rigorous as the ones they expect from those they teach, to avoid, forestall and delay monitoring of their activities.

Encouraging change among staff who have not studied educational or open learning theory presents major challenges. Many of the case studies in the Commonwealth of Learning Trainers' Toolkits (Commonwealth of Learning, 2000) refer to the problem of gaining the commitment of teaching and support staff to such fundamentally different pedagogy, technology applications and work patterns and to the idea of quality assurance as a standard developmental procedure. Materials have to be developed and delivered on time and staff must give the same prompt attention to the off-campus students' mailed assignments, e-mails or telephone calls as to their internal students' questions in class or the knock on the office door. At the same time, it is important to be sensitive to the fact that many staff have to undertake this work in combination with teaching, tutoring and assessing the work of on-campus students, research and administrative duties. Many institutions are also experiencing staff 'downsizing'. Innovation cannot depend upon the 'heroic individual innovator', working late, over weekends, and in addition to all their other duties. It is therefore important to establish realistic timelines and workloads and put in place support networks that will help develop morale, motivation and performance. In some institutions there is the additional problem that those responsible for managing open and flexible learning lack the authority or means to help the overworked teaching staff who are then understandably more inclined to yield to the requests and demands of their teaching departments and internal students.

Open and flexible learning calls for the development of many new capacities – in administration, course and materials development, student support, computing and media production and library and information services – and requires multiple specialists to collaborate in developing learning infrastructures, systems and programmes. It is therefore vitally important to invest in helping staff at all levels face up to these changed responsibilities. It is also important to establish high professional criteria for recruitment, policies and procedures for enhancing teaching quality, standards-based performance assessment, resources and advanced accreditation for on-going staff development, and incentives and career paths for good teachers.

Cunningham *et al* (2000) predict that the dual legacies of the fast-growing, for-profit higher education sector will be the professionalization of university teaching and its simultaneous disaggregation and that such commercialization will have profound implications for academics in conventional universities. Part of the for-profit institutions' intense customer focus has been an insistence on training for their teachers, followed up by unparalleled and constant monitoring of their teaching. Growing numbers of teachers are developing course materials for new technologies, using computer-based delivery and engaging in open and distance education. But in most cases, they are having to learn as they go and many are finding that such work makes significant inroads into their work time. The extent and depth of staff development and support needed for busy teachers who have never had the time or opportunity to study educational theory or the principles of open and flexible learning to experiment with alternative teaching methods or master new technology must never be underestimated. Far more is called for than occasional, short, self-contained and voluntary workshops. Staff development and support have to be ongoing, aligned to the institutional strategic plan and embedded in an institutional strategy for the short-term orientation, medium-term training, and long-term developmental needs of all administrators, academics and support staff (Koul, 1998). It needs to be informed by 'best practice' and reliable evaluative information. It has to be experiential, based on the concept of critical reflective practice (Schon, 1987), and must build a personal and local body of knowledge and aim for continuous performance improvement. It needs ample incentives and support. It cannot simply serve those few individuals who are the 'early adopters'. It must address hard-core resistance and support change by entire faculties and support groups (Latchem and Lockwood, 1998).

In universities and colleges, an increasing proportion of teaching staff is on limited-term contracts or employed on a part-time basis. Such staff are usually not paid or able to make themselves available to take part in orientation, induction and professional programmes or to fully familiarize themselves with the culture of the workplace, open and flexible learning and the needs and circumstances of their students. One way of addressing this problem is to provide staff familiarization and development programmes through online or packaged learning, face-to-face tutoring and mentoring and assessment of a personal teaching portfolio (CeHEP, 1999). For example, this approach has been adopted by the UK Open University's Institute of Educational Technology and Centre for Higher Education Practice for OU teaching staff, as part of a nationwide move by the United Kingdom to accredit all lecturers in higher education. The Commonwealth of Learning Trainers' Toolkits (Commonwealth of Learning, 2000) are a first attempt to provide training packages at the global level.

The staff development cost of translating ambitious visions of open and flexible learning into reality and quality practice can be high – the UK Open University spends at least US$2 million annually on training its 7,000 associate lecturers to ensure that they provide highly skilled and dedicated support for the OU's students (Daniel, 1999b). However, such expenditure must be seen against the advantages of having a workforce that has a commitment and capacity for change based upon accumulated knowledge and experience.

For those practitioners or prospective practitioners who wish to develop their roles and expertise through formal study, there are a number of certificate, diploma, masters and doctoral programmes offered through distance education and/or online. The UK Open University, Athabasca University, Indira Gandhi National Open University and the University of Southern Queensland offer postgraduate programmes in open and distance learning. The Pennsylvania State University masters programme in adult education, which is available worldwide through their World Campus programme, has a substantial focus on distance learning. The University of Wisconsin-Madison offers an online advanced certificate in distance education and the University of Maryland University College (UMUC) offers a master's degree in distance education. In addition, UMUC offers online programmes in information technology, technology management, telecommunications and e-commerce.

Recognition and reward

Public educational institutions and their constituent departments are usually funded on the basis of budget allocations rather than results. There are few incentives for these institutions to operate more flexibly or responsively. Operating as governmental entities, they are typically guaranteed students and paid a fixed price for those they enrol, by government grants or through student fees. There is no differentiation between those institutions that are forward looking, reformist, striving for improvements in quality, access or equity and pursuing opportunities for growth, and those that perform poorly in these regards. Restrictions on public funding, governmental controls and regulated environments are further disincentives. Within institutions, the extreme laggards are rarely penalized. Those faculties showing enterprise or with growing enrolments often end up subsidizing those that are stagnating or have decreasing enrolments, and there has traditionally been little inducement to be innovative or enterprising in teaching and learning.

It is important to recognize, both at the governmental and institutional levels, that such inflexible budget-based systems make it difficult to abandon unproductive and obsolete working practices and that 'off-the-top funding' and performance-driven incentives are essential strategies for change. There is nothing like granting greater autonomy in spending or income generation, or instituting grants, salary supplements, staff release, or other performance recognition systems to demonstrate high-level commitment to educational development and innovation within the educational or training system or institution.

Ernest Boyer (1990) has written about the wide gap that exists between the myth and reality of academia wherein lip-service is paid to the trilogy of teaching, research and service, but in judging professional performance and promotion, these three are rarely assigned equal merit. In the university world, research is often more highly valued than teaching and scant regard is paid to evaluating or formally rewarding staff effort in open learning or technology-based innovation. Hammer and Stanton (1995) suggest that where staff are told to re-engineer but are then held accountable by the old measures, they are placed in an untenable bind and Munitz (1997) observes: 'If you don't mesh the recognition and incentives and reward structure to your stated programme and objectives (staff) will go where the money is, not where the rhetoric is. I would argue for you to fight this battle early.'

Open and flexible learning as a scholarly activity

Open and flexible learning calls for a major re-definition of the academic role to embrace and connect research and practice. Boyer (1990) argues that we need to progress beyond the tired old restrictive 'teaching versus research' debate and redefine the work of college and university staff in ways that more inclusively reflect today's academic and community expectations. He does this by using the familiar and honourable term 'scholarship', but he gives this a broader, more capacious meaning, suggesting that it covers four equally important and overlapping academic functions.

He calls the first of these 'the scholarship of discovery'. This comes closest to what is meant by 'research', the freedom to inquire, wherever this may lead. The second function he describes as the 'scholarship of integration'. This work is interdisciplinary, interpretative and integrative; it involves seeking meaning in research findings, making connections across disciplines and putting findings into broader perspective. The third type of scholarship he defines as the 'scholarship of application', where new understandings arise in the very act of application, where theory and practice vitally interact, inform and renew each other. The fourth and final element in his model is the 'scholarship of teaching'. This is not merely a

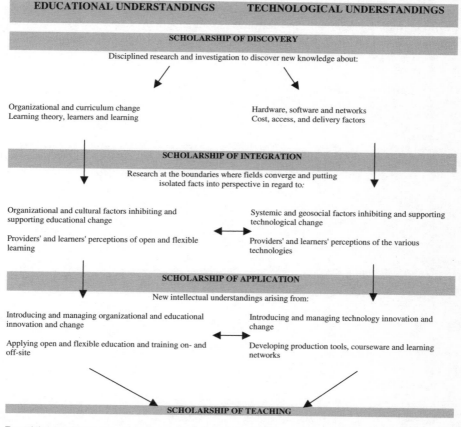

Figure 4.1 *The scholarship of open and flexible learning (with acknowledgements to Boyer, 1990)*

routine function but a continually examined and scholarly enterprise that both educates and entices future scholars. Boyer concludes that those who teach must be both steeped in the knowledge of their fields and capable of stimulating active learning, critical creativity and a capacity and enthusiasm for lifelong learning in their students.

We can adapt this model to develop a more inclusive, scholarly view of what it means to be involved in open and flexible learning and for teachers, researchers and technologists to move beyond their traditional disciplinary boundaries, communicate with each other, create a common ground of intellectual commitment and establish connections between theory, research and practice to inform and improve their work. Figure 4.1 summarizes some of the key functions which institutional managers, teachers and support staff need to address to gain greater understanding of the organizational, educational and technological dimensions to open and flexible learning. Embedding these functions within the organizational planning, staff development and reward systems may help to prove the merits of educational and technological development and bring about revolutionary change.

Chapter 5

Leadership in open and flexible learning

Colin Latchem and Donald E Hanna

Leaders and managers

Whether working in 'brick' or 'click' environments, CEOs, senior managers and professionals working in education and training face a head–spinning rate of change in customer demands, methodologies and technology. The 'dotcom world' is re-defining geography, communication and customer groups. Leaving behind the certainties of the traditional classroom, the traditional student and the traditional means of passing on circumscribed bodies of knowledge, bold leadership is needed to chart the way. Change is messy, complicated, involves conflicting demands and often occurs out of sync. Change is both political and personal. Like learning, change cannot be forced on people; most people only like it when they are in charge of it themselves. Mere management is no longer enough to guide and shape organizational behaviour. Organizations need leadership. Robbins and Finley (1997) declare that no change ever succeeded without talented leadership, whether at the top levels of the organization or at the team level. But what is a leader?

Schein (1992) suggests that the significant difference between leaders and managers is that the former create and change cultures, while the latter live with them and work for acceptable compromise. Zaleznik (1996) suggests that managers hold the view, 'If it ain't broke, don't fix it', whereas leaders understand that, 'When it ain't broke may be the only time to fix it.' Leaders are the living embodiment of the idea that mental attitude dictates performance. They create visions of exactly what they want to achieve, believe that they will succeed and often even 'see' the steps to realizing their goals. Leaders are also people who have the capacity to motivate and inspire others to think beyond their current frameworks to what is desirable, necessary and possible. They inject spirit and energy, creating optimal environments for innovation, quality and enterprise. They change mindsets and practices and gain collaboration and commitment, even in environments initially characterized by low trust and low morale. They redefine and reform organizations. They do not like to be constrained by rules or traditional lines of thought – they know when it's time to break with old systems and practices and set up new ones.

They point the way ahead and also have the courage to say: 'That is not the way to go.'

Leadership can take two forms – 'top down' (by far-sighted institutions and senior and middle managers) and 'bottom up' (by far-sighted sub-units or employees in these institutions who express needs and propose and implement solutions). In an ideal world, these two sets of directional drives will be complementary.

The characteristics of leaders

Leadership is essentially about getting people excited about moving in a positive direction. But it goes far beyond simply promulgating grand plans and engaging in empty rhetoric. It certainly doesn't stifle criticism, inquiry and debate and isn't blind to the principle of transparency. It capitalizes on the intellectual, administrative and technical capital in the institution and asks:

- Whatever our current circumstances, how shall we position ourselves strategically in the future?
- What will distinguish our institution?
- How do we make sure that we do better than the others?
- How do we ignore or clear all hurdles?

The popular view of leaders is that they are individuals with a strong sense of mission, the ability to envision what will bring success in the future, charismatic qualities which attract personal loyalty and commitment, determination and staying power, and the capacity to stand up to scrutiny, present a calm front in adversity and face up to hard and unpopular decisions. In practice, leaders vary markedly in personality and behaviour but they all act as role models for the kind of culture they wish to create. Some are revered as gurus and cult figures. Some are reviled. Some are master tacticians and brilliant negotiators. Some gamble their careers on 'crash or crash-through' reforms. Some are thoughtful and soft-spoken. Some are flamboyant, aggressive and self-promoting – Ted Turner, former CEO of CNN, reputedly has the motto, 'Lead, follow or get outta the way.' Some leaders are idiosyncratic while others avoid theatrics, seeing themselves as sharing the values of the common person or as 'backroom' strategists and planners. Some favour concerted action for system-wide change while others adopt a more incremental approach. Many leaders disappoint, some are found to have feet of clay and some, unchecked, become arrogant, reckless, intolerant of any criticism and delusional. And at some time, all leaders find that leading means becoming the target for blame and the place where the 'buck' stops.

Leaders need to be motivated for reasons beyond money and status. They need to control their own impulses, think before acting and be coherent, consistent and effective in managing interpersonal relations. They need to cope with a multiplicity of mandates and reporting lines. Collaboration and consultation are important, but sometimes leaders need to deal with those who will not cooperate or measure up to expectations.

Such traits suggest that leadership is closely associated with masculinity, perhaps not surprisingly, given the predominance of males in top management positions. However, as a consequence of affirmative action, more and more women are becoming CEOs, particularly in the United States where the management schools stress the value of such diversity. Schein (1992) suggests that women in leadership positions may in fact find it easier to accommodate a range of perspectives and methods in arriving at solutions, a view supported by Grant (1992), who suggests that women can often bring to their leadership roles such attributes as empathy, communication, conciliation and conflict resolution. Uren (1999) cites research showing that women are more participative, team-oriented and supportive of bosses, colleagues and subordinates, pay more attention to providing service and are more considered in their decision-making than males who are more event-driven. James (1996) argues that the world is gradually giving way to more androgynous ways of thinking and that it therefore makes little sense for our ideas about leaders to be bound by gender stereotypes, while Robbins and Finley (1997: 172) suggest that the new movement of leadership has the leader as 'emotionally in tune with others, a nurturer of ideas and aspirations, a sharer of information, a teacher, a helpmeet and a friend' – qualities often associated with a more 'feminized' role.

Leaders steering educational institutions through a fluid, fast-changing environment need to do far more than deliver a few glib phrases and platitudes. They really need to be public intellectuals because their constituencies, the politicians and their academic colleagues are extremely well informed and more than prepared to discuss the merits of contending ideas and ideologies. There is therefore a need for leaders to outline and articulate their vision and blueprint for action and show consistency in the substance and tone of their policies and actions. Australian Vice-Chancellor Don Aitkin (1998) stresses that CEOs like himself are often called upon to speak or act at short notice and cannot do this convincingly unless they believe in the vision or product themselves.

Ultimately, however, the proof of leadership lies not in the words but in the actions; everything the leader may do, however casual, will be taken by staff as planned and meaningful. James (1996) suggests that the quality and consistency of leadership in an organization may be judged by comparing the organizational vision, values and goal statements with the realities: the issues the leaders give priority to, their responses to crises, the organizational structures, systems and procedures they put in place, and the recruitment, selection, promotion and reward systems they create or condone.

Bogue (1994) suggests that effective leadership is as much a test of character as a test of intellect. As they forge new paths to the future, leaders have to take risks, learn from their mistakes and those of others, and re-address problems from new perspectives. They must avoid erratic behaviour, back flips, backroom deals, vagueness and vacillation, all of which undermine confidence and respect, cause confusion and inhibit change. They must avoid creating an environment in which people are rushed off their feet or fearful of downsizing, outsourcing or cost-cutting, all of which also inhibit the generation of good ideas. As more than one leader has found, 'it's tough to build morale while cutting budgets'. Another action that really puts organizations on the back foot is constant management change and restructuring. Every time this occurs, there is a consequent lowering of morale, professional continuity, corporate memory, trust and commitment to the organization. Another failure of leadership is to initiate endless reviews, setting in motion widespread consultation and speculation and then, because of lack of vision and true commitment, casting aside all the recommendations. Many potentially valuable open learning and flexible initiatives have failed to achieve their potential, drifted into oblivion or otherwise been fatally damaged by leaders adopting such methods.

The role and process of leadership

Many commentators find it more useful to consider leadership from the perspective of *role* and *process* rather than from the purely psychological perspective.

The leader's role is centrally concerned with persuasion. To summarize Bennis (1989) and others, the prime expectation of leaders is that they will provide clear, energizing visions and define or redefine the core values and goals of their organizations. Chris Patten (1998), who as the last governor of Hong Kong, overcame considerable opposition from the Chinese, Hong Kong and British authorities and introduced a measure of democracy before the handover of the colony to China, writes of the importance of having a clear plan and giving a firm and clear lead. He states that any community, and particularly a community in flux, needs to know what is intended, needs articulate and coherent messages, directions, justifications and explanations that correspond to the goals set, and needs a firm and unhesitating steer. He suggests that in such situations, leaders are unlikely to achieve or convey much sense of direction if they constantly consult with their staff and conduct surveys and focus groups to find out what they wish to do; the finger to the wind is no leadership strategy in times of turbulent change.

Ross Paul (1990), formerly Academic Vice-President at Athabasca University and now President of Laurentian University in Canada, stresses that the real effectiveness of leaders is tested in the face of conflict and argues that in the inevitable chaos of complex organizations such as universities, the responsibility for open learning initiatives must rest right at the top. Australian Vice-Chancellor Don Aitkin (1998) holds that today's institutional CEOs must be leaders who have excellent managers working for them and should leave the management to the managers. However, he also remarks that there can be conflict between the managerial levers to get things done and the collegial rhetoric and what he calls 'the languid feedback loop of academic boards and committees', both of which tend to stop things from happening. He notes that much of the budget is already fixed, so the capacity to use this as an instrument of change is often very limited. He suggests that if the power of the office is to be used effectively, the vice-chancellor must provide a sense of mission, a vision and an agenda for the university and must spend a lot of time building and nurturing the university as a political community. He suggests that this will come from the leader's experience, reflection and personal values harmonized with the needs of the university, and that the leader must spend a lot of time working through 'the big picture', bringing together the people who exercise delegated powers, building them into effective teams and sorting out territories. Ultimately, the CEO is the only person who can extend the zones of possibility, concentrate efforts and resources and give staff the space, means and opportunities they need for innovation and meeting new challenges. And as Viljoen (1994: 24) points out, 'Non-visionary CEOs are constant demotivators and cause perpetual frustration in potentially innovative organizations.'

Conversely, too much power at the top and an over-reliance upon charismatic leadership and extrinsic human motivation entails many risks and fails to realize the human capital. So leaders also need to concentrate on developing their institutions as 'learning organizations', developing a sense of 'collective leadership' or forward thinking 'leadership groups' who are continuously renewing their know-how and committed to leading the field in whatever they do. These groups will fulfil hybrid roles in open and flexible learning, providing *institutional* leadership, *academic* leadership, *administrative* leadership, and *professional* or *technological* leadership.

It is critically important for leaders of open and flexible learning to specify whether the ideology is that of access and equity and serving changing student demographics, or driven by political and economic expediency, market demands, commercial potential, or some combination of these. The leaders must also instil a sense of mission, fire the imaginations of the staff and champion the means of implementation. How they do this depends upon their personal philosophies.

Badaracco and Ellsworth (1989) suggest that leadership roles are guided by one of three philosophies: *political, directive* and *values-driven*:

1. The *political leader* holds a clear vision of the future but being aware of the inherent inertia and resistance to change within the organization, works to broadly defined goals, incrementally, flexibly and tangentially.
2. The *directive leader* objectively assesses the organization's strengths and weaknesses and directs the organization towards clear, specific and compelling goals, taking personal responsibility for key decisions, challenging conventional wisdom, and relying upon structure and systems to control decision-making and confront internal conflicts.
3. The *values-driven leader* provides leadership that serves the purposes and reflects the values with which the followers can identify but energizes them towards the overall organizational purposes rather than their own self-interest. The essence of this philosophy is to create the trust and a positive shared vision and then 'walk the talk', leading by example.

Drawing on his experience as a university president, Paul (1990) suggests that leaders can only achieve real and lasting commitment to change by adopting this values-driven approach, which is similar to what McGregor Burns (1978) calls *transformational leadership*.

Sayles (1993) argues that organizations cannot function effectively without senior and middle managers who are 'working leaders'. Binney and Williams (1995) and Behling and McFillen (1996) also stress the importance of leaders demonstrating their operational credibility and ability to achieve great things. A member of the University of Melbourne's governing council is quoted as saying of Vice-Chancellor Alan Gilbert, whose ambition it is to transform this $600 million institution into a $2.5 billion world player through the Universitas21 alliance described in Chapter 1 and a $300 million private adjunct to the public university: 'From day one, his vision seemed on the outer edge of credulity. But the council has backed him and, boy, has he delivered' (Gluyas, 1999: 37).

Blanchard *et al* (1987) argue that there is no single optimal leadership style and that leadership is *situational* or *task-specific*. They suggest that the effective leader has the ability to diagnose the competence and commitment of those who are to operationalize particular goals or tasks and respond accordingly:

- Where staff are inexperienced in the priorities, policies and practices, but committed, a *directive style* is needed. Here the leader is quite specific about the goal and how the task is to be accomplished.
- Where the staff are relatively inexperienced and uncommitted, he or she needs to build their competence and self-esteem by adopting a *coaching style*. This is still high on direction but involves explaining decisions, soliciting suggestions and encouraging staff participation in the decision–making.
- Staff who are highly experienced but variably committed need an even more participative *supporting style* that gives them shared responsibility for decision-making.
- Those who have both high competence and high commitment are best served by a *delegating style*, which provides little supervision or support for day-to-day operations.

Robbins and Finley (1997) suggest that there are four ways of leading for change:

1. Pummel ('We'll tell you what we think you need to know. If we didn't say it, you didn't need it'), an approach which dates from 'the bad old days'.
2. Push ('We'll explain what you have to do to survive'), which uses fear to galvanize action.
3. Pull ('Let's stay in touch. If you have a better idea, speak up'), which is what achieves the best long-term results.
4. Pamper ('Any time you want something explained, just ask us and we'll explain it to you'), which is essentially 'pull' but without any accountability.

Leadership is not something that is 'done to people' but 'done with people' and leaders need to be sensitive to people's concerns but positive about what they can achieve, and encourage creativity, innovation and risk-taking.

Robbins and Finley (1997) suggest that there are seven unchangeable rules of change:

1. People do what they perceive is in their best interest, thinking as rationally as circumstances allow them to think.

2. People are not inherently anti–change. Most will, in fact, embrace initiatives provided the change has positive meaning for them.
3. People thrive under creative challenge but wilt under negative stress.
4. People are different. No single 'elegant solution' will address the entire breadth of these differences.
5. People believe what they see. Actions speak louder than words, and a history of previous deception octuples present suspicion.
6. The way to make effective long–term change is to first visualize what you want to accomplish and then inhabit this vision until it comes true.
7. Change is an act of the imagination. Until the imagination is engaged, no important change can occur.

Abdullah (1998) describes moves into distance education by a conventional Malaysian higher education institution whose staff were experienced only in face-to-face teaching. The Rector had previously managed major change in another large institution and was well aware of the tensions this created. He announced his vision of enrolling 50,000 on–campus and 50,000 distance education students at a time when the institution had 37,000 on–campus and 8,000 off–campus students. He urged all of the staff to think seriously about how to achieve this target. He recognized the need to transform the second level managers and enlist their help in achieving the desired changes across the institution. He constantly advertised his vision and the strategies needed in formal and informal discussions with staff and students. He made clear his expectations that all of the staff would master the new skills of distance education and work to a quality assurance model. He also acknowledged the self–concern and unease the staff would inevitably experience during the transitional stages and assured them of his and the institutional support. Such awareness–building, motivational input, counselling and interaction with staff at all levels is critically important to judging the mood of the staff and sharing concerns and priorities in the process of change.

Aitkin (1998) argues that while it is essential for the CEO to establish the sense of mission and main agenda, to impose new directions without any awareness of the history and power of the institutional ideologies, myths and icons is to invite early failure. He suggests that leaders should seek to reshape these myths to contemporary purposes and weave new responses into them by using prevailing ideas and ideologies. However, as James (1996) observes, myths may be based on self–interest, prejudice or stereotypes. They may, for example, sanctify traditional teaching, research–related responsibilities, academic autonomy and ethnocentricity, particularly when people are anxious about the changes proposed, and James argues that it is important to let go of those myths that no longer serve our aims.

Leaders have to be able to manage the 'formal organization' (the official internal and external hierarchies) and the 'informal organization' (the unofficial lines of communication, gossip, innuendo, etc). They also demonstrate their leadership capacity by selecting and adding value to the managers and teams of professionals who have to take over ownership of the problems and by nurturing 'change activists' who can lead, steer, coach and empower others. Where leadership for change and development is wholly outside the teaching departments and far from where teaching and learning occur, traditional institutions will be slow to embrace change and take advantage of new opportunities. One of the most important, immediate and intensively challenging tasks for the conventional institution is to develop additional strategies for building leadership capacity to support change at the staff level (Hanna, 2000).

Leadership and open and flexible learning

Chattell (1995) suggests that tomorrow's leaders need to be capable of handling dynamic agendas of possibilities and see the future as discoverable rather than predictable. When leaders have a clear vision, they may not be able to foretell the precise form the opportunities will take, but they will certainly recognize them as soon as they present themselves. Former California State University Chancellor, Barry Munitz (1997) tells how he was once listening to the Chair of his Foundation Board, a senior executive with Chevron, describing the problems the company was experiencing in gaining approval from the 137 southern Californian municipalities affected by a new underground natural gas pipeline. Asked about the safety factor, this senior executive explained that there was a fibre optical cable running along on top of the pipe which monitored the temperature, leakage and speed of flow. Chancellor Munitz then asked about the percentage of cable capacity needed for this monitoring and when informed that this requirement was less than 1 per cent, put forward the following proposal. CSU, which needed a network to support its off-campus delivery throughout the same region, would survey the educational services required by those communities, design the delivery structure and provide the courses in return for Chevron funding this and permitting the non-proprietary use of this cable. They struck a deal over this.

Leaders need to envision for the long term. The transformation of organizations, and in particular large educational systems and institutions that have a lot of momentum and embedded self-interest, is generally reckoned to take at least 5 to 10 years. It actually took Japanese manufacturers 20 years to achieve the mature quality movement capable of delivering sustained competitive advantage for which they are now renowned (Cole, 1995). This transformational process can be derailed at any moment by a discontinuity of leadership. Very few CEOs or heads of department hold their positions for more than five to seven years, but successful organizations are often able to acknowledge the contribution of outstanding leaders who, in their formative years, saw the potential, invented the means to exploit it, and played a galvanizing role by instilling a 'can do' culture.

It is critically important that leaders familiarize themselves with the resources, structures, systems, people and history of the system or organization before making any decisions about new strategic directions. To do this, they need to work with people as equals, clarifying goals and achieving a working consensus on the ramifications and means of achieving change. A desire to make history without doing this can kill initiatives.

Evans (1999) describes how in the late 1980s and early 1990s, the Canberra politicians and bureaucrats convinced themselves that the large number of Australian universities offering distance education represented 'unnecessary duplication'. They decided that this was a 'problem' that could be resolved by limiting the number of university providers (nominated as 'Distance Education Centres') to eight. The government's plan was to concentrate the necessary resources and expertise in these DECs and require all other would-be distance education providers to develop 'collaborative relationships' with these institutions and contract with them for their course and materials development. The aim may have been increased equity, professionalism and innovation but the proponents of this model totally failed to comprehend its shortcomings. First, as Jakupec and Nicoll (1994) note, they failed to explain how this restructuring could create a distance education system that went beyond the production and delivery of distance teaching material. Second, they under-estimated the concerns of the 'non-DEC' universities, most of whom were keen to adopt flexible delivery and some of whom were concerned about their viability, and their capacity to maintain their distance education operations by stealth, collusion and subterfuge (Johnson, 1996). Third, they had hopes that distance education could achieve savings of 25 per cent, hopes that were quickly dispelled by an independent report revealing that the DECs could only substantiate discounts of 1–10 per cent over on-campus teaching. The government was soon forced to abandon the DEC model. This episode serves to show that change can only be meaningful and sustained where there are shared understandings and commitment.

It is of course impossible for governmental or institutional leaders to have the instincts, skills, sensitivities, judgmental capacities and technical knowledge to be on top of every agenda in open and flexible learning. They must therefore seek out the most knowledgeable professionals within or beyond their system or institution. They must also be capable of achieving an accommodation between new ideas and recommendations and existing subcultures (or defence mechanisms). While leaders must be open to suggestions, they must also avoid entrusting major decisions to experts where this may be perceived as leadership lacking in direction or essentially concerned with administration. Decisions by particular subgroups can be ill informed, short-term, based upon self-interest or otherwise negative for the organization.

Leadership development and succession

Great military leaders are typically seen as having magnetic influence over those they command, strategic brilliance and the highest levels of commitment and political persuasiveness. Great corporate leaders are often perceived as tough, energetic and having outstanding business acumen. Great conductors know how to achieve harmony and rhythm and the heights of musical achievement. It might be argued that today's educational leaders need all of these capacities as well as a firm grasp of academic agendas. Such leaders are not born, they are developed.

However, in education, leadership development is rarely conceived in terms of career development. Many are placed in leadership positions based in large part upon previous academic achievement and prestige. When training is available, it usually comprises short courses for specific purposes (Middlehurst, 1995) and is more concerned with raising awareness of issues and developments than with transferring learning back into the workplace (Davies, 1995). So how are these leadership capacities to be developed in senior and middle managers?

Sadler (1997) suggests that leadership training programmes are often seriously flawed, being focused on management rather than leadership skills, and that such programmes cannot by themselves develop leadership potential. He argues that leadership is developed through an organizational culture that nourishes vision and creativity, provides challenging workplace assignments that require influential rather than positional power, encourages training and self-development and rewards those who encourage leadership in subordinates. Le Grew and Calvert (1998) suggest that non-formal development activities and problem-based programmes in work settings have far greater value than short courses in enabling executives, planners and decision-makers to develop and manage new paradigms and modes of education. Brown-Parker (1996) shows that this can be done through mentoring, shadowing, special projects, job exchanges, structured placements, networks and action groups. Senior executives also learn a great deal from their peers who are often the only people to understand the issues well enough to discuss them in depth. Gordon Moore, one of the founders of Intel, says he spent little time studying management theory – he had already learnt enough by studying his former bosses' mistakes! (Lenzinger, 1995).

Organizations get the leaders they deserve. The prevailing culture can nurture the right leadership behaviour in staff, or can stultify it. Succession decisions are critical to the renewal process. Appointing leaders from within the ranks can raise questions about institutional complacency. High-profile searches from across the sector signal that substantial change is needed, and a leader who can fundamentally challenge all of the basic assumptions and ways of doing things. An even more extreme course of action, recruiting leaders from outside the sector, signals a lack of appropriate talent or significant change of direction within the sector. Whatever method of recruitment is used, if innovation and change are to be maintained, the new leadership must truly personify these.

In the following chapters, we follow up on these ideas on leadership by interviewing outstanding leaders and innovators in the fields of education and training. These individuals come from many different countries, cultures and backgrounds, and are called upon to exercise their leadership in many different organizational and community contexts. Their reflections and experiences serve to demonstrate the vision, commitment and intellectual strength that are called for in helping to achieve educational transformation and reform.

Chapter 6

The University of South Australia: providing leadership in flexible learning

Professor Denise Bradley, Vice-Chancellor of The University of South Australia (UniSA), an institution that places flexible learning at the heart of its mission, discusses the leadership issues she has confronted in achieving such change.

Q. UniSA places great emphasis on 'flexible learning'. Why and how was it decided that this was strategically important?

A. The University of South Australia (UniSA) came into being in 1991 as a consequence of sweeping policy changes at the national level, which abolished an earlier binary system of higher education and resulted in the merger of two Adelaide-based institutions. Its statutory obligations were that it provide high quality, accessible and equitable education for the professions and also meet the needs of groups traditionally disadvantaged in access to higher education. These obligations harmonized with the history and mission of each merger partner.

Almost immediately it was acknowledged that a consistent academic policy framework across the merged institution was necessary. Review, discussion and agreement to such an approach in each academic policy area (eg, admissions, course structures, assessment and appeal procedures) began in earnest in 1992 and proceeded relatively smoothly.

One critical difference in institutional cultures was highlighted, however, in an early debate at Academic Board – about what constituted a student workload for a year. One of the merger partners, because it was a distance education provider, had already accepted that neither staff nor student workload could be measured by the surrogate of staff/student contact hours each semester. The other, which had only the experience of teaching on campus, found the assumptions underlying the debate very difficult to address. This debate was the first to open up the mix of views about what constituted 'good' teaching and how and by whom its quality was judged.

Nevertheless, despite such differences, in hindsight, all of the early debates about the academic programme within the new institution largely concentrated on what was taught rather than what was learnt. Perhaps the greatest change over the 10 years has been a shift in emphasis in policy and strategy from what is taught to what is learnt.

By 1993, UniSA was ready to debate the quality of the learning environment with consistent academic policies in place. Later that year it made a broad and relatively open policy commitment to move towards a new learning environment. In so doing there was general agreement that the decisions we made in future about the use of technology in teaching should be driven by the institutional mission, which emphasized quality, accessibility and equity, rather than by cost. Thus we committed ourselves to a form of flexible delivery defined as 'the provision of learning resources and the application of technologies to create, store and distribute course content, enrich communication, and provide support and services to enable more effective management of learning by the learner. In particular, the concept involves a view of learning in which a teacher does not predominantly mediate the student's experience' (King, 1999: 271).

The decision to move in this direction was driven by three major strategic considerations:

- Our experience in distance education was a strength as we began to address the impact of new technologies and new patterns of demand for lifelong learning.
- A multicampus 'new' university needed to provide some alternative to traditional institutions if it was to have any strategic advantage.
- Traditional patterns of student teacher interaction would be affected by the emerging wave of change in communication and information technologies far more than they had been by any earlier technological changes.

In order to support this new direction we began a comprehensive process of institutional planning intended to put more resources into infrastructure to improve the working and learning environment and help us reach the conditions we considered appropriate in 2003, the year in which we aimed to realize a new learning environment. Of course there were many impediments to the realization of our lofty aims. For example in 1994 it was clear we needed to address:

- How to coordinate and mount systematic programmes of professional development to assist academic staff to gain the skills required in the shift from teacher-centred to student-centred approaches.
- The implications of teaching in a multicampus university where the same subjects could be taught on more than one campus and where distinctions between on- and off-campus study were disappearing.
- Differences within the university in familiarity and comfort with less traditional forms of teaching.

- Different levels of provision of equipment to support innovative teaching approaches between and within schools and faculties.
- A decrease in academic staff numbers and the need to plan for more efficient forms of teaching within the framework of a commitment to student-centred teaching.
- Inadequate access to the communications network for some areas within the university.
- Confusion about the responsibilities of support units in the provision of academic staff development to permit more flexible teaching approaches.
- Lack of coordination at faculty and school level between equipment purchase and provision of systematic staff development assistance. (Where equipment is purchased to support innovative practice there is an inevitable related demand for professional development to support both understanding of the innovation and the best use of the equipment to meet that end.)
- The balance between institutional responsibility for providing students with access to ICT resources in contrast with individual student responsibility.

As I write, early in 2000, the structural issues have been successfully addressed, the ICT infrastructure is enormously improved, staff losses have been much greater than we ever anticipated in 1993, students have adopted the new technologies enthusiastically, and we are trying to manage huge demand for support from academic staff as they make innovations in their teaching.

Q. What roles have you played in establishing the new strategic directions for UniSA?

A. As Deputy Vice-Chancellor from 1992 till 1996 I was responsible for leadership of the University's academic programme. Over that period, however, understanding of what that meant changed radically, both at UniSA and elsewhere in Australia.

At the beginning of the 1990s most Australian universities considered that leadership in this position was exercised through chairing working groups that refined relatively well established academic 'rules', and refereeing arguments between faculties and schools about course delivery. By the end of the decade the position was seen both as that of chief strategist for the university's approach to teaching and learning and as the position with management responsibility for overseeing the maintenance of quality in that approach. However, from my appointment in 1992 I believe that the Council and the Vice-Chancellor saw me as undertaking these two roles, although I do not believe that this view was necessarily accepted within the University until 1995. Two factors that made my contribution more critical at this time were the new national Quality Audit process, which highlighted the need for more systematic and strategic approaches by universities, and the drive for quality which resulted in UniSA achieving first ranking in the 1994 teaching and learning audit.

With this mandate from the University's governing body and support from the Vice-Chancellor, Professor David Robinson, I initiated and oversaw sweeping policy change, comprehensive external review of every aspect of our academic programme, structural changes in academic and administrative units and establishment of a new direction for the University – the move to a flexible learning environment. All of these changes were debated and adopted by Academic Board after wide discussion within the University. All, however, required my initiation of a review process and the production of discussion papers, policy analyses and environmental scans. I wrote a lot between 1992 and 1996!

My role in developing the proposal that the university move to a flexible learning environment is a good example of how I generally proceeded. Having seen the need to establish a more holistic framework for what we were attempting to do, I initiated discussions with and between key staff in our Distance Education Centre (DEC) and our Centre for University Teaching and Learning (CUTL), worked with them on the first draft of a paper, took that paper to the Senior Management Group where I argued for the approach and then released the paper into the formal consultation processes. These processes led to debate at and adoption by Academic Board.

My role in establishing the Flexible Learning Centre (FLC) in 1995/6 was more directly managerial and interventionist. I considered that there were symbolic, educational, structural and resource reasons for merging the DEC and the CUTL. I argued for this outcome in a paper to the Senior Management Group, outlined the rationale to the affected staff and oversaw the merger and restructuring. This was the first support unit of this kind established in an Australian university and is discussed more fully in Yetton and Associates (1997).

As Vice-Chancellor, I have, of course, had a less direct hand in shaping the University's approach to teaching and learning. However, in 1998 I undertook a major intervention. I became concerned that, because of senior staff changes and a financial crisis in 1996/7 we had lost both our strategic focus on teaching and learning and our position as a leader in this area in Australia. I called together a small group of key staff and carried out a review of our progress against the 1993 statement and identified what we needed to do each year from 1998 to 2003 to achieve our vision of 1993. The outcome was a formal statement of the University's Strategy for Teaching and Learning, a set of agreed actions for the next four years and a clear understanding within our planning and budget processes of what this meant, particularly financially. This process also clarified our need to have a distinctive approach to the provision of an online learning environment. By March 1999, UniSAnet, a common and universal online environment scaleable to all staff, students and courses of UniSA was in operation and by December 1999 over 200 of the University's subjects had an online dimension.

Q. What theories, principles or experiences have shaped your leadership style?

A. I believe I've been shaped by two main influences. One is very idiosyncratic – I don't think I'm afraid of change, indeed I think I quite like it. Also, I have largely had a positive personal experience of organizational change because in broad terms I have not been a victim in the four institutional mergers I have been involved in during the last 20 years. However, that is probably less significant than the other influence – feminism. I have been a committed feminist since the late 1960s and have had extensive experience in both state and national policy bodies. In those positions I have been involved in policy development to bring about change in both the educational experiences and employment opportunities of Australian women. I have been committed for most of my working life to bringing about change in opportunities for women and, indeed, other groups who are disadvantaged in their access to education and employment. As well, I was operationally responsible for policy implementation in the late 1970s as South Australia's first Women's Adviser in Education. These commitments and experiences mean I:

- See leading change to policy and approaches as a central responsibility of senior managers.
- Believe that senior people are responsible for having command of the 'big picture'.
- Expect my ideas to be in front of opinion wherever I am working and thus accept I will need to be leading every stage of the process of change from the front.
- Assume I will be a controversial figure wherever I work and that I will need to take that into account as I manage change.

Q. How do you and your managers encourage and support innovation and change across the organization?

A. UniSA has always operated within an explicit strategic planning framework but the challenges we've faced have led to constant review of the processes within which planning occurs. While we operate within a 10-year framework with a three-year planning cycle, we have found that careful annual review and planning have become increasingly critical. Review in particular has assumed greater significance since 1997 as has a greater reliance on quantitative measures of performance. Nevertheless, while I had no doubt that the annual Corporate Plan directed the activities of the central administrative units very tightly, until 1997, I was always sceptical about how tight the fit was between our Corporate Plan and school activities.

But since then, tight performance targets for the whole University, capable of disaggregation to the school and unit level have been introduced; annual performance management agreements are being implemented for all staff including those below management level; our own survey of student satisfaction has been initiated; Divisional Academic Plans which make explicit what subjects and courses they intend to develop (and bring online) in the next cycle are required; and formal service contracts between the Flexible Learning Centre and the divisions must be negotiated as part of the process. As well, from 2000, divisions and schools receive a percentage of their budget directly tied to their performance against some key performance indicators. Student satisfaction with teaching is one of these indicators. The institution is increasingly organized around this planning cycle as it attempts strategically to direct scarce resources to areas where we judge we are most likely to meet our longer-term strategic intentions. A broad strategic framework which allows us to set clear annual targets, fine-tune our tactics when circumstances change, determine with clarity how we are progressing and identify areas of strength and weakness is all we want!

Various programmes for reward of innovation in delivery, for good teaching and for service to students are in place. However, we are still grappling with shifting our culture from one of goodwill towards students to one where the students' learning is at the centre of our approaches to teaching and administration.

Q. What qualities of leadership do you see as necessary and seek to encourage in your managers, teachers and support staff?

A. I believe that people leading others to change need to demonstrate:

- broad contextual understanding;
- flexibility;
- comfort with risk-taking;
- a capacity to work in teams.

However, the reality is that in most universities at present a Vice-Chancellor is confronted with enormous external pressure to change, little choice about who you can use to help you to achieve that change and considerable scepticism from academic staff about the necessity to alter the way they do things.

Professional development of university managers is necessary, but I am not convinced that universities have been very successful in this area. At UniSA we have adopted a comprehensive approach to performance management, have been a consistently heavy user of various national professional development programmes organized by the Australian Vice-Chancellors' Committee and implemented our own targeted programme for managers in 1999. However, we found in 2000 that it was not meeting their needs and are now moving to a new approach – using organizational learning as the key concept.

Q. What lessons have you learnt about changing university teaching and learning?

A. Two perhaps surprising lessons are that every opportunity must be seized and that, as Vice-Chancellor, I cannot afford to remain aloof from the detail.

The statement, 'The Qualities of a Graduate of the University of South Australia', which we now require to be addressed formally in every subject in all under-graduate courses, is an example of the importance of seeing and seizing an opportunity. The coincidence of both a special Working Party established by the Chancellor to consider the broader dimensions of the University mission and my visit while Deputy Vice-Chancellor to Alverno College in the United States, where I observed the implementation of that institution's Ability-based Curriculum, led to my seeing how we could begin to address a range of issues related to teaching and learning which initially appeared unrelated. In particular, I thought a systematic approach to stating our intentions about the qualities our graduates demonstrated would move the debate within the University to the critical issues about student learning rather than teacher intent. We had spent far too much time arguing about what we planned to do rather than finding ways to gauge what we had achieved. Like all universities we asserted that we produced graduates who could demonstrate a range of broad and deep learnings, but I was concerned that we could not reach agreement on what these learnings were and could do no more than assert the presence of particular generic attributes in our graduates. At the same time there was genuine concern among members of University Council about both the purposes of university education and UniSA's role in the education of the next generation of our leaders.

I set in train a broad consultative process to achieve a formal statement about the attributes the University wished its graduates to demonstrate. This was informed both by the Report of the Chancellor's Working Party and documentation of practices in Alverno College and other institutions. In so doing, I was aware that many of my colleagues saw this as a public relations statement. However, I believed it could be used to address some endemic problems in teaching practices. When Academic Board passed the statement and later adopted an implementation strategy that made plain that the statement would drive major change, I was not sure that many saw this as likely.

I regarded the adoption of this policy statement and the first attempt at implementation as an opportunity to shift the emphases in teaching from a preoccupation with content and assessment towards the processes of learning. There had been a series of debates at Academic Board on such issues as the nature of assessment and the need to broaden the curriculum to ensure we were producing graduates with a capacity for lifelong learning. However, in my view, the opportunity for real change which would be to the advantage of students and employers had been lost in these debates. They always foundered on strongly-held and differing views about the nature of university education and it proved impossible to move Board members beyond the conventional preoccupations of their different disciplines to consider the more fundamental general questions that turned on the very purposes of university education. The radically different dimension to the debate about Graduate Qualities is that it necessitated a focus on university-wide concerns about the ends of higher education rather than discipline-specific means to those ends. This, in turn, permitted a subsequent focus on new means to those newly agreed ends.

It has been my experience that you need to know the organization well in order to judge when to act. While you must have a personal vision as well as the institutional vision for which you are responsible, you have to be able to judge how far and how fast you can push a collegiate culture. That means that you must understand what is happening within it. The introduction of Campus Central, the single point for all student queries established on each of our campuses, is a good demonstration of this. The Campus Central initiative began in mid-1998 and was operational for the start of Semester 1, 1999. It was not part of our Corporate, Quality Improvement or Capital Plan for 1998. So how did we establish an operation which required movement of staff physically and functionally, which needed space to be identified and new facilities built, and which cut across the responsibilities of several central administrative units, all schools and the then faculties? The answer lies in our planning and review processes. It also required someone with considerable authority to see an opportunity and seize upon it with some resolution.

From late 1996, our corporate planning documentation had been emphasizing the need for the University to establish processes to support the development of what we called a service culture. The review phase of our planning cycle in 1997–98 had shown that while there were some excellent examples of areas in the university modifying their practices to meet student needs, there was not enough sign of cultural change generally. A particular concern highlighted was the lack of cooperation between areas to address complex service issues. We had various projects in place and there was some progress, but it was incremental rather than transformational. What we needed was a breakthrough.

When the University's Council accepted my proposal for a major change to our structure and organization I knew I had three months when neither academic nor administrative heads were clear about the future because the restructuring was occurring. Thus they had little time or inclination to fight over modification to some aspects of their span of control. Our quality officer was an enthusiastic advocate of centralization of all services to students at one service point on each campus and, luckily, an excellent process manager. Our capital programme for 1998–99 was also capable of being reshaped, given that we had identified improvement of service to students as a priority in 1997 and 1998. However, it is my firm view that, for the intervention to succeed, it needed both the power of the CEO's position and acute judgement about what was possible. Nobody else could have redirected effort and resources so rapidly, decisively and holistically. An account of the introduction of Campus Central can be found in Schulz *et al* (1999).

Q. How far do you feel UniSA has come in realizing its goals?

A. There are two answers to this question.

First, not as far as we might have expected in late 1993 when we determined to work towards a more flexible learning environment with the learner rather than the teacher centre stage. The cost and complexity of implementing change in teaching technologies was much greater than we expected. However, the learning environment has been transformed. In late 2000 we have a universal online environment allowing all staff and students to enter and be successful in e-learning. Eight hundred subjects have online resources in place and 'Learning Connection' provides access to learning support for all students. Our focus has shifted from teaching to learning as we implement curriculum approaches that embed our agreed graduate qualities into our courses. Technological change has affected every aspect of the university's operations. We have found ourselves revisiting our budget distribution models, engaging in major shifts in resource allocation, restructuring the institution (several times) and constantly interrogating our approach to planning, review and quality improvement.

But second, further than we dreamt. As we teach overseas, offer virtual libraries to students in each of the University's divisions, go online, and systematically work to improve the learning environment for students through our integrated review, planning and budget allocation processes, we are living a future most of us would have thought was further away than it has proved to be.

Q. What skill sets do you see as necessary in CEOs and managers introducing or renewing flexible learning systems?

A. Resilience and persistence are vital if you want to change delivery methods and organizational cultures and practices. There is plenty of change rushing down at us and the trick is to change the university in ways that complement its mission and directions. That means you must understand how:

- Broad institutional directions can be achieved in the circumstances at any particular time.
- Who to trust when, on what, and how far.
- Specific technological advances may or may not meet the University's broad strategic intents.
- The job will never be finished – all improvement is the move towards something, not the achievement of the ideal!

Chapter 7

The University of the South Pacific: leading change in a multinational, multimodal university

Professor Rajesh Chandra, Deputy Vice-Chancellor of The University of the South Pacific (USP) describes the leadership issues facing a university owned and operated by 12 island nations and functioning across 33 million square kilometres of ocean, islands and atolls.

Q. How does The University of the South Pacific's multinational mandate affect the institutional leadership, priorities and strategies?

A. USP is one of only two universities in the world serving a geographic region comprising a number of island nations, the other being the University of the West Indies. Founded in 1968, USP is owned and operated by 12 member countries that largely financed it: Cook Islands, Fiji, Kiribati, Marshall Islands, Nauru, Niue, Solomon Islands, Tokelau, Tonga, Tuvalu and Vanuatu. Students from all of these countries attend the university and staff, campuses or University Centres are located in all of these countries and the multicultural nature of the staff and students give USP an exceptional character.

The governance of the university recognizes this regional nature and ownership in that the Council, the highest governing body, is made up primarily of representatives of the member countries. It includes five members nominated by the government of Fiji, two by the government of Samoa, and one each by the governments of the other 10 member countries. It also has two representatives of the donor governments, Australia and New Zealand, an appointee of the Privy Council, representatives of the associated Fiji School of Medicine and University of Papua New Guinea, the Pacific Islands Forum – the apex political and economic organization for the region – and the Pacific Community, and six co-opted members. Heads of other organizations in the Council of Regional Organizations of the Pacific attend as observers. The University's representatives are the Vice-Chancellor, Deputy Vice-Chancellor, three Pro Vice-Chancellors, four professorial and two elected academic staff, and three members of the Student Association. The Heads of Schools, Bursar, Director of University Extension and Director of Physical Facilities and Planning are in attendance. Council is presided over by a Pro-Chancellor, appointed by Council, who serves for a maximum of two consecutive three-year terms. It meets twice yearly, once at the USP Laucala campus in Suva, and once in another member country, each country hosting this in turn. Council has a number of Committees and Joint Committees, the most important being Finance and General Purposes.

The chief academic authority of the University lies in the Senate, which is also large, comprising USP's senior management, the heads of schools and departments, professoriate, University Librarian, Directors of Institutes, University Extension, and Centre for Enhancement of Learning and Teaching, two elected academic staff, and six Student Association representatives.

It is a basic requirement that the regional mandate be a prime consideration in setting priorities in the University's Strategic Plan, which we developed throughout 1998. We thought long and hard about how to produce this Plan, how to ensure that the needs and aspirations of the 12 member states and other stakeholders were fully considered. The answer was found in organizing national planning seminars in which the major stakeholders in each country and USP's senior management could openly discuss the human resource development needs of that country and its expectations of the university. We also organized seminars for our staff and students, who represent some of the best human resources in the region, to indicate how they saw the university's future. We then convened a regional consensus meeting to reach an agreement on what should finally feature in the Strategic Plan and through this, settled on the key priorities. Council then approved the Plan in October 1998, secure in the knowledge that the views and aspirations of all member countries had been taken into account.

The priorities we arrived at reflected the overriding multinational needs. We identified six academic areas for concerted future development: Agriculture, Marine Studies, Tourism, Teacher Training and Environmental Management and Sustainable Development and, overlaying all of these, Pacific Studies, which is expected to relate to all of our courses and activities.

The USP School of Agriculture located in the Alafua Campus in Western Samoa has very small student numbers, and is not strictly viable. However, it was planned to give this more support, partly because of the harm that would be caused by its closure, but also because agriculture still supports the largest component of the labour force of many member countries. Another indication of regional influence was the emphasis on environment and sustainable development. The Annual Communiqués of the South Pacific Forum have expressed major concerns over climate change and sea level rise and the university has responded to this in its future development plans. Another important feature of the Strategic Plan in response to need for equity and a fair distribution of educational benefits was the priority given to open and flexible learning, the development of the University Centres into mini-campuses, and the upgrading of the University's satellite-based telecommunication system.

Q. USP is multimodal, serving a vast area encompassing many different peoples and cultures. What challenges does this present and how does USP respond to these?

A. USP was founded in 1968 and has been offering distance education courses since the early 1970s. Distance students already comprise 43 per cent of our students and this share is set to increase sharply. The Strategic Plan projects the future of the University as a flexible, multimodal learning institution. Our main challenges are how to provide educational services to dispersed and isolated communities across an area more than three times the size of Europe with a total landmass equal to the area of Denmark; how to cater for the varying levels of educational development and need; how to cope with the different fee-paying capacities, language skills and human resource and management capabilities; and how to deal with the growing national aspirations for national postsecondary institutions.

Our response to the first of these challenges was to replace the limited, unreliable telecommunication system and dependency upon a number of providers that dated back to the 1970s with our own satellite-based USPNet 2000 system. This US$7 million system, launched in March 2000, is probably one of the most important strategic initiatives ever taken by our university. It provides more comprehensive, reliable, economic and integrated voice, data, telephony and video services for the whole USP system. We can now broadcast live interactive video lectures from our three campuses in Fiji, Vanuatu and Samoa to all of our University Centres, we can use our own videoconferencing system for tutorials, meetings and administrative support, and all of our campuses and Centres are connected continuously into the University's management information system. USPNet 2000 is achieving greater participation and sense of ownership among the non-Laucala campus sections and giving a major boost to distance learning. Audio tutorials are now compulsory for all courses and a few courses are already being taught by Internet and Intranet and being broadcast live.

The second major strategic initiative has been the further development of the University Centres. These now cover all 12 countries and they are all equipped to handle video broadcasts and videoconferencing and with computer and science laboratories.

The third major initiative has been better articulation of national postsecondary awards with those of the University. Senate has established a Committee on Accreditation specifically to promote this objective, to work closely with these national institutions, achieve a seamless system of postsecondary and higher education in the region and maximize returns to member countries' resources.

Q. What has been your role in these planning initiatives?

A. I have been deeply involved in all of these developments, both in my previous role as Director of Planning and Development and during my term as Deputy Vice-Chancellor. I worked closely with the Director of Planning and Development and Vice-Chancellor in establishing the approach to be taken in developing the Strategic Plan. I participated in the national planning seminars. I helped in the overall development of the Plan and wrote those sections of the Plan that were part of my portfolio, for example on staff development, quality management, research, and environment and sustainable development. I presented the draft Plan to staff to win over their support. And today, when we welcome our new students and the new staff at our twice-yearly induction programmes, even when the Vice-Chancellor is present, it is my task to speak about the Plan, to communicate USP's vision. I am also responsible to Council for the overall development of what we call Support Plans – the plans of schools, institutes and other sections and for areas such as quality management, flexible and distance learning, communications and information technology and staff development – in line with Council guidelines. We have developed 15 such Plans since October 1998.

In terms of on-campus teaching programmes, my role is to ensure that any new courses and programmes are developed in line with the Strategic Plan, and that there is academic and practical support for these. We have also pressed sections to review their current courses and programmes to see if some of these could be terminated in favour of newer programmes responding to emerging opportunities, especially in good governance, environment and sustainable development and information technology/information management systems. In terms of off-campus teaching, I chair the Distance Education Committee and as well as ensuring that the Flexible and Distance Learning Support Plan reflected fully what we had outlined in the Strategic Plan, I also made sure that this Plan detailed how we would implement our intentions, was output-oriented and contained measurable performance indicators.

Finally, it is my role to enhance the quality management system of the University beyond its current reliance on external advisers.

Q. What strategic planning and management processes have you found useful in establishing priorities, policies and procedures change?

A. One of the practices I find particularly useful is capturing the viewpoints of a range of stakeholders by soliciting reactions and contributions to position papers that I have prepared from those colleagues I have found to be progressive thinkers and knowledgeable on these matters. This is in addition to the circulation of these papers to the respective committees constituted by the University; I may also seek the concurrence of members and co-opt these individuals on to these committees. Being the chair of so many key committees is also helpful. I believe in being an engaged chairman, pursuing the agendas I am responsible for. I find that to be effective is to lead the process of change, to argue the case, to persist, and to network for the success of the ideas. This enables the committees to take a coherent approach and to situate policies within an overarching philosophy.

I also find it useful to broach the general approach of our initiatives with the USP University Grants Committee, to gain the benefit of getting their reactions early on. Sometimes the UGC adopts these ideas in its recommendations, which makes the task of implementation much easier; sometimes we use the backing of the UGC to promote the ideas in the various committees.

Universities consist of highly educated people who often feel that they have the right solutions. Many good ideas are defeated, not because the ideas themselves are not good, but because the staff members are unhappy at not being fully consulted. So it is important to spend time in discussion and consultation. However, it is also our experience that the average USP academic is neither change-oriented nor attuned to the need for student satisfaction and feedback from the labour market. In general, our staff are not yet fully aware of the global transformation of higher education and the consequent challenges to our relatively small institution.

Q. What theories, principles or experiences have helped shape your particular leadership style?

A. In my approaches to change management, I have benefited from an eclectic borrowing from the management literature, but particularly from Michael Fullan's (1993, 1999) writings.

My basic guiding principle is that a leader should drive the institution rather than mediate among competing positions, should proactively, constructively and energetically shape people's views, should work to develop the vision for the institution, work hard to win support for that vision, and work hard for its implementation. In taking such a position, there is always the danger that one might try to impose a vision or idea that is not shared by others or that might be totally inappropriate. I deal with this by ensuring that there is genuine dialogue before major ideas are put to committees and by being open to new ideas and suggestions during the discussions, particularly from key individuals whose commitment and judgement I respect. The experience of often having taken positions that were opposed and later being proved right has given me confidence to push for change, for particular measures.

I am also guided by the principle that we need to spend time to convince people about new policies and then communicate effectively to disseminate these policies. I regularly use e-mail to reach all staff, not just selective staff in management positions, to share position papers I have prepared or talks I have given. This allows me to foreshadow changes and elicit responses.

My experience as Head of the School of Social and Economic Development during the difficult and unsettled periods of the military coups of 1987 also shaped my leadership and management style. We had just returned from a Council meeting in Tonga the night before, and I had just settled down to work, when one of my staff came running, saying that there had been a military coup. There had never been a coup in the Pacific islands, and this was a completely new experience for us. In the wake of that coup, and the other that followed soon after that, there was unprecedented turbulence and uncertainty in Fiji. The military came onto the campus and shut down the telecommunications system we used for distance education. They also took some of our staff and beat them. There was an atmosphere of apprehension and fear. Our staff and former staff members in the School of Social and Economic Development had been at the forefront of the deposed government. To keep staff from leaving, and to keep the school and the University from undertaking any activities that might prompt the army to act against us even more, I spent a great deal of time counselling, cajoling and pleading with the staff. I also spent a lot of time with the Vice-Chancellor's management group, working out strategies to deal with the uncertain and unprecedented situation.

One of the severest challenges I had to deal with was the possible reaction of the many indigenous Fijian students and staff members. I believe that what helped me in the end was my steadfast adherence to the universal values of democracy and human rights and my unwillingness to accept racism or compromise on the issue of academic freedom. The fact that I had been teaching these students for a long time and had never been seen to take any political position, helped. I got no adverse reaction against me from students or staff. Finding that I had that ability to deal with uncertain and unprecedented situations gave me a lot of confidence in my subsequent management roles. I am also helped by the fact that I believe I have the trust of the staff.

Q. USP's teaching staff are a mix of regional and expatriate staff and tenure does not exist. Given these circumstances, how do you mobilize people for change?

A. These staffing factors undoubtedly present problems for the University. However, despite these, we have managed to introduce many innovations across the campuses and Centres, driving from the top where necessary, and we have managed to enlist or create groups who have assisted in:

- establishing the Centre for the Enhancement of Learning and Teaching in 1992;
- developing the Mission Statement in 1994;
- developing the Strategic Plan in 1998;
- developing 15 support plans by May 2000;
- introducing a staff appraisal scheme in 1997;
- gaining approval for teaching evaluation in 1998, to be applied from 2000;
- overhauling the performance management system in 1999;
- launching USPNet 2000 in March 2000 and the concept of multimodal, flexible learning;
- introducing a comprehensive system of staff development, including a formal system of staff induction, from 1997;
- introducing a Certificate and Diploma in Tertiary Teaching in 2000;
- establishing USP Solutions in 1998 as the entrepreneurial arm of the university.

An important change strategy has been the provision of leadership training highlighting the university's mission statement and strategic plan. These sessions have enabled our managers to move from a culture of system maintenance to a culture of change and innovation and have given them effective and up-to-date management and leadership tools.

Deployment of resources has also been an important change strategy. New resources are going into areas identified in the Strategic Plan and related innovations. All new courses and programmes are scrutinized from this perspective.

Our review of staff performance is now more focused and systematic and takes specific account of teaching quality. This has led staff to take teaching far more seriously. In terms of distance education, there is close monitoring of assignment turnaround times and the Director of University Extension is required to provide these data and comment on the staff review forms of all those teaching our distance students.

Another mechanism to promote acceptance of change and innovation has been the stance taken by the management that it is better for the university community to change on its own terms than to be changed in response to outside consultants, which is not uncommon in some universities. Our staff are now beginning to realize that we cannot maintain the status quo and that it would be better if they make an input to change.

The rotation system for Pro Vice-Chancellors has also helped, in that these staff go back to their sections after their two to three years in office, having seen the University from the perspective of the total institution and having experienced the pressures for change from the University Grants Committee and Council, and they often become change agents.

Q. How do you measure and reward quality in USP's distance teaching and support services?

A. USP aims to provide degree programmes comparable to those awarded by universities in the UK, Australia and New Zealand. Since its inception, it has used external advisers to assure academic quality. Each department has an external adviser, appointed by the External Advisers Committee for two-year terms. These external advisers, mostly eminent scholars from reputable universities in Australia, New Zealand and the United Kingdom, review the courses and programmes and report on these to the Vice-Chancellor. In terms of distance education, the course development cycle itself assures quality through the employment of competent course developers and editors. Staff are encouraged to work as teams and practise self-evaluation and review. The materials are again reviewed by external advisers. Quality in service delivery is measured by turnaround times of assignments and by randomly checking the extent and quality of comments on assignments. In addition, we undertake periodic reviews of distance education itself, to assist us in quality management and in our future planning. The latest of these reviews, held in 2000, was by an international team comprising experts from the UK Open University, International Extension College, and the University of Southern Queensland.

We are now planning to introduce a more comprehensive quality management system, one that goes beyond the use of external advisers, perhaps adopting a team approach and encompassing the entire University rather than just teaching and learning. We also plan to place more responsibility on sections for developing and maintaining quality management systems.

Rewarding staff for their performance is done primarily through contract renewal, incremental progression and promotion. There is explicit recognition of work in distance education and associated summer schools. The contributions of staff are also taken into account when sabbatical, conference and special leave are being considered.

Q. What lessons have you learnt about changing university teaching and learning and improving distance education?

A. First, and most importantly, that many academics are likely to challenge attempts to improve teaching and learning. I remember vividly the opposition of the staff when the creation of the Centre for the Enhancement of Learning and Teaching was mooted, and many staff did their best to discredit the emerging Centre. This emphasizes the need to have people in top management who can not only innovate but also persist in the face of opposition and expose the often tenuous arguments that are advanced to thwart innovation and change.

Secondly, that one needs to use a system of incentives and disincentives in this process. At USP, the three-year contracts have helped in that we can take account of these expectations during these reviews. Staff who demonstrate a clear inability to accept the university's core values either leave of their own accord, or do not have their contracts renewed. There are in fact very few non-renewals of contracts, but these do demonstrate to staff the importance of accepting the university's goals and policies.

In the case of technology, again, innovation has not always come from the practitioners. Some new technologies have been introduced through the encouragement and support of the University Grants Committee rather than the enthusiasm of staff members. However, patience with staff and robust training programmes can help to win staff over. We have to watch very closely the introduction of new technologies to ensure that staff do not simply introduce technologies that are personal to them and cannot be sustained if they leave. To assure sustainability, all new technologies have to be considered and accepted by departments and sections. We also monitor the utilization rate of these technologies – it is all too easy for investments to be under-utilized.

Q. What skill sets do you see as necessary in CEOs and senior managers faced with a need for change in higher education and, possibly, organizational and individual resistance?

A. The most important requirement for leaders in this situation is in fact not a skill but an inclination – acceptance of a proactive rather than a mere mediation role. CEOs should be prepared to scan the environment for emergent needs and trends and then push for change, energetically and persistently searching for the best solutions, not merely accepting those that are adequate or to hand. Major changes normally have to go through various external and internal bodies or committees – for example, in our case, through the University Grants Committee and Council respectively – so strong-networking skills are vitally important. CEOs also need to build teams committed to change and enthuse them. To help sustain the culture of change, CEOs and senior managers also need to have a broad understanding and appreciation of the required competencies. Staff are more likely to accept leaders' ideas if they can see that they are knowledgeable and genuinely interested in developing their capacities.

Given the rapidity of change and unexpected challenges facing universities worldwide, CEOs must be committed to continuous self-learning and reflection, keeping in touch with international trends, studying influential reports, attending conferences and networking. These stimulate new ideas and instil confidence. Universities, and especially the world of distance and flexible learning, are being transformed by developments in ICT. Success will be closely tied to the ability to come to grips with managing technology and a strong grounding in these areas will be essential in tomorrow's leaders. Finally, leaders must be able to communicate effectively, regularly and horizontally to all staff members, not simply vertically to management and administration. With the new technology, this is both fast and feasible.

Chapter 8

Alverno College: transforming the institution to an ability-based curriculum and flexible learning

Sister Joel Read, President of Alverno College since 1968, describes the circumstances, philosophy and events that have led to this US institution being internationally renowned for its on-campus flexible learning and ability-based curriculum.

Q. Alverno College was an early adopter of ability-based and flexible learning. How did this come about?

A. Since the early 1970s, we have worked to transform the liberal arts curriculum. Instead of assuming that abilities develop naturally as a by-product of mastery of subject matter, we explicitly teach students to develop abilities that facilitate the application of what they know and enable them to reflect upon and take responsibility for their learning. We have identified eight broad areas of ability that we believe characterize the liberally educated adult: communication, analysis, problem solving, valuing in decision-making, social interaction, global perspective taking, effective citizenship, and aesthetic responsiveness. We have specified six developmental levels for each ability and we describe these in behavioural terms so they can be taught and assessed across the curriculum. Both instruction and assessment in each discipline and area of professional studies employ a wide range of technologies – video, computers, internships, projects, collaborative learning, self-assessment protocols, presentations in multiple formats. Students become active participants in all technologies within two semesters. This approach has a long history.

Alverno College came about as a consequence of a 1948 merger of three incorporated institutions founded by the School Sisters of St Francis: a Teachers College, a Music College and a Nursing Programme. The educational philosophy of the Teachers College was expanded into the liberal arts and professions. This shift was significantly accelerated in the 1960s. We then had the women's movement with its emphasis on women choosing their own careers rather than those that society assigned them. Concurrently, the School Sisters of St Francis decided that any people wishing to join the congregation should already hold a baccalaureate degree. No longer required to educate prospective members for the congregation, the college was free to introduce a range of new majors attuned to the careers to which women were aspiring. There was also at that time a noticeable decline nationally in college entrance test scores (such as the Scholastic Aptitude Test) and some students entering the college lacked the academic rigour to which the faculty were accustomed. Faculty were also exercised by the Free Speech movement at Berkeley, the bombings at the University of Wisconsin, and the student takeovers at a number of universities. Our feeling was that these were due to a perceived gap between the students' classroom experience and street experience. Finally, we couldn't ignore technology. Computers were still the size of a room and the chip was not invented until 1973, but it was clear that the world of work would soon be re-wired and substantially different.

Our monthly staff discussions took note of these events. And because our staff were used to debating pedagogical questions in substantive and sophisticated ways, they sought solutions that would lead to the development of effective learners. The Alverno tradition highly valued and researched teaching. Years before Boyer's (1990) insightful book articulating a *scholarship of teaching*, we espoused that philosophy.

Q. What strategies did you use for such a transformation?

A. The changed mission initially lost us some 300 or so students. But having a new mission and, for the first time, a lay Board of Trustees, really liberated us and engendered a mood of optimism. Optimism does not of itself lead to solutions, but it creates a far better climate for analysis and decision-making than pessimism!

The new Board set about demanding data from which to forge solutions. I was the first President this new Board selected, so we partnered with the staff in shaping the new institution. Given the strengths of the staff, the Board was able to depend on them to bring forth recommendations on what kind of institution Alverno College should be. The Board, meanwhile, instructed me to make recommendations regarding the administrative structure of the College, which had formerly operated much as a family business, with family (ie, Congregation) members holding joint appointments. We had to establish an Admissions Office, a Development Office and a Marketing Office and structure or restructure various functions to take the College forward. We mounted an 'Alverno 76' Campaign, anticipating the build-up in public consciousness of the American Bi-centennial, and aiming to change the image of the institution from a school for nuns to a college for women, increase enrolments, and lay the groundwork for annual fund-raising to meet the increasing costs.

We accomplished the first of these goals through a brilliant series of full-page ads using striking photographs combined with text to promote the new kind of learning environment we were offering. These actually won an international award for the *Milwaukee Journal*.

This campaign led to some improvement in enrolment, but not significantly so. The real spike in enrolment came with the introduction of our Weekend College in 1977. Planned initially for 50 students, it attracted 250 enrolees in that very first year. Did they come because of the ability-based curriculum or for the convenience of the timeframe? Hands down, it was the timeframe. So we increased our enrolments by offering greater flexibility and aiming for a new market. We also increased our funding through significant grants received in support of the ability-based curriculum. The college became well known in the foundation world and various federal government-sponsored programmes and the attendant publicity of receiving grants has contributed to the image of the college as being at the cutting edge of educational theory and practice.

Q. What does it take to achieve such fundamental institutional and cultural change?

A. As I recall, there wasn't the body of change literature around at that time, nor a 'change language' – 'is this negotiable or non-negotiable?' – and so on. We had this sense of new beginnings, which was in itself exhilarating, but we had also a number of inherited problems. Problems are normal; they go with the turf. So, what does it take to achieve cultural change? The same as it takes to adopt on-campus open and flexible learning or an ability-based curriculum – will and perseverance and a senior administration that will help shape or find solutions, and then use them.

The dictum holds that 'the problem is in the process not the people', but it's equally true that it's often not the problem that is difficult, but people involved with it. What this says to me is that one needs to listen to what people are saying, hear what they are not saying, and try to understand what they are feeling. If it is necessary to change something, it will affect people. Leaders need to set an example by being open to things being done differently, and create or help to shape an environment in which different ways of doing things are accepted even if they're not always welcomed. The managerial lingo is that human capital is the most important aspect of any institution. That is so abstract and bloodless. There must be trust and respect that can only be built up through constant listening and hearing and the administration's 'batting average'. In other words, are the outcomes of the decisions positive for the institution? Are students enrolling? Are the fund drives succeeding? Are the staff receiving the benefits of such efforts? Are the facilities attended to and improved? Is the technology adequate or being updated? Are the policies and procedures simple and fair? Are the personnel consulted and involved in decisions related to their areas of responsibility? Do the people talk, consult and collaborate with each other, or is 'all the bowling done alone'?

Q. How do you help teachers joining Alverno from conventional institutions make such radical shifts in their teaching and learning?

A. We recognized from the beginning that staff would need to collaborate closely to implement the new curriculum, so we concentrated on providing faculty with structures to support ongoing discussion, refinement, implementation and assessment, to help staff reflect on their experiences and learn from each other what works and what doesn't. This was necessary for those staff who were there from the beginning and even more important for those who came after. Our staff development programme has explicit goals:

- constancy of purpose;
- focus on student learning;
- collaborative inquiry;
- commitment to continuous personal and professional development;
- measurement against explicit, meaningful standards;
- commitment to continuous improvement.

The built-in collaborative dimension is its most powerful aspect and contributes most directly in assisting new staff in assimilating the Alverno approach to education. The programme has two major components that offset the traditional, often isolated condition of teaching in higher education. First, the programme integrates the abilities requirement into the curriculum with a 'dual-matrix' structure. Staff hold joint appointments in an interdisciplinary department within an ability area, and in an academic department in their discipline. Each 'ability department' is responsible for refining and increasing its staff members' understanding of a particular ability, and oversees how it is taught and assessed across the college. We also make extensive use of a team approach that gives staff a sense of shared ownership and responsibility for the curriculum and offering the students the best possible combination of intellectual challenge and engagement.

Second, to provide opportunities for staff to meet regularly and exchange ideas, we have restructured the academic calendar to include significant blocks of time when all staff can attend 'college institutes', before the fall and spring semesters and after graduation. At these working sessions, faculty review and evaluate timely issues such as new approaches to teaching and advising, improvements in assessment theory and practice, and research findings and their implications for students. Friday afternoons are reserved for weekly meetings alternating between discipline and ability departments. Once or twice a semester, we hold all-college workshops on such topics as professional ethics and responsibilities, teaching for group problem solving, and questioning as an analytic technique for teachers and students. A two-day orientation workshop and special workshops throughout the year help new staff members incorporate the ability-based curriculum and performance assessment into their teaching and a seminar series addresses their special needs and provides a mentoring system. The Alverno 'culture of change' is sustained by this 'culture of collaboration'.

Q. What major opportunities and challenges do you now see for Alverno College and how do you plan to address these?

A. Our major opportunities almost always present themselves first as challenges. When the college changed its mission 30 years ago, we were challenged to find a new and appropriate infrastructure. Today, we need to realign or expand our departments to undertake new or expanded functions. Over the last 30 years, the Weekend College and efforts to foster international studies have led to increases in students enrolling from beyond Milwaukee and Wisconsin and, to some degree, from abroad. But in an increasingly globally interconnected world, geographic and cultural diversity should be a part of every student's education. Through technology, there are multiple ways of achieving this, although technology will never substitute for personal interaction. For Alverno College to break out of its local market and achieve a geographically diverse student body will require the reorganization of our Admissions Office and a new Division of Enrolment Management. We must also break out of our local donor base and develop a national base of friends built upon increased knowledge of Alverno's educational excellence. This will likewise require a reorganization of the division.

Students have begun acting like customers, and the student watchword for education has become 'quick, cheap, and easy'. Market-driven programming, including one-year baccalaureate degrees and distance learning programmes are changing student expectations for the bachelor's degree. The degree is presented primarily if not exclusively, as an economic advantage – the key to promotions and financial well-being. But for the development of an educated person, quick, cheap, and easy are not appropriate or effective strategies.

To best educate students in the 21st century, we must maintain and strengthen the coherence of Alverno's dynamic curriculum but ensure that the opportunities we provide our students are multiple, flexible and responsive to their present and future needs. This means we have to:

- Expand our understanding of the liberal arts and the professional majors as complementary parts of an integrated curriculum in order to serve our students better while resisting the national trend of narrowing of the majors, on one hand, and the lack of coherence in the first two years of undergraduate education, on the other.
- Design varied and coherent prior learning assessments that will enhance our curricular coherence while serving the needs of our highly mobile and older student population. In this regard, we also believe that we can make a contribution to the higher education community where credit hour rather than curriculum coherence determines transfer credit and prior learning considerations.
- Support staff in developing innovative distance education strategies. Our staff believe that distance learning opportunities coupled with student-centred teaching and learning principles have the potential to enhance the learning of a substantial portion of our adult students by providing the flexibility that they need to achieve outcomes they might otherwise be unable to achieve.
- Systematically integrate ICT across the entire College to support course delivery, administration and management.

Continuous staff development in ICT is a *sine qua non*. This, in itself, is a difficult leadership challenge. Assisting people to change their mindsets is always taxing.

Having to enter into a mode of continuous change because technology demands it is even more trying. But an equally difficult leadership challenge is the reconceptualization and reorganization necessary to make time available for staff to participate in such continuous education. Such changes require the acceleration of a leadership culture at all levels of the organization.

Q. What principles and experiences have shaped your leadership style?

A. In one's job, it's always difficult to separate who one is from what one does. My most fundamental principles stem from my religious beliefs and my family. In regard to shaping experiences, I expect problems and find them to be a normal part of life. In solving or resolving them, I always find it helpful to involve others. Ruminating about things alone is often akin to chasing one's tail. Talking with people with different perspectives enables you to gain new insights and see where a solution or resolution may be found. For that reason, I've always found management by walking around to be very helpful. I often offer to meet people in their own offices. I walk around campus a lot so that people can see me out there and know they're cared for. I keep my eyes 'wide/shut' – seeing or not seeing things as appropriate. I've learnt to wait until some things are brought to my attention, and that I don't have to take care of every problem immediately. Some situations are inherently capable of self-cure; others will not improve and are to be endured but ameliorated.

Experience has taught me that the excellent or the perfect may well be the enemy of the good. That's an important point in working with people (faculty, in particular) whose search for truth is always elusive. There is often a tendency to want to keep discussing, debating and deliberating until the thing is right or perfect. But that only prolongs the same base line of ignorance. There is a kind of knowledge that comes only by trying a different approach, to break out of that circularity. There is wisdom in the comment, 'one of the first principles of perseverance is to know when to stop persevering'. In my experience, perseverance is not a well-established virtue in higher education. It was once said of the Peace Corps that Africa is littered with two-year projects. So too is academe. So, experience has taught me that playing 'back-bone' to an effort is part of my presidential role, particularly if it's an institutional issue.

I believe in getting the process of decision-making as close to the level of the implementer as possible. That implies another operating principle – open administration. If we advocate open and flexible learning for our students, we must have an open and flexible learning environment for our staff. The late Robert K Greenleaf, of Servant-Leadership fame (http://www.greenleaf.org/), promulgates a philosophy which supports people who may or may not hold formal leadership positions but choose to serve first, and then lead as a way of expanding service to individuals and institutions. He has written that the measure of an institution is whether or not the people in it grow as a result of living and working in that institution. I believe this to be true and try to achieve this for Alverno College. But, I also assume that on any given day some 5 to 10 per cent of personnel and students have their noses out of joint about something. As Walt Whitman observed in *Leaves of Grass,* every success is the source of the next set of problems. Therefore, I see principles and pragmatism in permanent and enduring tension, which makes every day different, interesting, and worth facing.

Q. What leadership qualities do you look for and seek to develop in those who work with you?

A. I look for people with particular expertise in their chosen field or profession; highly developed communication skills; a track record as problem solvers; insightful perseverance; a love of and respect for people; the ability to see simultaneously 'the large' and 'the small' picture; the ability to 'wing-it' and take risks when necessary; and who see the daily surprises of the job as par for the course. I look for contrarians who have learnt to be team players; people who are good at taking individual as well as group institutional pulses. I look for people who can 'get to yes without saying no', people who accept human foibles as normal and understand how to deal with them and keep them from becoming more than they are.

I believe leaders today need more help than ever, so they need people who, working together, bring multiple perspectives to bear and who through both highly analytic as well as intuitive skills can enable the CEOs to keep on course by 'tacking with the wind' as necessary.

These are the leadership skills I expect in the people I hire. No one has all of these attributes but they can be developed by a climate of expectation that anticipates, supports and rewards such behaviours. Diana Trilling, in her 1983 editor's foreword to her husband Lionel Trilling's book *Speaking of Literature and Society,* published by Harcourt Brace Jovanovich, New York, wrote that what kept him writing even when he felt he couldn't was 'not the will of imposition (but) the will of freedom and individual affirmation, the will that mobilizes itself against all despotisms, even those of our own temperaments'. I think that sums up what every leader needs to understand and do. It's what I look for in others, and what I attempt to encourage and sustain in myself as well as in others.

Q. What else has sustained you in this leadership role over all these years?

A. Being involved in fundamentally important work. Having the opportunity to support and sustain the educational innovations of Alverno College on behalf of women, especially women who are minorities or the first in their families to obtain a degree, is the opportunity of a lifetime. Did this come without cost? Of course not! But the criticism that comes with change is all in a day's work.

The people I work with also sustain me. They are true colleagues who do not hesitate to tell me off when necessary. I also keep a permanent appointment with myself. This allows and assures me of daily moments of sanity and balance – a time to remind myself, as the scriptures note – that sufficient for the day is the evil thereof. In other words, don't add to it; instead find the fruitful solution that benefits the most people. That's not always easy, but a daily reminder of the obligation to do so does wonders for one's sense of balance and proportion. Problems shrink in importance and suddenly are more manageable than they seemed.

I learnt early on in life that paradoxically, to be truly passionate about something, to really believe deeply in something means that you'd willingly give it up, if its success required that. The work is greater than the individual. So one has to be involved and detached simultaneously. That's how I've been sustained over these 30 years. I don't need to be President but for as long as I accept the position, I need always to be searching for what appears to be best for the institution, based on the needs expressed by those whom the college serves.

I'm where the buck-passing stops but I'm not expected to be the source of all insights or connections the college needs. I am expected to assist the institution to be its most creative self by setting forth a clear and consistent picture of the changing reality of education and what I think it needs to become to serve the learner – the business we are in. But there is great wisdom in Lao Tzu's saying, 'When the leaders have led well, the people say we did it ourselves.'

Freeing people to become all they can become – students and staff – is one of the most exhilarating jobs one could have.

Q. What skill sets do you see as necessary in the CEOs and managers of the future?

A. If the pace of change continues to be as rapid or even more so in the future, I think one of the prime requirements will be tolerance to live with ambiguity even as one searches for clarity of direction. Such tolerance can only be sustained if one has a high degree of self-knowledge and is as free of self-deception as possible. That's why it's necessary to select co-workers who see themselves as one's peer and at times, mentor or conscience.

Given the enormous amounts of information that come across one's desk or at the click of a mouse, CEOs need insatiable curiosity but the ability to make connections with people who can rapidly digest and synthesize such information in ways that are useful. So the CEO of the future needs clarity on all dimensions of the business he or she is in and must factor that in, in selecting the personnel they work with. No person leads alone; either they marshal critical human resources well and lead as a team, or they fail.

Leaders must not only be able to assess their co-workers' strengths but their weaknesses. Knowing how to keep people's weaknesses from interfering with their strengths enables a manager to more quickly make use of and to heighten their best talents. To ignore weaknesses is to lessen a person's strengths, albeit unknowingly.

Leaders need highly developed communication skills. I believe that this is an ability that can be learnt. Fear of public speaking, like fear of flying, can be overcome. With time and space obliterated by technology, CEOs and managers need the improvisational skills of the actor.

They also need to be good time managers, not simply to be effective and productive, but for self-preservation. Every CEO or manager worth her or his salt needs to regularly set aside 15 minutes or so to reflect on what they are doing and why. Without a regular garnering of one's inner resources, one's job can eat one up. For the sake of the institution and oneself, I would say, be serene and check all challenges for opportunities.

Chapter 9

Leading and managing innovation in UK university contexts

Roger Lewis, formerly Professor of Learning Development at the University of Lincolnshire and Humberside and now Regional Consultant with the UK Higher Education Funding Council, discusses his experiences and views on leading and managing educational change in UK higher education.

Q. You have worked in the University of Lincolnshire and Humberside, a 'traditional' university moving into open learning, and before that, with three distance education institutions – the UK Open University, National Extension College and Open College. What differences have you found between these institutions?

A. I have always worked in 'development'. This implies innovation and an element of risk. But few jobs are totally developmental; there is almost always also a requirement for innovation to become part of ongoing activity, consolidated and/ or extended. Maintaining the balance is a constant challenge. The 'fizz' of the early days of a major venture tends to fade as it becomes established: the leadership and managerial challenge is then to keep the original vision alive or find a new or modified vision to re-focus energy and re-kindle creativity. I found this a challenge when I was working at the UK Open University as a staff tutor in arts in the 1970s and I suspect this is still an issue there.

Between 1980 and 1986 I was assistant director and then deputy director of the National Extension College, which runs correspondence courses, publishes learning materials and takes on specially-funded innovation projects. Prior to that I had been a part-time tutor and course writer for the College for 10 years. Under the leadership of Richard Freeman, its then director, the College balanced creativity with maintaining the mechanisms of a correspondence college and publisher. A group of innovators in course development, basic skills education and open learning had gathered around Richard's quiet but charismatic presence, and the organization's varied activities were held in successful tension through a shared vision and commitment.

Between 1986 and 1992 I worked at the UK Open College in a variety of capacities, including deputy director of student support and director of corporate services. The Open College was set up in 1987 to meet the skills gaps identified in UK industry. It was expected to attract individual adult students via broadcasting and multimedia packages. It was also expected to generate sufficient income to sustain its activity beyond a short initial period of government funding. This was a difficult mandate and, faced with the need to become self-financing, the College cultivated the corporate market: employers able to pay for customized training. It experienced the difficulties of many such ventures: an over-estimate of income, under-estimate of costs and acceptance of impossible targets in order to gain commissions and funding. It started with a great developmental thrust but then, as its start-up grant ran out, lost its way and nearly foundered. It remains to be seen whether the UK University for Industry (UfI), set up with similar aims to those of the Open College, will succeed where the College failed: in attracting a mass market and the resources to continue satisfying the needs of its students.

At the University of Lincolnshire and Humberside, a 'traditional' face-to-face teaching institution, the difficulties stemmed from uncertainty over its mission. In the early 1990s this fast-growing polytechnic was interested in entering distance education and in learning innovation. I was appointed inaugural BP Professor of Learning Development in 1992, a position partly funded through an endowment by British Petroleum and intended to stimulate and support new learning methods. Much development work was undertaken, but in a strategic vacuum. Senior managers never defined the core question of our activity. Was it to transform mainstream 'conventional' teaching? To build our capacity to handle overseas students via 'distance' learning? To improve the learning experience of existing on-campus students? To develop more cost-effective approaches to teaching? Clarifying these issues would have focused our innovative energy and the way we shaped the curriculum, learning materials and technology. As it was, we had this vacuum, and development was steered by short-term or hidden agendas and the ebb and flow of managerial manoeuvrings.

Q. Many 'conventional' UK universities are now adopting open and flexible learning. How do you feel they're going about this?

A. Distance education literature tends to refer to 'on-campus/conventional' and 'off-campus/distance' delivery as if these were two separate sets of activity. Such categorization constrains development. Witnessing the success of the Open University in reaching new markets, 'conventional' universities have over the past 10 years been trying to put into place 'distance' systems quite separate from their mainstream activity. This is inevitably costly and creates ghetto provision, with no creative interplay between two approaches to learning that should be feeding off each other.

Rather than starting with systems, we should be asking: what learner groups do we seek to reach and where and how will they wish to learn? The answers to these questions will help us determine which systems will best meet which learners' needs within available resource limits. Such analysis of learners invariably reveals that they are rarely at either end of the on-/off-campus spectrum. Hence the increasingly complex mix of methods used by the Open University and some 'dual-mode' or 'mixed-mode' universities. Most universities need to do far more to analyse their markets and develop technology applications, learning materials and tutoring systems that serve the learners wherever they may be on that spectrum. Many current developments in dual- or mixed-mode provision are opportunistic rather than strategic and piecemeal rather than systemic, and the challenges of new types of student, constrained funding and changing technology are leading universities to tinker with existing ways of doing things rather than completely rethink the learning environment. The situation was very different for the Open University – it was able to start afresh, with the student at the centre of its planning and operations.

Q. How do you see the role of senior management in such change?

A. Senior management support is vital to success in working for educational change. I referred earlier to Richard Freeman's leadership at the National Extension College. Richard was able to energize teams to work towards a vision. His credibility as a practitioner was also vital. Richard excelled in just about every aspect of open learning: defining new learning systems, developing courseware, tutoring, running workshops, and acting as a consultant.

The Open College's second CEO, Michael Colenso, also led through demon-strable expertise. Previously a consultant and trainer operating at a strategic level within major companies, he took over the College at a critical time and had to turn it around from certain disaster. He had an unusual mixture of 'hard' and 'soft' skills. He took tough business decisions, involving some loss of jobs, but at the same time he released a lot of energy and imagination to enable the Open College to move to its next stage. He also developed a number of new business management systems. One of these was appraisal, carried out every three months, linking performance to payment and providing all staff with training as appraisers and/or appraisees. This had a remarkable effect. It enabled fine-tuning of the business, permitting three-monthly steering. It guaranteed everyone high quality feedback and thereby created a corporate learning environment rare in my experience. It helped staff understand where they were – or were not – adding value. It helped them develop the skills they needed and it demonstrated the Open College's commitment to investing in this development. Some people left the organization, but more positively than would otherwise have been the case. Michael practised what he preached – his appraisals could take two to three hours and he was capable of recalling particular incidents with great vividness, to illustrate his feedback. As with Richard Freeman, as a leader he demonstrated excellence in areas central to the core business – in these cases, learning and development.

Q. You once described your educational development work as managing conflicts of expectations and remits. What did you mean by this and what lessons have you learnt from this?

A. There is always some degree of conflict inherent in educational innovation. This is professionally stretching and rewarding. Other kinds of conflict, such as the wearisome infighting which is seemingly endemic within organizations, simply drain energy. I am always reluctant to engage with colleagues who are motivated by political rather than educational objectives. When I do have to play this game I am usually unsuccessful: I recall losing a significant budget allocated to learning development to two deans of school, united in a tactical alliance against me. So I tend to eschew institutional politics, concentrating instead on delivering in defined areas and negotiating specific issues to enable innovations to proceed. For example, at the University of Lincolnshire and Humberside I led a team developing a skills and capabilities curriculum. I chose to do this because it was central to the University's mission and compatible with national and international trends. At the political level, I contented myself with managing the interface between the curriculum development teams and senior management, to ensure continuing funding and support. At the professional level, I concentrated on leading the teams, ensuring synergy between them and creating a curriculum that could be supported either on campus or via electronic means. It took five years to design and implement this framework (20 per cent of the undergraduate curriculum), including learning materials/technology and a tutorial system. The end product was externally evaluated and considered a leading example of the integration of skills into the curriculum.

Q. What other strategic planning and management processes have you found useful in helping institutions and faculties to change?

A. When I was at the University of Lincolnshire and Humberside, the vice-chancellor was known to have an interest in new learning technology and methods. My immediate colleagues and I saw the opportunity for a major strategic initiative and we drafted a discussion paper defining the attributes needed in our graduates and the learning environment needed to develop these. We gained informal support from the vice-chancellor and his team and the paper proceeded painlessly through the university's committee structure. The vice-chancellor thought, correctly, that formal committee endorsement was insufficient and that I should discuss the proposals, not only with academic departments but also with the library, computer and other learning support services and those responsible for quality assurance, planning, finance and marketing.

In all, we involved 337 people from 27 departments in 40 hours of intense and open discussion on the need for new forms of learning and teaching (Lewis, 1995a). There was much questioning and criticizing of the university's intentions. Some staff felt that in reality improving learning and teaching came a poor third to expansion and cost-effectiveness. They observed that the new learning environment would require considerable investment and that the university had hitherto failed to invest adequately even in the conventional teaching methods and systems. It was feared that the new learning environment might be just another way of cutting costs. Reactions to the proposals varied: a few staff were enthusiastic, a larger number wanted to believe it was possible but were sceptical, most were indifferent, and a significant minority was overtly hostile (Lewis, 1995b).

We realized that this did not augur well, given that these would be the very teams responsible for leading the students into the new learning environment. On reflection, we also realized that it had not been a good idea to begin in this way. So we tried another approach. A major report (UK Funding Councils, 1993) had just been released, outlining the changes needed to ensure that university libraries responded to the digital age. This report included vignettes of a day in the life of an undergraduate, an academic and a librarian in the year 2001. These spoke far more eloquently about the future than the rest of the report's measured discourse. So we conceived the idea of workshops to enable our colleagues to envision a day in the year 2000, at that time seven years into the future. We asked them to describe who their students would be, what they would be learning and how, what the physical environment would be like, how technology would feature, and what they and others would be doing to support learning. We had 60 staff working in curriculum teams, which included both academic and learning support staff, albeit all at the more enthusiastic end of the spectrum. It was interesting to observe how long it took the participants to get started – it always seems that academics are happier analysing and criticizing present arrangements than envisioning the future. Nevertheless, 23 lively scenarios were produced by these teams (Healey, 1995), there was a strong measure of agreement and the environment defined was realistic and achievable, given institutional commitment. This exercise gave us a strong basis on which to develop the resources, staff skills, student approaches, technology and curriculum needed to bring to fruition the envisioned learning environment.

A further piece of personal learning – subsequently reinforced by my observation of a wider range of UK universities – relates to implementation. It is all very well to have a strategy but an accompanying implementation plan is essential. We invited our sponsors, British Petroleum (BP), to set up an audit team to report on the University of Lincolnshire and Humberside New Learning Environment (NLE) initiative. This team searched in vain for an implementation plan and concluded that: 'staff have been given a vision but no implementation process. . . the university is not yet in a position to specify what has to be done, by whom and when. The NLE needs to move from strategy mode to project mode' (BP Audit Team, 1995). The audit team pointed out that in industry, when an organization wishes to achieve a particular goal it draws up a comprehensive plan, including monitorable targets, earmarks resources and responsibilities, and appoints a project manager to pull everything together. How often do we see this in education?

Q. You have observed elsewhere that the current climate in UK higher education is one of low trust and low energy. What should leaders do about this?

A. Although it is proving a more gradual process than might have been expected, the UK higher education institutions are increasingly taking a strategic view and seeking to transform the learning environment. This transformation demands not only new roles and skills sets in the academics but also the reorganization of academic support services. But the climate for such change is poor. Pay remains depressed. Academic staff in particular are wary of what they see as increased managerialism in the universities and bureaucratic and constraining quality assurance systems. Educational innovation demands time and effort and offers uncertain payback. And the innovating academic runs the risk of indifference or even hostility from his or her colleagues. So leaders need to consider the key ingredients for motivating staff in difficult circumstances.

Our colleagues like to see the results of their efforts – in contemporary language, the value they've added. And they like to see these endorsed by their peers, senior managers and students. Another motivating factor is the quality of the innovatory experience. This should be positive, warm and, though strenuous, should release energy. Teamwork and humour are also important. Broader 'human resources' issues also need to be considered. The process of change begins with recruitment: selecting the right people for the task. And without a clear vision, one cannot know what skills are needed in the appointees. Then there is the need for induction, not only at the general institutional level but also into particular departments and teams. This helps the newcomer, it helps their colleagues see what the newcomer has to offer and vice versa, and it makes it more likely that the unique and particular contribution of the new appointee will be released and applied.

Our colleagues need to negotiate the form their contributions to the organization should take and how these will be assessed. Individuals and their managers often need help in formulating appropriate targets for activity. Regular feedback on performance, both formal and informal, is as important for us as professionals as it is for our students. These processes should be opportunities to consolidate the views of different people, to address contradictions and to determine the best ways forward. In a good appraisal process, such as we had at the Open College, the manager becomes mentor. Not only does action need to be agreed on but also the support to be provided, including, but not limited to, 'staff development'. The UK's Investors in People scheme, which encourages organizations to 'invest' in the development of their employees, has promoted good practice in this regard.

Institutions are increasingly using part-time tutors. This leads to a further motivational problem: part-timers who mark assignments for students they never meet and according to criteria they cannot influence. Such staff may perceive their role as peripheral and may become disengaged and disenchanted. Managers should recognize, and take steps to address, the needs of this group – for example, by giving them some role in course design and review, and maintaining dialogue throughout the year.

Q. How do you think we should measure, assure and reward successes in university teaching and innovation?

A. We need to look at the two terms in this question: 'teaching' and 'innovation'. The first word needs to be broadened to 'teaching and learning': there is not necessarily a connection between the two – as our students often point out. We've moved in recent years from referring to 'teaching' to 'teaching and learning' and now, for example in documents published by the UK Funding Councils, to 'learning and teaching': an interesting and encouraging evolution in terminology!

Innovation is a word to pause over, too. According to the dictionary, it means to make changes in something established. It begins with, but goes beyond, invention: it implies testing out and then successfully exploiting new ideas or ways of working. In botany, an innovation is a newly formed shoot which hasn't completed its growth, with the older parts dying off behind. Hence the association of innovation with exposure, with being premature or being ahead of one's time. Commitment to innovation risks unpopularity because it involves the pain of change in what people do or how they do it, and it implies the possibility of failure and the death of some older practices. Hence the inevitable conflict referred to in the answer to an earlier question.

Innovation should thus be seen as a continuum, beginning with invention and moving through to translation into the mainstream. Rewards, including encouragement and support, need to be attached to each of these stages and yet, as a recent report comments: 'lack of recognition and rewards for innovation are still common issues in most HEIs' (HEFCE, 1999a: 1).

Following the Dearing Report into higher education (National Committee of Inquiry into Higher Education 1997), the national Institute for Learning and Teaching (ILT, http://www.ilt.ac.uk) has been established to define 'good teaching', to create in effect a national standard. The UK Funding Councils are also taking initiatives to raise the profile of learning and teaching and reward good practice. These relate to institutions as a whole – for example, requiring all universities to have a learning and teaching strategic plan; to subject communities – for example, setting up networks of subject centres to identify and disseminate good practice; and to individuals – for example, funding teaching fellowships administered by the ILT (HEFCE, 1999b). Such national activity is raising the status of learning and teaching and ensuring that all universities have in place arrangements to encourage and support excellent practice.

The universities themselves are also taking initiatives to promote good learning and teaching – for example, by creating promotion opportunities for outstanding teachers to parallel those open to researchers, introducing readerships, chairs, fellowships and other senior positions in learning and teaching, providing funds for innovation and support for conferences, planning seminars and publications to encourage and disseminate best practice in learning and teaching. Such activities inevitably stimulate further definition and achievement in excellence in teaching and there is a need to mirror these at the faculty and departmental level.

There are also national quality frameworks for learning and teaching. The Quality Assurance Agency in the United Kingdom regularly reviews subject provision in higher education and its criteria include curriculum design, assessment and feedback practices and the provision of learning resources. Opinions differ on the effectiveness of these reviews; their critics argue that they can easily become mechanistic, degenerate into paper chases and focus on regulation rather than enhancement, thereby stifling rather than fostering innovation. In addition there have been various attempts to establish standards and assure quality in open learning. These have included guidelines for delivery, such as *Ensuring Quality in Open Learning* (The Training Agency, nd) and frameworks to identify good practice in tutoring, materials writing and other performance. These frameworks have also provided an opportunity for individuals to gain certification (Lewis, 1993). The tendency more recently, however, has been to treat open learning as part of the broader activity of learning and teaching. In this, as in other senses, open learning has thus entered the mainstream.

Q. What do you see as the main challenges to universities in the new millennium and how should these guide strategic planning?

A. I see the main challenge as basing planning on the analysis of markets and the creation of learning environments to support the students in those markets. As I stressed earlier, planning needs to start with a vision, a vision that releases the energy of those who have to implement it and that builds on the strengths of the particular institution. Universities need to identify those markets where their strengths can be applied. Most universities remain unsophisticated in their approach to market analysis. The energy of academics goes into defining the curriculum, the content they would like to teach, rather than analysing their students, what they would like or need to learn, and the contexts in which they are studying.

Underlying this is the question of how universities view their students. Traditionally, students have been treated as passive, 'undergoing' the experience of higher education. We now tend to look upon students as customers or consumers whose needs must be satisfied. This is perhaps a step forward and universities still have far to go in becoming 'customer-friendly'. But this view of the student as customer is ultimately limiting; students should be regarded as participants, with responsibilities to play an active part in creating the environment in which they can learn (Fitzgerald, 1996).

Q. What do you see as the essential requirements in educational leaders confronted with the need to reform their institutions?

A. Two points can be made in conclusion. First, we need to focus on learning as the core activity of everyone in higher education. In this sense leaders need to be student-centred. This simple fact is nevertheless often ignored. Only last week in discussing major rebuilding in one of the UK's best-known universities, the senior managers were surprised at the suggestion that students should be consulted over this. And secondly, the learning the senior managers should focus on is not limited to the students: staff too need to learn. Fortunately, the conditions for learning are the same for both groups: clarity over objectives, rich feedback on performance, and a high level of involvement in decision-making.

Chapter 10

The University of Twente: leading and managing change via a Web-based course-management system

Professor Betty Collis, *Faculty of Educational Science and Technology and multidisciplinary Centre for Telematics and Information Technologies at the University of Twente in The Netherlands, discusses leadership in introducing flexible learning and telematics into European universities.*

Q. What do you see as driving traditional universities to introduce ICTs into on- and off-campus teaching?

A. The many interviews we have conducted with university decision-makers in Europe, North and South America, Australia, New Zealand, Japan, India, and South Africa (Collis and Moonen, 1999) reveal a shared sense of inevitability about using technology for new forms of educational delivery, in order to maintain existing markets or to gain new ones. We can summarize many of the responses as: 'You can't not do it.' Telematics applications, the term used in Europe to indicate the combination of information and communication technologies, most familiarly the Web, are seen by universities as a strategic tool.

We also find that economic motives underlie these telematics-based strategies: to find new cohorts of students because of dangerous drops in enrolment among traditional intake sources; to avoid the drain of students to competitors; or to regroup after forced reorganization due to reduced funding. Fisser (2000), analysing motives for telematics policy making in traditional universities, found a nearly even split between economic and social concerns (reaching the disadvantaged, offering re-entry possibilities and supporting lifelong learning). However, from our interviews, we conclude that the social concerns in turn relate to economic incentives: more students, more subsidies, and more funds. Also, universities are sensitive to their public image. Telematics adds to the modern cachet of the university; not doing so suggests falling behind, not leading in the information society. Such image aspects are nebulous but important in competing for students and regional, national and international positioning.

Our analysis shows that all traditional universities support some level of telematics for teaching and learning and public communications (institutional Web sites as an information portal and advertisement). But it is particularly interesting to note that despite the economic motivations, very little economic analysis has been carried out to investigate costs versus payback, short- or long-term.

As a final observation, we have found that policy makers generally assume that telematics applications will be used for the addition of some form of distance education. However, for pioneering instructors, the motivation is typically better teaching and learning for their current students, not necessarily those at a distance (unless distance learners are already part of their current loads). The considerable telematics development within traditional universities is not usually something evolving out of university policy but rather from grassroots initiatives in in-house courses. It is our observation that the bottom-up use of telematics in an institution provides a context conducive for a top-down strategy for telematics to develop, but that the motivations for the two may be quite different.

Q. You have worked with many European universities. What do you find are the critical issues in gaining staff and student commitment to telematics-based change?

A. Using technology in teaching for most instructors represents a major change in working, a change they may not be particularly interested in making. We have developed a '4-E Model' (Collis and Pals, 2000; Collis *et al*, 2000) as a framework for gaining staff commitment. This model says that the likelihood of instructors making use of a telematics application in their teaching is a function of four global variables: perception of educational effectiveness, ease of use, environmental conditions, and personal engagement.

Educational effectiveness includes expectations of improved learning by the students, improved outcomes for the institution, and improved circumstances for the staff. *Ease of use* refers to the time and learning curve involved in instructors learning to use the new hardware and software and applying these to tasks which are meaningful to them, accessing computers for preparation and teaching, accessing networks which are robust and reliable, and generally integrating telematics into the ways instructors and students work. *Environmental conditions* covers the institutional history of technology-change initiatives, the vision of senior management and the endorsement of key people to the proposed change, the educational and technological support within the institution, and the implement- ation strategies used in the change. *Personal engagement* relates to the subjective reaction of the individuals concerned to the change.

We have found that if we express each of these 4-Es by a standardized vector, and then consider the vector sum and its height in comparison to a normative value (obtained relative to scores of technology users; Collis *et al*, 2000), we have a simple-to-apply method to predict likelihood of use and to steer a change process (see also the Web site of the 4-E Model project, at http://projects.edte.utwente.nl/ 4emodel/new/). And this is the approach that we have used in our own faculty. Our recommendations for addressing the 4-Es are:

- *Educational effectiveness:* find arguments for technology-related change that are concrete, and set realizable and measurable targets; be explicit about the benefits to the institution and why these are important.
- *Ease of use:* provide adequate support staffing, computers and software and a user-friendly, flexible and expandable platform; commit to such a platform as soon as possible to develop a common frame of reference; subsidize at-home connectivity, so that staff can work and communicate with their students from their office or home; continually upgrade internal networks and servers.
- *Environmental issues:* provide funding and recognition for faculty, focusing on instructional issues rather than technology; ensure leadership, recognition, funding and personal engagement in the innovation by key figures in the institution.
- *Engagement:* involve as many stakeholders as possible in the consultation process; choose implementation strategies that respect and build upon instructors' concerns and current ways of teaching, facilitate initial engagement and success and acknowledge the users' limited time (and possibly interest); appoint a strong figure with experience and internal credibility to lead the implementation, and provide funding for this person to appoint his or her own support staff; reward and recognize participation by providing extra financial support, release time and other payoffs such as funding for conference attendance and incorporating such participation in staff evaluation and promotion procedures. These mechanisms are well within the control of institutional managers, but not often utilized.

This 4–E Model can also guide strategies for student acceptance. It should not be assumed that students automatically welcome change and the use of telematics. They are pragmatic and busy. They typically only want to engage in what is necessary to meet their course requirements, for example only using computer conferencing if it is a graded part of their coursework. And many distrust change, presuming there is a hidden agenda to reduce services, require more time than they had planned for, or force them to be more organized and public in their work.

With respect to leadership for planning telematics infrastructure and support, it is important to involve a range of well-informed people – and not necessarily use the head of computing services as chair. University computing services can be surprisingly conservative (change is for them, disruptive, especially when initiated by those outside computing services) and computing service managers are not necessarily implementation strategists or educational specialists. The priorities of educators and technologists can be quite different; however the determining voice should be the educators'.

There is a substantial literature base behind these recommendations, which we have reviewed in Collis (1998; 1999a) and Collis and Pals (2000).

Q. Encouraging whole faculties to adopt telematics in all courses is rare in traditional universities. But you've achieved this at the University of Twente. How have you managed this?

A. In the Faculty of Educational Science and Technology at Twente, we have successfully implemented a faculty-wide change process facilitated by a Web-based course-management teaching system called 'TeleTOP', which stands for Tele-Learning coupled with the initials of the Dutch name of our faculty. With this, we have integrated a new cohort of students – part-time adults, working and at a distance – with our regular students in virtually all of our courses and our master's courses for international students with our regular courses. And all of this has been accomplished in a remarkably short timeline by technology-change standards.

TeleTOP began in 1997–98. I became its leader, funding was provided to recruit five of our best recent graduates onto the TeleTOP team, an implementation plan and technical platform were developed, faculty cultural change was jump-started and all instructors of first-year courses were prepared in the use of TeleTOP. In 1998–99, we supported these instructors and their students, prepared all instructors of second-year courses, and, because of a university decision to change the curriculum, revised the content, length and representation of all the first-year courses in the TeleTOP system. In 1999–2000, we supported all these courses as well as many of the remainder, and prepared our international masters programmes for TeleTOP and our new teaching methodologies. In 2000, the university officially adopted TeleTOP as the course-management platform for the entire university and allotted a large sum of money for its implementation. In 2000–2001, we are moving more into a research role, leaving the implementation to others across the university. So in less than three years, we have achieved the institutionalization of our innovation; TeleTOP is now a mainstream operation.

Such speed, and such instructor acceptance, occurred, I believe, because we worked to our 4-E Model. Faculty management was clear on its educational goal and targets. Announcements were made in the national press and a public relations campaign was mounted to recruit working students to the new programme. Everyone teaching a first-year course had to participate as did the students regardless of physical location. Most innovatory projects begin with volunteers, hoping that a critical mass will emerge in time. We did not have time for this. Faculty management entrusted the TeleTOP team with the development of a technical platform that we believe is exemplary in its ease of use. Special funding enabled incoming students to receive a fully loaded, high-quality multimedia computer with writable CD-ROM, modem and ISDN capability. The idea is that students pay off these subsidies over four years but that each year, if they maintain reasonable grades, they do not have to pay back what they owe for that year. This may seem a costly incentive, but we calculated that it would pay for itself through less call for help desk support, less disruption at the beginning of courses, fewer technical problems and frustrations for the students, and a higher pass rate – all of which have proved true. Instructors are also subsidized for ISDN home connections, so they can work with TeleTOP whenever and wherever they like.

With respect to environmental conditions, the faculty's leadership supported the TeleTOP team and its leader/manager fully, not only in words, but also by their deeds, showing up at staff sessions and most importantly, using the system themselves. The Dean made efficient and creative use of the TeleTOP system in his own teaching and used his course as a demonstration tool. He came to know what the system and the new approach to teaching was all about, and this fed into his role as policy-leader.

The TeleTOP team developed an efficient and effective eight-point implementation strategy using a specially designed TeleTOP Decision Support Tool for the instructors (Collis and De Boer, 1999a; 1999b). This enabled each instructor to adapt and use the TeleTOP system according to his or her course and style and stimulate new ideas by showing colleagues what they were achieving with the system. The experience, credibility and personal characteristics of the TeleTOP team were also critical to the start-up and on-going implementation.

In summary, I believe the key factors for our success were having:

- clear and measurable change targets;
- consistent support by faculty leadership;
- a strong figure with institutional stature as the change leader;
- exemplary team implementation and spirit;
- a custom-built system, tailored for instructor control and ease of use;
- concern for all issues affecting implementation, not only the technology.

Q. What principles and strategies do you apply in your leadership role?

A. Several years ago, I co-conducted a study into the skills needed in change leadership in technology compared to those needed for managing an institutional technology support group (Collis and Moonen, 1994). Two points I believe are particularly important to my leadership style in both the change and management roles.

First is what I call my 'bi-polar approach': I try to combine research and practice, leadership and management and vision and implementation in my thinking and working. I'm concerned about how to make ideas work in practice. If I cannot see a feasible way of implementing an idea, I go back to see how to reconceptualize it – or even abandon it. This continual two-way process is, I believe, critical for success. Also, I've been extremely fortunate in working with a team who can also think in these bi-polar loops, often faster than me.

Second, I do not advocate anything I have not tried myself in Web-supported teaching and learning. I am the 'pioneer' for each new idea or version – in my own teaching, not just under laboratory conditions. When it comes to new ideas, I only preach what I have practised. It has been my observation that many leaders and managers of technology-related instructional initiatives in universities are not actually users of the technologies they promote. This is a serious deficiency in insight and credibility and in my opinion a major reason for the lack of mainstreaming of many initiatives.

Q. What qualities of leadership do you seek to develop in managers and in staff engaged in such change?

A. Flexibility and consistency, although these may seem also to be bi-polar. By flexibility, I mean we must be sensitive to new ideas or circumstances indicating new opportunities or variations, and how to interpret these so they can be incorporated into our current procedures and directions. We also need to be flexible in terms of time, usually in terms of finding more time to do something faster than one would think possible.

But consistency is also important. Senior managers and staff must not lose track of the key principles. We need to plan our implementation activities so that they are dependable and instructors know where to find help when they need it. We need to have things ready for when they are needed: new course sites, reports, feedback for our students, information in course sites, and so on. And we need to be confident of the support of our leaders, our team, our instructors and our technical support staff.

Combining flexibility and consistency is not always easy. We find that we need to keep our mainstream tasks and ideas flowing smoothly even as we respond to new possibilities. We use different project-management tools to help us in this, but it is often hard work being both stable service providers – being in the place where the instructors expect us to be when they have last-minute problems – and creative innovators. Also, those who have already changed do not want to quickly change again; sometimes our new ideas are more a cause for concern than a source of delight to our colleagues.

Q. Telematics seems to be a tool for collaboration among European universities. What has been the catalyst for this and what leadership challenges have arisen?

A. I have reflected quite a bit on this question, both in preparing an article I wrote on telematics-supported education in traditional European universities (Collis, 1999b) and in a study concerning international trends in ICT in higher education conducted for The Netherlands Ministry of Education, Culture and Science (Collis and van der Wende, 1999). We found that several factors push universities into participating in ICT-based learning consortia:

● Funding opportunities, particularly those of the European Union, which make inter-institutional collaboration a prerequisite.
● Complexity. Few universities have the in-house experience and skill to carry out TeleTOP-like projects. Sharing costs and resources, a consortium has more likelihood of achieving realizable change.
● Competition. In Europe, a number of institutions have formed consortia to gain a market and reputation in lifelong learning or other delivery or organizational innovations. It is hard for single institutions to compete against the combined institutional strengths of such consortia, and so they need to join, or form, one or more strategic alliances – the University of Twente participates in several.

Consortia thus have many motivations and synergistic interactions among their partners. Certainly they are key vehicles for university leaders to feel they are moving forward and improving the visibility of their institutions. However, consortia and other multi-partner special projects have some serious drawbacks in terms of real effect on practice. Studies in Australia, the UK, Belgium and other settings indicate that the results of projects are difficult to integrate into mainstream institutional practice. Special projects, such as those carried out within a consortium framework, are typically developed and organized by people other than deans and departmental heads. Alexander and McKenzie (1998), reviewing over 100 specially-funded projects involving telematics applications in Australian universities, many of which involved university–university or university–business partnerships, noted that 'in a surprisingly high number of cases' the issues that motivated the individual participant to become involved in a project were 'not always shared by their department or faculty. Very few projects were linked to departmental or faculty strategic plans, and this in many cases, appears to account for their lack of mainstream implementation' (1998: 250).

Because of this lack of diffusion, I believe there is more of a future for multi-partner collaboration within a shared discipline than there is for consortia that do not share a common discipline base. Discipline-specific collaboration can thrive across institutional boundaries if the deans and departmental heads are open to collaboration. One example in which the University of Twente is involved is the EUNICE Consortium, focused on European universities teaching information technology and telematics. Because of this shared interest, the partners have a common discussion topic and have recently succeeded in acquiring support from the EU to see how to use technology to better share instructional materials. TeleTOP will be one of the technical platforms in this sharing process. By contrast, the University of Twente is involved in several other consortia where the common link is less clear and here it is more difficult to actually arrive at collaborative activity that fits the procedures at the different universities involved.

Thus my advice to those in leadership roles in such multi-partner endeavours would be to see if the collaborative project can be translated into a direction that is meaningful in the home institution, and to involve as many of the key players in the home institution as possible. Otherwise, approach consortia initiatives as an interesting learning experience, good for network building and new experiences for junior researchers, but only give them as much time as can be justified by concrete institutional relevance.

Q. The EU has supported telematics innovation and collaboration. How useful is such regional and national government intervention?

A. The EU is in a position to facilitate, but not actually interfere in, education. Thus one of its major objectives for the support of telematics innovation is better contact among players in the different European countries. The telematics projects it has promoted are very useful in this sense. But in terms of pay-off in the local institutions, it is my impression that there has been much less success. In my experience, the major proportion of time spent on such projects is concerned with maintaining the project itself rather than grappling with the issues of implementing technology-based change in the institution. The procedural aspects can sometimes be quite overwhelming in terms of time and management, even years after a project's completion. The cost–benefit balance of such project participation is therefore often not favourable. Our report to our Ministry of Education (Collis and van der Wende, 1999: 96) recommended that regional and national governments should pay more attention to providing funding to 'stimulate implementation developments within institutions; not special projects involving multiple institutions but rather initiatives that are sustainable over time and within the ordinary procedures of the institution'. In making this recommendation, we challenged the general constraint in The Netherlands that funding for telematics innovation in higher education must involve at least two institutions. However, to date, this policy has not changed.

Q. What lessons have you learnt about costing and quality assurance in telematics applications?

A. Here I'll draw on the long-standing national and international research by my colleague Jef Moonen (Moonen, 1999; Moonen and Peters, 1999) some of which I have contributed to. He concludes that:

● Decisions made on the basis of cost-effectiveness of technology use are highly speculative. Accurate data are not available or cannot be disentangled.
● Costs are more appropriate to consider than effects, which are not only entangled with more than technology use but also typically long-term. Costs, especially those related to the time and strain on the instructor and institution, have a direct bearing on whether technology use continues.
● To contain costs, students need to become more involved as producers rather than consumers of learning resources. Students augmenting course material by finding up-to-date Web references and adding them to a course Web site is not only an interesting idea pedagogically, but a way to expand course material without cost to the institution (although student time should be regarded as a 'cost').
● The integration of support services – libraries, computing services, information services, and tutoring/counselling services – would reflect the convergence of tasks and technologies and provide a mechanism for costing control and quality assurance (Moonen, 1999: 87–8).

Q. What advice would you offer CEOs and senior managers of traditional universities on adopting telematics for learning?

A. I would say that telematics-based learning should be regarded as a new approach to make the learning process more flexible for all students, regardless of how much time they spend on campus. In my opinion, the term 'distance' is losing functional and organizational value in higher education. CEOs and senior managers in traditional universities need to be much more flexible in preparing for increasingly diverse learners and those who do not want a full programme or course, but a 'just-in-time' learning opportunity. It is mainly the operating procedures of the traditional universities that constrain this development; and these can and must be changed – by a profound mix of leadership and management skills and psychological and institutional insights.

Chapter 11

Washington State University: a US rural land-grant university responds to its changing environment

Dr Muriel Oaks, *Associate Vice-President for Extended University Services at Washington State University (WSU) in the United States, discusses leaders and staff responding to political, economic and demographic forces by changing from a single to a multicampus institution and embracing distance education.*

Q. How has Washington State University been able to establish itself as a national leader in telecommunications and distance learning?

A. Our changed or extended role resulted from a number of converging events. Internally these included a new institutional vision, a supportive institutional culture, and mid-level managers willing to work as part of cross-unit teams. These combined with external factors, including an emerging market of place-bound adult learners, new technologies to reach this audience, and increasing political and social pressures to respond to these new realities.

The two-way interactive microwave system WSU initiated in 1985 with 142 enrolments in 14 courses has grown to a state-wide broadband interconnection serving 7,000 students with 250 courses from our institution alone, with significant additional use by the state's public two- and four-year institutions. We've gone from being a single-campus institution serving almost exclusively traditional-age students to having three branch campuses in Spokane, Richland and Vancouver (WA) serving an older, more part-time population. We've established learning centres in 11 communities around the state, providing expanded access to WSU's distance education degree and non-credit training programmes. We've also come to provide six degree completion programmes (the last two years of a four-year baccalaureate degree) in a totally asynchronous manner and additional distance degree programmes using various synchronous methodologies.

Q. Could you expand on the political and demographic pressures that have impacted on WSU and how you've responded to these?

A. The political and economic condition of the state in the early 1980s was quite negative. The economy was weak and WSU had had to absorb significant funding cuts. Also, we had a narrow political support base, limited to the small number of legislators from the rural district immediately around our Pullman campus. As a primarily state-funded university, these conditions threatened our stability and funding base. However, our leaders recognized these conditions as opportunities for WSU, realizing that change is always more acceptable in a crisis situation. Our subsequent statewide expansion broadened and strengthened both our political and financial support.

The state's changing demographics was another key factor. Our main campus is in Pullman, a city of 25,000 population located in a rural part of the state, 300 miles from Seattle and the other major population centres on the west side of the state. We've always had a strong base of traditional-age students, but over the past 15 years the older population has become an increasingly important customer base for all of our higher education institutions. However, it was always a challenge to attract these older students because in order to attend our Pullman campus, they'd need to uproot their families and leave their jobs.

The demographics of Washington confirm that there are large numbers of people in the state who have started college, but have not completed a baccalaureate degree. In 1990, Washington ranked third nationally in the per capita enrolment in two-year postsecondary education programmes. Conversely, it ranked a dismal forty-ninth in the per capita enrolment in four-year degree programmes.

This disparity arises from the fact that Washington has a strong community and technical college system, with 32 campuses spread strategically around the state. Thus, it's relatively convenient for residents to complete the first two years of college. On the other hand, the state has only six public baccalaureate institutions, and only one of these is based in a highly urbanized location.

These political, economic and sociological conditions moved us to devise ways of taking our programmes to the people, rather than assuming they'd come to us in Pullman. We did this by developing branch campuses, through the two-way audio-video telecommunications system, and by establishing distance learning degree programmes and learning centres.

Q. What changes did WSU have to make organizationally to do this and how did you persuade faculty to accept these changes?

A. Organizationally, we moved from a single-campus system to a four-campus system within which our academic programmes were geographically dispersed but operationally within a single departmental structure. This is an unusual configuration for an American university and we modelled it on the cooperative extension and experiment station structure common to most land-grant colleges, and particularly their Colleges of Agriculture. This structure deploys faculty from single departments within various locations around the state. WSU's creativity was to apply this concept to the delivery of academic programmes from across the spectrum of its academic colleges and this has certainly positioned us well to meet our land-grant mission of providing for those previously denied educational opportunity.

Throughout planning for this change, we invited all faculty, staff and administrators from every academic and administrative unit to express their ideas, concerns and suggestions and all of this input was combined with our findings from a nationwide study of multicampus systems to develop a model that people were confident would work for WSU. Because of this broad input from the university community, we were able to initiate a workable system in a relatively short timeline.

As you'd expect, we've all learnt from our experience what works well and what doesn't and there've been modifications to our operations over time. But the basic model remains intact, the core being to keep academic departments in control of academic issues, even when the administration, faculty members and student support staff are in multiple locations. The major strength of this model is that WSU is able to offer degrees that don't distinguish between locations, with faculty charged to assure that the quality of all programmes remains the same, whether offered in a classroom in Pullman, at a campus in Richland, synchronously via videoconferencing, or asynchronously via the Internet.

Having successfully developed and implemented this 'one university, geographically dispersed' model, the transition to providing asynchronous degree completion programmes was probably easier for WSU than it might be for institutions that have retained more traditional approaches to educational delivery. Our faculty had already accepted the equivalence of courses offered at branch campuses and delivered through videoconferencing. Even so, developing the first programme wasn't easy when we broached the idea in 1990. The concept of distance learning was harder to sell at that time than it is today, when it's more universally understood and when so many successful programmes nationwide can be used as models. Our success came from a modification of the inclusionary model we'd used in our development of the multicampus system a few years earlier. The design committee for that inaugural programme was composed primarily of faculty, co-chaired by an associate dean and an administrator from the Extended Services (continuing and distance education) Unit. The goal was to develop a totally asynchronous degree completion programme that was of the same quality as our campus-based programmes and appeared the same on the diploma. The programme we developed with that faculty committee and initiated in 1992 has gone on to enjoy great success and has been used as a model for all the subsequent programmes we've developed at WSU.

Q. What other strategies have you used at WSU to achieve such a dramatic philosophical and organizational shift in such a relatively short time?

A. If success can be considered a strategy, then I'd cite achieving success as the most important of our strategies. The fact is that we've had a relatively flat rate of growth on the Pullman campus, while enrolment increases in the extended degrees (degrees from WSU extended to a state-wide and national customer base) and branch campuses have been much stronger. Those who initially feared that the new campuses, learning centres and distance education programmes would draw state funding away from Pullman have come to see that the reality has been just the opposite. By spreading our programmes around the state we've considerably broadened our legislative support, which in turn has resulted in increased funding state-wide for the entire system, including the Pullman campus.

Faculty were also initially concerned collectively about the quality of distance education programmes and individually about their ability to convert their courses to a technological delivery format. Our strategies here were to assure that the faculty themselves took ownership of the quality control issues, and to provide faculty training and a cadre of support personnel to help them with their course development and delivery.

We've also found inculcating a culture of inter-institutional collaboration to be an effective strategy. As state resources to higher education have declined, our institutions have begun working together rather than competing for state resources. For example, the baccalaureate and community colleges, together with the public school system, have made a successful joint request to the legislature that resulted in a US$42 million appropriation to expand the state's technology infrastructure for education.

Q. How does your university assure quality and measure and reward success?

A. Our institutional philosophy puts faculty in charge of quality regardless of how, where and when courses are delivered. Also, and here I summarize from the findings in WSU's recent accreditation process:

> Academic standards, faculty expectations of student performance and admission standards are the same for all programmes regardless of location or mode of study.
>
> All programmes delivered to the campuses or in distance mode undergo review and approval by the academic department, college, Faculty Senate, Board of Regents, and Washington Higher Education Coordinating Board.
>
> Regular, tenure-track faculty are utilized as much as possible to develop and deliver courses.
>
> The assessment plan for all programmes includes input regarding student performance outcomes, student and faculty satisfaction, and, where possible, employer satisfaction.
>
> Opportunities are provided for regular programme feedback to academic departments.

Faculty recognition and reward are seen as critically important, and most importantly, the inclusion of faculty effort in distance education as part of the regular tenure and promotion review process. We've found that the weight given in our review process to the faculty members' activities in developing and delivering distance courses, integrating technology into their teaching, and supporting non-traditional students has had a direct impact on the willingness of all faculty in that department to participate.

Now I would have to admit that at WSU, as with most institutions, the extent to which this is done varies across academic departments. But its inclusion is increasingly the norm as our department heads come to understand and appreciate the value of staff motivation and commitment in the distance learning programmes. We find that faculty members frequently use examples of their contributions to distance education courses as part of their teaching portfolios, which they're required to assemble for the purposes of tenure and promotion. Faculty also publish articles about their distance teaching experiences, and a number of our colleagues are involved in research projects on the impact of technology on student performance. Several faculty members have been nominated for local and national teaching awards as a result of their successes in distance education, and we always make sure that such awards are widely publicized. Some of these staff have subsequently been invited to discuss their experiences at state and national conferences, further enhancing the impact of the awards and nominations.

Q. How important do you find the support of your leaders – for example, the Board of Regents and the President – in achieving the kinds of change you've described?

A. I'd have to say that the support of our top university leadership has been absolutely critical to getting others within the academy to regard these activities as important and we've been fortunate to have had such support at WSU. The importance of this was brought home strongly to me when carrying out some research in 1988. I visited a number of institutions with the aim of identifying the factors critical to the successful adoption and maintenance of telecommunications-based degree programmes. My hypothesis was that the administrative structures would be the most important factor, and that some structures would be more conducive to success than others. What I found was that it mattered very little what the administrative structure was, how talented the programme administrators were, or even what technology was available. What mattered most was how supportive the central administration was. I've never forgotten that.

One of the critical leadership challenges we've had to face at WSU over the past 15 years has been gaining and maintaining adequate state support for our institution. As I mentioned earlier, our success in developing and delivering degree programmes state-wide has resulted in a broadening of our legislative support and increased funding for all aspects of our multicampus system. From a base of three local legislators in 1985, we now have 66 who have a major part of WSU within their districts. So an important aspect of leadership is the capacity to gain external political support for and through new initiatives as well as the internal political support.

Another critical leadership issue has been the willingness of the WSU senior management to take a financial risk in initiating new systems and alternative programmes. Because they recognized the importance of these programmes to the institution's future, our leaders were willing to let new programmes like our initial extended degree programme and our interactive video system to initially run at a loss. Such risk-taking, allowing new ventures time to become accepted and educationally and financially successful, has made a big difference in our ability to become a leader in distance education.

Q. Are there particular strategic planning or strategic management processes you've found useful in helping your managers and faculty understand the need for change?

A. First, it was important to build and communicate our understanding of the external politics, pressures and demand for higher education services delivered at a distance. We needed to know more about the emerging programmes and actions of other leading universities across the country and we needed to share this with our colleagues. To accomplish this, we joined other institutions as members of organizations and consortia exploring distance learning, for example, the National Universities Degree Consortium, National University Telecommunication Network and Mind Extension University. We found it very important to communicate intelligence to the campus on what other major universities were doing and we certainly found that our ideas gained credibility when we could say knowledgeably: 'Here's what Maryland, Colorado State or other respected institutions are planning to do.'

Our second strategy has been to build an awareness among faculty of the educational needs of the distance education students and that the numbers were significant. We found it important to put a real face, with real human stories and successes, into the planning structure. We did this by using our extended degree students as advocates. The average age of these students is 37, and most are combining their studies with working full- or part-time. They're most articulate in speaking about their needs and the value of our distance programmes in meeting those needs. We've used their testimony – in person, on video, in teleconferences and in print – to communicate with faculty, legislators, or anyone else who needs to know, just how important it is to look at new ways of meeting the needs of these adult learners.

Our third strategy has been building strategic alliances within our state and nationally. For example, we've worked with the state's community colleges to develop articulation agreements and 2+2 programmes (articulated degree programmes in which the community college provides the first two years) to meet the needs of specific groups of students. We've subsequently worked together to promote these programmes, not only to potential students, but also to the faculty who will serve them and to the administrators and legislators who will support them.

Our fourth strategy, and this has been most critical, has been to build a collaborative working culture. We've made presentations at orientation sessions for new faculty, to the Faculty Senate, to various Senate committees, and to the Board of Regents about our distance education programmes. We've explained the value of the state-wide investment WSU has made in technology and we've described the various ways in which the administrative infrastructure, learning centres and branch campuses can and must support these students. We've also worked hard to develop alliances with other WSU administrative units to address the unique needs of adult learners. Extended University Services (EUS) has assigned staff members as liaison persons with other non-academic and/or academic units to promote communication and a team response to problem solving. For example, we have a staff member who spends part of every week in the Admissions Office, helping to facilitate the admissions process for students in our distance degree programmes.

And finally, from the initiation of the first asynchronous degree programme in 1992, we've had an Academic Advisory Committee, consisting of associate deans, department chairs and faculty from each college offering degrees overseeing all academic aspects of WSU's distance degrees.

Q. What qualities of leadership do you look for in those you work with in pursuit of innovation and quality in distance learning?

A. Our leaders need to have vision. We need people in charge who can see the 'big picture' and describe this to others in a language they can understand and in ways that inspire them to get on board and contribute. Leaders in pursuit of innovation and quality have to be more than just administrators – they have to be advocates and they have to show a passion for open learning. People respond to passion.

Those of us who've been involved in WSU's distance education programmes know just what a difference these programmes can make in improving our students' lives, and we've been committed to their success from the beginning. Our zeal helped win initial approval for our first programmes from sceptical state officials, and our enthusiasm continues as we improve and expand our offerings and services.

Open learning requires open minds. We won't succeed in the future with what we've done in the past, and we all need to keep our minds open to new ideas, to new approaches to learning, and to new target groups for our programmes.

Q. What principles and experiences have helped shape your style of leadership and what advice would you offer university leaders and managers in regard to integrating distance learning and technology into campus-based institutions?

A. Several principles have shaped my style of leadership, and I've mentioned these previously. One is that results work. We worked hard to make our first courses a success, because we recognized that it was those pioneering faculty who would persuade their colleagues to get involved. And we involved our inaugural students in selling the programme to others. This principle applies to so many things. Even when your first effort isn't totally successful, you can build on those aspects that worked, and take lessons from those that didn't.

Second is to keep academics in charge of the academics. In an institution like WSU, where distance education programmes are part of the basic mission and integrated into the goals of the colleges, faculty 'buy-in' comes through the academic units taking responsibility for the design and the quality of the programmes. Our role in EUS is to be supportive – we help with the needs assessment, with modifying the programmes for distance delivery, with providing support services to the distance students and with marketing the programmes. But we make it clear that the academic units and Faculty Senate are in charge of the curriculum and policy issues. Working at WSU has also helped me realize the value of cross-unit teamwork. Much of the success we've enjoyed in EUS is the result of working closely with other units and avoiding a natural tendency to maintain administrative control and become an autonomous unit. By providing staff liaisons to administrative offices, by working on course development teams with staff from the Center for Teaching, Learning and Technology, and by sharing equipment and staff with the university's telecommunications unit, we've been able to accomplish our goals in a more efficient, effective and collaborative manner.

I recognize that each institution's culture is somewhat unique, and that senior managers have to develop leadership styles that fit their particular institution. On the other hand, each of us can influence those around us, and so all of us have to take responsibility for moving our institutions towards the best possible future.

Q. What skill sets do you see as necessary in our future educational leaders?

A. It's certainly no exaggeration to say that those of us in higher education face a considerable challenge in the competitive environment of the future. I can identify a number of skills that will be crucial.

Our leaders need to be able to identify emerging political, social and economic trends and support their institutions in addressing these trends. In other words, they need to be visionary. We were fortunate at WSU to have a president, Dr Samuel H Smith, who provided just this kind of visionary leadership when he came to the institution in 1985. His vision for the institution, honed by his years as a faculty member and administrator in land-grant institutions and his early awareness of demographic and political changes in the state, helped move WSU in new directions.

However, good leaders need more than just a vision for what needs to change. They also need to possess the skills to persuade others to move with them in a new direction. They need to be able to influence, lobby, negotiate and bargain as necessary to get support to actualize the vision. Our success has largely been built on our skills in convincing others of the value of distance learning.

The persuasive power of leaders is dependent on a related skill, that of developing a network of effective relationships. The trend we've seen in Washington of an increase in institutional partnerships and consortia is being echoed worldwide. The higher education leaders of the future will need to be able not only to develop working relationships within the academy, but beyond, forging connections to business, government and any other agencies that can support their programmes.

Leaders also need to have the ability, and the willingness, to take risks. The ways we've worked in the past won't necessarily guarantee success in the future as we face new customers, new competition, and a decrease in our traditional financial base. Our leaders will need to be open to offering different kinds of programmes, working with a broader range of partners, and investing in new ventures.

Finally, I'll reiterate the point I made earlier – that leaders need passion. We need to really believe in the value of our distance learning programmes and to articulate this passion to others, to persuade them to share our vision and to rally their support in making our preferred future a reality.

Chapter 12

Western Governors University: a competency-based virtual university

Robert C Albrecht, *Former Vice-President for Academic Affairs and Chancellor Emeritus, Western Governors University (WGU), discusses the inception and development of this unique US institution, and contrasts WGU's philosophy and operations with those of the more traditional universities.*

Q. WGU was proposed in 1995. You were named as its first chief academic officer in 1996, and later became its first chancellor in 1998. What led to the creation of WGU, what was the initial vision, and how was this articulated?

A. At a meeting of the Western Governors Association (an organization of the governors of the Western United States) in 1995 the Governors discussed those aspects of higher education that they believed to be of particular concern, including rising college tuition costs, declining state monies available for higher education, the lack of funds to build new campuses, and the growing numbers of learners that couldn't be accommodated in public institutions. Governor Michael Leavitt of Utah led these discussions around the issues of cost, budget allocation and bricks-and-mortar capacity; Governor Roy Romer of Colorado argued for the reform of the system of seat-time, student credit hours. Romer suggested that an institution based on competency would revolutionize higher education, making it more responsive to the marketplace and more attractive to students. The Governors agreed on the need for a new educational institution and in November appointed a design team to report by June 1996, meeting to create a virtual university that would address many of the issues discussed.

The subsequent report, 'From Vision to Reality: A Western Virtual University', included 11 criteria for the new institution. These criteria express the rationale behind the basic concept and the purposes. The new institution would be:

Market-oriented	Non-teaching
Independent	High quality
Client-centred	Cost-effective

Degree-granting	Regional
Accredited	Quickly-initiated
Competency-based	

It would be a non-profit institution supported initially by private funds. Since it would have no teaching faculty and offer no courses of its own, it would rely upon the courses offered by 'provider institutions'. WGU students who needed coursework to acquire the competencies required by the curricula would receive that instruction from the offerings of those providers. The complex design and implementation plan for what came to be called Western Governors University, was produced for the Governors primarily by two organizations, the National Center for Higher Education Management Systems and the Western Cooperative for Educational Telecommunications, a division of the Western Interstate Commission on Higher Education. These two organizations provided a variety of planning and consulting services to colleges and universities; the latter focused on assisting universities in delivering educational programmes at a distance. My own role was implementing an academic design adopted by the Governors. I was especially interested in the possibilities for extending learning to new audiences that were not served by traditional institutions. The virtual university offered a 'location' where learners could be credentialed for the skills and knowledge they possessed, whether that learning was acquired in the classroom, the workplace, the library or via the Web.

Q. *WGU is organized around a revolutionary competency-based curriculum. What was the impetus for this and do you believe such a curriculum will become more commonplace in US universities?*

A. WGU's competency-based degrees are built upon curricula designed by Programme Councils comprised of respected faculty members (from other institutions) who determine the competencies a student must demonstrate in order to earn a degree. These faculty members (accompanied by other professionals for some degrees) are drawn from those who teach in the discipline. The Council agrees upon the requirements for the degree in the same way faculty members discuss the course requirements in a traditional setting. For example, members of the WGU Associate of Arts Programme Council agreed upon the inclusion of a composition (writing) requirement and on the specific competencies required of each student.

Each WGU student enrolled in a degree programme must demonstrate through individual assessments the competencies required. The assessment instruments are chosen by the Programme Council that designs the degree and the Assessment Council, a group of measurement professionals. The assessments are reviewed for validity and reliability as well as for their appropriateness to the WGU requirements.

The time, place and source of the student's learning are irrelevant to the process. WGU does not offer courses, and courses taken in traditional universities are valuable only to the extent that they help the student demonstrate the competencies specified for the WGU degree. Where the student acquired the learning, when they acquired it and the identity of the educational source is not relevant to awarding WGU's degree. The portability of learning is a recognized principle for WGU. The WGU transcript records the assessments of the students, not the learning experience.

Competency-based degree programmes are similar to a variety of degree and licensing structures that require students to demonstrate their knowledge and expertise and/or the outcomes of their studies. For example, nurses must pass licensure exams before receiving their professional credentials. The emphasis on competency, on outcomes, on what the student can actually demonstrate, is common among professions.

Much of the impetus for organizing the WGU curriculum came from the discussions among the Governors who initiated WGU. The university serves students who are unable to attend classes in traditional campus settings and who have acquired competencies through work experience or through prior academic experience. To diminish the time required to earn a degree, the design avoids the unnecessary repetition of academic experience. If a student has the maths skills required in the curriculum, he or she should not be required to repeat a learning experience. Incidentally, the well-known Advanced Placement Programme of the College Board is a very successful version of a competency-based programme. Students in this programme earn college credit through examination and are not required to complete a particular course before taking the AP exams. Having been involved in the AP programme in English literature for many years, I found competency-based structures a viable alternative to the traditional learning models.

The increased emphasis on outcomes in accreditation procedures and elsewhere, including the workplace, suggests a growing realization that we can't measure learning through 'input', or 'seat time'. Governor Romer often tells of his experience as a flight instructor, remarking that no student could be licensed as a pilot until he had flown a plane. The number of hours spent studying the various requirements for flying a plane is finally irrelevant if one can't fly the plane.

Will competency-based degrees become more commonplace? The increased numbers of learners in outcomes-based or performance-based programmes suggest a major shift. Many corporate training and education programmes, including such leading programmes as that of Andersen Consulting, rest upon outcomes-based learning. Few new programmes replicate the seat-based education programmes. A number of states have moved towards performance-based programmes in K–12. University of Maryland Chancellor Langenberg wrote in the *Chronicle of Higher Education* that K–12 is rapidly moving towards performance-based education while higher education remains tied to the seat-based model. Accrediting associations are also moving from input to outcomes criteria in assessing institutional quality.

Q. WGU has developed a number of critical relationships with large corporations such as Cisco, Microsoft and Sun. What are the benefits and risks of such partnerships and what are the lessons for others?

A. Corporate participation in WGU began very early as representatives of that sector sat with the Governors in their meetings of 1995 and 1996. Having corporate representatives on the National Advisory Board and the Board of Trustees provides better and faster communication with the corporate segment. Since WGU has a particular mission to serve the needs of that community and its employees, the connection has been essential. The relationships with the corporate community, like other partnerships, hold risks. The common risk in any relationship – corporate, educational, profit or non-profit – is the loss of control to the partner. Universities have often feared such relationships as a threat to their autonomy, fiscal responsibility, or academic freedom. Rather than being such a threat, the corporate partners have been quick to insist that WGU become a respected academic institution in order to meet the expectations of the corporations as well as the academic peers. Their continued interests rest upon the promise of education for employees, better understanding of the potential of distance learning, communication within industry, and the opportunity to influence distance learning and its direction.

What, then, can be learnt from the relationships WGU has developed? These relationships have provided models for other institutions. WGU's academic programmes have been formulated with the help of corporate participants to advance students in their careers, and the long-term plan is to provide information from students and employers on the efficacy of those programmes. The Assessment Council regards the measurement of student success in employment as part of their charge in designing the evaluation of student outcomes. Certainly as a private institution, WGU relied heavily upon corporate support for funds to begin. And early attempts at collaboration did not always succeed; for example, WGU was unable to mount programmes quickly enough to meet corporate needs.

Few corporations want to be in the learning business, as it is called, but many want to collaborate in shaping the programmes that help their employees. There are risks on both sides. Learning institutions need to be independent of the corporate winds of change, and corporations must recognize that need for academic independence. Corporate participation in educational and research programmes in universities has been growing very rapidly in recent years; the WGU partnerships are simply one aspect of that development. WGU's collaboration with Micron and with Microsoft, for example, has resulted in strong academic programmes that provide workers to the industry.

Q. What have been the most significant challenges faced by WGU and what challenges does it face in the longer term?

A. In 1995, the year WGU was initiated, the state of distance learning and its acceptance differed considerably from what it has become in just a few years. Online learning was uncommon; distance learning was often confined to divisions of continuing education; computers in the home were less common; older students were thought to be resistant to using the computer; and virtual universities were unknown.

A primary challenge for WGU was to become known and accepted within an academic community unfamiliar with what this innovative university offered, how it worked, and what it proposed to do. Until WGU achieved some recognition within that community it couldn't successfully reach students, faculty and institutions, or be accredited. The institution needed credibility within higher education for acceptance, enrolments, transfer articulation, accreditation and provider contracts. Of course acceptance of competency-based credentials (portability) is also necessary in the consumer marketplace, among both students and employers. Another challenge was the implementation of a very complex design including an electronic catalogue of courses, programmes and services, a competency-based curriculum, an accompanying set of assessments, a marketing plan and a realistic business plan. Finally, the institution needed to find ways of appealing to and recruiting consumers unfamiliar with online learning and competency-based credentials.

Thinking back to its origins, we may have relied too heavily on university models in the early months; certainly the need to recognize the importance of e-commerce models for the business of the university came slowly. In 1996 building the electronic catalogue seemed critical; only later did an off-the-shelf solution seem wiser. Developing partnerships with other educational institutions has been more difficult than anticipated. These challenges, while simply stated, represent some of the major obstacles of the first period of WGU's history.

For WGU the market niche of competency-based credentialing has been clearly defined, but that has not been widely accepted by the learning public. Corporate training and corporate education have increasingly recognized outcomes-based learning and performance-based learning, and traditional education recognizes a variation of this principle in the licensure of students. The distinctions among these labels are also not widely accepted or understood.

Q. Many universities and colleges provide courses that are 'mapped' to WGU's competency-based degrees. What barriers or challenges did you encounter in establishing these relationships and how were some of these overcome?

A. Accreditation, state licensing, tuition, student credit hours, transfer policies and traditional views of faculty functions constituted some of the policy barriers to establishing WGU and marketing its programmes to students. Among the early challenges was the construction of the 'Smart Catalog', which was intended to be a portal to distance learning delivered by any means. Teaming with universities to provide the offerings listed there and to offer courses 'mapped' or matched to the WGU-required competencies became significant hurdles. Partnering with universities to accomplish this required working with administrators at several levels as well as with the faculty members offering the 'mapped courses'. In the early months, even the number of available courses offered online, for example, were significantly fewer than we expected. Eventually WGU actively recruited selected institutions and worked with their faculty to 'map' courses to competencies.

Although WGU has from its inception been reliant upon the traditional institutions for courses for its students and for many services from their faculty, concerns surfaced almost immediately over competition for students. The traditional public institution is funded by state government according to the number of students it enrols; hence, the creation of an apparent competitor for those students is a threat to the existence and well-being of the public college. Although WGU was founded to serve students who could not attend traditional residential institutions, some perceived it as a threat to their own enrolments. Articulation agreements and other collaborative efforts are diminishing those issues. For any new institution, accreditation represents a significant barrier; WGU has successfully moved through the traditional process of regional accreditation with IRAC, the Inter-Regional Accrediting Committee, and has been awarded the status of candidacy.

Several changes have reduced participation barriers for the institution and its students. WGU moved to a model of revenue sharing in which the tuition revenue was split between WGU and the provider institution. Articulation agreements have been signed with a number of institutions.

Q. Are there particular strategic planning or strategic management processes you've found useful to help leaders and faculty understand the mission, goals, structure and operations of WGU, change work cultures and motivate institutions to work with you?

A. Early in the history of WGU, the meetings with pilot institutions, essentially one from each of the participating states and two corporate providers, facilitated ties with partners that led to significant exchanges on the design and implementation of WGU. However, we soon learnt that the divisions (and their leaders) within the institutions had to be dealt with directly. While decentralization within universities and corporations serves internal needs, it often provides a substantial barrier to outside partnerships. In every case, identifying the key leader within an institution was critical.

Also effective were the scores of discussions concerning the design of WGU, accrediting issues and transfer issues held with groups of faculty, administrators and other university personnel. For example, in one major public university, discussions with faculty leaders over transfer policies between the two institutions led to a more general conversation about university evaluations of performance-based high school transcripts.

The self-governing processes of the traditional academic institutions remain critical to the basic functions of higher education. While these may need redefinition in a world of part-time faculty and changing employment arrangements, the governance and control of curriculum are basic to the academic success of American institutions. WGU, in unbundling the faculty functions, was designed to retain the traditional process even while rearranging the elements. We found that individual faculty members from other universities serving on programme councils and other WGU committees shed their institutional identities and enthusiastically fulfilled their academic functions of curriculum design, etc. They quickly engaged in the challenge of the new structure.

The student-centred learning upon which much of the WGU design is based offers common ground for institutional collaboration. The portability of learning experience and credentials benefits students and institutions, as most undergraduate students now attend three or more institutions before receiving a baccalaureate degree. WGU was designed to maximize the resources of existing institutions; collaborative agreements that encourage the provider institutions to see WGU as a marketing ally in serving larger numbers of students can draw upon the strengths of both institutions. While the outsourcing of library functions has been successful, partnering with other institutions to maximize resources has been difficult. For example, early attempts to join in providing student services were not successful.

Q. What influences have shaped your style of leadership and what qualities do you look for or seek to develop and encourage in those you work with in pursuit of innovation and quality?

A. Years of working in traditional institutions have accustomed me to the usual academic structures and entrepreneurial qualities of individual faculty members. Working at WGU has required me to be aware of those characteristics in our partner institutions and yet to break from these in our non-teaching, e-commerce environment. A start-up business – even a university – must be more competitive, less collegial, more attuned to external forces, more oriented towards a financial bottom line and more committed to maximizing each employee's strength. Furthermore, the learner-centred approach to education reflects cultural shifts in consumer perspectives through much of today's economy. Distributed learning, online education, voucher proposals, collaborative learning and other developments also signal the changes in education. These changes are often described as if they apply only to individual learners, but other customers for education – employers, unions, companies – are also affected by and affect changing practices. The challenge to leaders in government and education is to embrace the fundamental shift in the public's expectation of postsecondary education. In dealing with WGU students, we repeatedly found that their readiness to embrace opportunities for online education, for example, far exceeded the willingness of the traditional institutions to provide such learning.

Helping new staff members to appreciate this and treat students as eager customers was rewarding; persuading other institutions to join with WGU in meeting the new expectations raised traditional doubts. In the past 15 years in the US, traditional higher education's share of the learning market has declined from 45 to 25 per cent. The demand for learning has increased and the sources for that learning have multiplied – corporate training programmes, corporate universities, virtual institutions, online offerings, learning portals, and so forth. New leadership requires not only vision and understanding but financial, technological and process skills to move institutions into the Information Age. No learning institution will be exempt from the demands that have caused businesses to transform themselves into 'new' businesses, the commercial norm of the New Age.

Q. What do you see as the main emerging issues and challenges for leaders and managers of open and distance learning in public universities in the US?

A. The integration of distributed learning with campus-based structures is a very significant challenge. Other issues – accreditation, credibility, quality, credentialing, student-centred learning and services – follow on from that issue. The rapid growth of distributed learning programmes suggests that many learners prefer the advantage of these programmes. What is in play here is fundamental institutional restructuring, not just modifying the 'edges' of institutions.

How do we assure quality? Critics have challenged the quality of the education delivered at a distance. They have rightly pointed to those areas where current technologies don't seem effective. Chat rooms, for example, don't truly replicate the culture of a seminar. While such criticism of distributed learning may avoid the issue of quality in traditional settings, it correctly raises the issue in regard to the new delivery systems and the teaching and learning strategies we employ in exploiting these technologies. Some of these applications can, in some instances, be more effective than the traditional classroom, but this needs to be demonstrated if we're to advance learning effectiveness – and counter institutional preferences and traditions. The insistence on high quality distributed learning can be unequivocal in organizations dependent upon such effectiveness yet that insistence is rare in universities.

Who's to be served and how are they to be served? While new institutions work to match the expectations of a market that favours modularized calendars, certificates rather than degrees, convenient hours and locations, access to faculty, simpler application and admissions processes, and more open financial aid policies as well as broader access to student services, issues of scale and productivity remain. Indeed, current practices in online education are a step backward.

How can the demographic explosion of learners be served? Just as the scale of the large 'multiversity' dramatically altered the integrity of learning structures based upon small institutions, distributed learning threatens to change learning without improving it. That is the challenge upon which higher education must focus.

Q. What advice would you offer to university leaders and senior managers involved in establishing new models and distributed learning systems and overcoming concerns about credibility and legitimacy?

A. One challenge for leaders and managers is to change the bureaucratic structures to reflect the realities of learning, for faculty and for students. The line between on-campus and off-campus is blurring and does not in itself affect learning. Traditional classroom learning can be improved through the use of Internet presentations. Yet the distinction between on- and off-campus is built into many institutions through structures of finance, faculty identification, registration, tuition, credit and countless sub-structures. As institutions become more learner-centred, these distinctions become less viable. Only the issue of how students learn in a particular discipline distinguishes what can best be done face-to-face and what can be delivered through other means, and much of that distinction rests upon the student rather than the material. These challenges must be framed as educational challenges, not technological, financial or bureaucratic problems.

The differences between part-time faculty and full-time faculty, between part-time students and full-time students, between distance learners and campus learners are distinctions that have a history and a logic. However, the technologies that now serve learners lessen the importance and significance of those distinctions. In many instances, the distance learner has better access to the instructor in an online course than an on-campus student. Similarly, the distance learner is often better able to access information resources electronically than those available to the on-campus student in a classroom.

For the leadership seeking to establish new models of open and distributed learning systems, the rapid success of programmes outside traditional universities should be studied. Much of the growth in the other sectors – such as corporate and the new e-commerce companies – has been achieved with distributed learning. Significantly, the numbers within traditional postsecondary education have remained stable. So those leaders who seek to introduce changes may wish to look outside the traditional higher education institutions for inspiration, direction and new models.

We have the ability to improve learning as we alter the ways in which it is delivered. And we have the ability to assess that improvement. The challenge is to apply that knowledge for the benefit of the student, altering the institutional processes and culture as necessary. Such changes can lead to stronger institutions, better learning and increased access for students. Preserving less effective instruction, less effective delivery, more costly structures and bureaucratic barriers simply because they preserve institutional structures must give way to new practices. Higher education may experience the dramatic changes of other industries in moving to a new era of consumer demand, business practices and financial structures in order to maintain its primacy in the culture.

Chapter 13

The American Distance Education Consortium: from rural provision to virtual organization

Janet Poley, President of the American Distance Education Consortium (ADEC), a 'virtual organization' headquartered at the University of Nebraska-Lincoln, discusses leadership issues in constructing and running this international consortium of 58 state and land-grant institutions providing ICT-based distance education programmes in the United States and internationally.

Q. What leadership role have you played in developing the ADEC vision and mission and extending the membership from the original 27 state/land-grant universities?

A. ADEC was established in 1989 under the name of Ag★Sat and was, as this name implies, originally conceptualized as a means of offering land-grant university undergraduate and graduate-level agricultural programmes nationally via satellite. I've been told different stories about Ag★Sat's origins, but most agree it was generated by US Government employees in the Department of Commerce and a law firm involved in telecommunications, and that the original/charter members signed on because it provided an opportunity to gain matching equipment funds from the Federal Government. At the time of Ag★Sat's creation, and for the first years of its operations, relatively few institutions were involved, but the challenges of constructing numerous satellite uplinks and downlinks paled in comparison to the challenges of building a coherent and cohesive organizational structure to produce and share these distance education programmes.

I was the second CEO and I took over in early 1994 immediately following a 'Futuring Summit' called by the Board of Directors in which some key thinkers considered the case for providing programmes other than agriculture. As a consequence of this, the consortium's mission was broadened to include the provision of programmes in natural resources, environment, health, nutrition, family and consumer science, and rural and economic development. In 1999, the Board further broadened this mission to include all subjects offered by the land-grant universities. So I started out as the CEO with an excellent platform from which to eventually launch the more comprehensive American Distance Education Consortium (ADEC).

But back then I hadn't seen the financials. Now I caution others: 'Beware when accepting positions in non-traditional organizations!' It took me most of that first year to straighten things out in finances, audits, federal reports, staffing, processes and procedures. Fortunately, I had grown up on a cash-poor farm and had spent more than 13 years working in international development, six of these in Tanzania, so I was well used to limited funding. I was also well aware that projects typically fail in the long term because of short-term artificial inputs – grants that cease when pilot projects end and temporary external appointees who develop their knowledge and skills but not those of those people who'll be there after they leave. Many would have thrown up their hands in despair at all the red ink on the Ag★SAT ledger, but I saw great potential in the organization, and it included some very fine people and learning resources, and to give up on that would have been wrong.

While I might have done this anyway, the shortage of money required me to think differently about staffing and operations. I replaced highly priced programme and technical staff with more economical but highly skilled management and accounting staff and I found a talented student to work with the Internet. To this day, ADEC is under-capitalized, but some of the great things we've achieved probably wouldn't have happened if we'd had more money.

A large number of people share my vision throughout the consortium. But, increasingly there are forces tearing at the fibre of cooperation. Some of the administrators in our non-profit land-grant universities are seeing big dollar signs in computer-assisted teaching and learning and pursuing the number one position in the nation rather than working to develop the knowledge marketplace. And some in the private sector are cherry-picking, only interested in the quick and easy profit and leaving aside troublesome questions about the digital divide and how to take education to the people, particularly the disadvantaged.

Q. ADEC now includes virtually all of the land-grant institutions, including the historically black universities and tribal colleges. What does it take to sustain such a consortium?

A. We certainly have varied membership in terms of size, budgets, technology, experience and capacities. But we use a lot of participatory leadership in ADEC and I try to listen carefully for good ideas from anywhere in the group and pick them up and help frame them so the consortium can go to work on them. One of my mentors taught me that good ideas are a dime a dozen, especially in higher education and government: the real differences are made by those who can put good ideas into action! Another of my mentors said that intelligent people enjoy talking about ideas but that the secret of accomplishment is exceptionally fine staff work. I firmly believe it takes really great vision *and* leadership *and* team management *and* passion *and* hard work to achieve anything of the magnitude we're attempting – not to mention quite a bit of luck.

I have my cynical days when I think only the power hungry and greedy finish first. But we keep trying. We know that some of these dimensions are out of our control. I try to be an honest broker, pushing for inclusion, encouraging partnering and creating opportunities for representatives from the different institutions to listen to each other. I try to encourage an inclusive, open, developmental, sharing, collaborative culture. I want us to embrace racial, ethnic and cultural differences because these differences fuel our creativity, our minds and our business opportunities. I also think the more quickly our governance achieves 50 per cent male and female, the healthier our entity will be, but we've still a long way to go on this. I want ADEC to be a learning community – how can we help others learn if we don't value the learning opportunities presented within our own groups? And I want our culture to embrace the world and the learning needs in other countries and cultures.

I'm also encouraging quality management and sound business practices. We have to respect the fact we're spending valuable resources – creativity, time, energy, money and materials – in pursuit of our goals. Financial transparency is essential. Nothing breaks down trust in a consortium faster than financial suspicions.

Finally, I want to encourage response, action and speed. It's often a real struggle moving from ideas to action and responding to new opportunities within higher education, but now many of our partners are recognizing they've a lot to gain from our consortium and are beginning to identify potential niches in the United States and overseas. They're realizing too that their resident students can also have a better education through technology. Some are asking for ADEC teams to help them with capacity building. ADEC is a successful programme developer and aggregator in our core mission areas. ADEC's online catalogue and e-commerce systems are well developed. The ADEC communication system with the Web home page at its core is central to all ADEC institutions. The consortium is a strategic mover and capacity builder in distance education.

Q. You're also working internationally?

A. Many of our land-grant university members have long-standing relationships with universities in Mexico, Honduras, Costa Rica, Brazil, Tanzania, Uganda, Malawi, South Africa, Thailand, India, Russia and Poland, to name but a few. In most of these locations we are building ADEC-like consortia or partnerships and now, with the Internet in place, we can plan for completely different ways of conducting research, developing curriculum and globalizing classes. I'm suggesting to our universities that in a few years time, we'll be rewarded not so much for what we send out to others, but for what we bring into our state or country from beyond the borders. We have to establish real partnerships. The United States may be wealthy and technologically and educationally advanced, but we have much to learn from others that can enrich our lives, imaginations, spirits and educational enterprises. We already have many international students attending our institutions and we need to look to new ways of achieving linkages to others.

We're taking time to work out relationships and design projects and programmes with our partners in other countries. We're certainly not trying to take our existing programmes and dump them someplace else in the world. We're sensitive to our member institutions' long-term relationships with overseas universities and we seek to strengthen these ties, not replace them. Also, we know we can't achieve a situation where every ADEC institution puts an equal amount in and gets an equal amount back. I want people to think more about what they can contribute – not what they think they'll get back in a material sense.

I've watched many types of organizations come and go over the last 10 years. I may be viewed as naïve for saying this, but I think getting up and going to work every day is the first prerequisite for accomplishing things. I'll be 55 years old when this book comes out. I've survived a lot of things including physical danger, investigation, malicious slander and breast cancer. I intend to continue working on the international promise of these new technologies for learning, probably to the chagrin of some and hopefully, with the support of others. There's a part of me that says – 'Just keep doing it!'

Q. What strategies do you use to gain the support of your Board, the university presidents and other senior personnel?

A. It's been fun watching the learning and growing every time someone new joins ADEC's Board. One of our Board members said that when she first joined us, it was if she'd come into a foreign country and we were all talking a different language. When you think of the speed of change in the deployment of the Internet and digital everything, it's not surprising that many of our leaders don't have the depth of knowledge about the technologies and their educational, financial and organizational implications to make really sound decisions on policy matters. Having said that, I've also been really fortunate to work with a subset of land–grant university presidents who are as interested in and excited about the possibilities of distance education and technology as I am.

One strategy I've used is videoconferencing to provide a platform for presidents to speak to faculty and each other. We've been fortunate to gain W K Kellogg Foundation funding for a series of national videoconferences supported by Internet/Web materials and collaborative activities on the future of the land–grant universities. We've also received support from the National Science Foundation for a series of such conferences focusing on improving college and university teaching. It helps when people have opportunities to work together on such projects. It also lets busy people like university presidents focus for a short period on what you're doing and aiming to do.

I spend a lot of time speaking, meeting and writing. Warmth, humour and personal connections are important in change. I always learn a great deal when I'm on-site at member institutions, seeing what people are doing, how they're set up, and the on-ground realities. I also try to help ensure that other people's conferences and projects work well. It's the old 'practice what you preach' approach, combined with reciprocity. I worry that today's young people aren't developing an appreciation for reciprocity. Perhaps it's my development within a large extended family and many years in Africa that make this such a strong value for me.

Q. What are ADEC's goals and strategies for the future?

A. Right now, we have three really important goals. First, we want to push for more affordable access to the Internet for learning purposes. We're very concerned about the digital divide issues, about under-served rural areas and inner city communities, about racial and ethnic minorities and about disparities of gender. We're interested in the wireless options – but more concerned about competition, regulation and money than what this technology will or won't do.

Second, we want to see new openings – like direct broadcast service (DBS) set-aside channels – for quality educational initiatives. We want to develop an ADEC channel using DBS and the Internet in combination. We want to encourage our members to contribute to this channel and shift resources to this type of delivery. And third, we want to develop an organization capable of forging strong international relationships or what I call a 'global community of interest'. Further than that, in 2001, we're going to hold another 'Futuring Summit' to chart new directions for the next three to five years.

Q. What has shaped your particular leadership style?

A. I try to balance an understanding of my own proclivities, strengths and weaknesses with learning from life experiences and the theories and principles of leadership developed by others. My most important experience bases come from growing up as the oldest child in a large extended family of five brothers and sisters and five double first cousins on a farm in Nebraska. We had to make up many of our own activities and one of my favourites was producing shows for aunts, uncles, visitors and anyone else who would pull up a chair and watch. I had to organize the content and the people for particular tasks, figure out who could sing, play the piano or other musical instruments, dance, tell jokes, read poetry, make the programmes, find the costumes, set up the chairs and do anything else required. Some of my relatives say that my early noticing of their talents helped shape the directions they took in later years. In many respects my work with the Tanzania Training for Rural Development Programme was similar to this. I had to use every resource available and work with others to make things happen. The joy of creating, collaborative learning, connection with others and achieving tangible outcomes is very important to me.

With respect to theories and principles, I use the Positive Power and Influence Model constantly, not simply to guide me in what I do, but to reflect upon what has worked or hasn't and why. I've learnt through such instruments and other training that I'm not a highly reflective person – 'Just do it!' comes pretty natural to me. So I find this self-appraisal model, which is complex and complete with respect to leadership and influence behaviours, very useful. You can use it conceptually to think about your behaviours strategically or as an energy model to feel how and where you direct your energy in influencing others. In the energy model, you're asked to self-assess your leadership behaviours and ask others – your supervisor, colleagues, subordinates and family members – to do the same.

You profile how you use these behaviours to move with, move against or move away in the energy sense. In the conceptual sense, you examine both the 'softer track' leadership behaviours such as visioning, goal setting, bridging, disclosing, communicating and empathizing with others, and the 'harder track' behaviours, such as persuading, reasoning for and against and bargaining. You learn that moving away from a situation, physically leaving it, joking about it or engaging in some other type of cooling off behaviour, can lessen tensions and allow people to begin anew another day.

The first time I undertook this self-assessment, I discovered that others didn't see me as using the behaviour of disclosing very often. On one hand, I think of myself as an open book – I am pretty emotional – but on the other hand, I grew up in a family that believed that we should bear our own burdens. When I learnt that sharing mistakes and failures with others was very important in leading, I began to consciously re-examine what I was doing. This is just one of the changes I've made in learning to use all of the behaviours at my disposal. Most of us over-use and under-use certain behaviours.

When I was doing a lot of training of leaders and managers in cross-cultural settings, I worked with motivation profiling tools such as Myers Briggs Type Indicator (http://www.aptcentral.org/aptmbtiw.htm), French and Bell's (1994) systems approach to organization development and other theories and techniques related to shared and collaborative leadership. These are now all ingrained in my thinking and actions. My leadership style is shaped by the fundamental idea that different people bring different strengths to an organizational setting and that as a leader, I have to find these best talents and motivate people according to their preferences. My experience tells me this will result in better outcomes than simply following my own ideas and inclinations.

I like to think that three of my strengths as a leader are vision, passion and high energy. However, I've learnt that I can sometimes seem like a freight train barrelling down the tracks. I know what I see and where I want to go and I push really hard. When I meet resistance to something I strongly believe in, my natural tendency is to push back – sometimes creating even more resistance. As I grow older – and hopefully wiser – I try to consciously make myself step back, reflect, consult with others and try something different. But I'll never find that easy.

Q. What do you see as the emergent challenges for open and distance learning in higher education?

A. I predict that global communities of interest will become more important, and that there will be an increasing blurring of distinctions between research, teaching and public service. We're already seeing a blending of off-campus and on-campus education around the world. I feel that our major universities with their roles in teaching, research and public service may have the greatest opportunity – they already have the legitimacy and many are working hard to open their doors to innovation. But they also face some of the greatest challenges – the biggest issue in these large organizations isn't programmatic, it's top-heavy management and administration. Some of the most expensive resources in our universities spend lots of their time sitting around in meetings rather than facilitating learning, conducting research, developing applications and engaging with the wider community.

I'm a strong advocate of open and distance education as a mainstream activity in our public institutions, not an add-on, not a cash-cow and not simply for-profit. And the model I advocate starts with the learners, their needs, the content and the methodologies, not with the digital distribution system. Providing more bandwidth doesn't necessarily mean increasing learning or opportunity for anyone. There are fantastic possibilities for improved learning in virtual reality, simulations, holograms and other as yet un-invented applications. But the biggest challenge for our existing institutions lies in shifting resources – people, technology and money – away from non-productive activities and into achieving these new environments for learning. Such is the scale of the task that much of this has to be done at the systemic level, through communities and through collaboration.

Q. What kinds of leadership do you try to encourage in those you work with?

A. I'm a strong proponent of the 'wysiwyg' style of leadership – what you see is what you get. Leaders are followed and respected because people know they can count on them for something or other – for their creative ideas, or strength in times of difficulty, or great organizing ability, or balance and wisdom. People don't generally follow erratic people. Being responsible, visionary, an excellent articulator, a hard worker on behalf of others and a sensible risk-taker are important. So are tolerance and inclusion.

Much of my career has been spent in male-dominated environments – in educational technology, senior government, and international education and development. I still find it irksome to occasionally encounter traditional expect-ations about gender roles and racial and ethnic stereotypes. And people fall into the same old trap of leaders who can be leaders because they look like leaders they've seen previously. All too often, big, tall, white and male describes the stereotypical leader. Sure, they can be excellent leaders, but so can short, stocky women or medium-sized non-Caucasian males. We must continue to work with governments, education and industry to open the doors, break the glass ceilings and welcome individuals to the table from many backgrounds, places and experiences.

It goes without saying that leaders must know a lot about the business they're in, in our case about education, distance learning and technology, and where to go to find out about anything they don't know. The number one priority for leadership in distance and open learning is understanding how people learn, what motivates them, and what keeps them learning. We'd think it ridiculous to have a sports captain or coach who didn't understand the fundamentals of the game. Unfortunately, some of our leaders and colleagues are seduced by the wonderful new technologies and the supposition that there's much money to be made and forget what this was all about in the first place.

Another leadership quality that's often overlooked is a sense of timing. I hypothesize that leaders that have this knack are intuitive, integrators and synthesizers. I like to think of the projects I'm working on as tents in a big circus complex. I can work on the detailed parts inside any tent, I can work between and among the tents, I can work on the superstructure, and I can even work on the external environment. And if things aren't working on the midway, I can always go to work on the animal cages for a time. This diversity keeps me from feeling trapped or stuck. I am also fascinated by the negative spaces, cracks, connections, relationships, networks and linkages in the things we do. Leaders often have to be able to see the things that others ignore or are blind to.

Q. What advice would you offer CEOs and others involved in changing organizations, cultures and practices?

A. Don't ever give up! Love your neighbour – your colleague down the hall and those around the country and the world. Learn as much as you can about your own business and something about everyone else's. Laugh – at yourself, the human condition and anything else that bugs you. Give as much as you can and know it's fine to expect reciprocity in return. Remind yourself that organizations really do change and that resistant individuals usually move on or are moved on. Remember too that most people do as well as they can. And always remember that the external environmental pressures are aligning to push very hard for more discovery, more integration, more learning and more sharing. As distance educators, if we ignore these forces, we'll perish.

Chapter 14

The UK Open University: managing success and leading change in a mega-university

Sir John Daniel, *who was knighted for services to higher education in 1994, discusses leadership issues in the context of his 16 years as Vice-Chancellor of the UK Open University (OU) and President of the Laurentian University, Ontario, and 10 years at vice-presidential level at Athabasca University, Alberta, and Concordia University, Québec. Sir John is now Assistant Director for Education, UNESCO.*

Q. The OU has as its mission to be 'open as to people, open as to places, open as to methods and open as to ideas'. What demographic, market or industry changes have affected the evolving vision and strategies of the OU since its earlier years?

A. That mission statement has provided the OU with a robust and unifying vision that has given the staff a strong sense of common purpose for 30 years. This has been helped by the participative and consensual nature of OU governance. Through regular discussions in its thousand-member Senate – which includes many students and part-time academic staff – the OU community has been able to update its understanding of its mission in the light of changing circumstances.

The slogan 'from second chance to first choice' summarizes the overall changes in vision and strategy over the years. When it opened in 1971 the OU was seen, both by its staff and the public, as the university of the second chance. Prior to the establishment of the OU less than 10 per cent of UK school leavers had the opportunity to go to university. This created a large pool of able and motivated people aged over 21 who were eager to obtain a degree if they could fit study around their work; 40,000 of them applied to be given this second chance when the OU first advertised in 1970.

There were then few other opportunities for part-time degree study. Indeed, one wag remarked that the effect of opening the OU was to close the other universities even more firmly to part-time and adult students. Not until the 1980s did part-time higher education begin to expand in other institutions. However, from the 1970s onwards the provision of university places for young, full-time students expanded steadily, accelerating in the 1990s so that by 1999 some 35 per cent of school leavers opted for higher education.

The number of working adults who feel the need for a degree increases as the participation of school leavers in higher education grows, which is why the OU's undergraduate numbers have grown steadily from 25,000 to 125,000 over three decades. Over that time, however, the profile of the student body has remained fairly stable. The average age of students on entry is in the mid-to-late 30s, although with a spread from the teens to the 80s. The demography of the United Kingdom will see a steady reduction of numbers in the 30 to 40 age bracket over the next decade, so the OU is targeting more of its marketing at the 18 to 30 age group which is providing an increasing proportion of OU students.

The trend for more people to use the OU for their first chance at university study has been reinforced by the large numbers for whom the OU is the first choice for professional development and graduate study. During its first decade the OU limited its offerings to courses in the traditional arts and science subjects. In the 1980s it developed a suite of programmes for the professional development of managers with the result that today the OU Business School is the largest in Europe. Since then professional programmes in Law, initial and in-service training for teachers and Health/Social Welfare have been developed and also operate at scale.

The OU is now the largest single UK provider of part-time university education at all levels and in most subjects because of the enviable reputation of the quality of its teaching. Interestingly, the first stakeholder group to be convinced of the OU's quality was the rest of the UK academic community. From the beginning large numbers of academics from the other institutions were hired to work part-time for the OU as tutors, course assessors, external examiners and guest contributors to TV and radio programmes. Thousands gained direct experience and a sense of ownership of the OU approach, which led to the widespread use of OU materials in the rest of higher education and helped other institutions to mount their own distance learning programmes when this became fashionable in the 1990s.

Students were the next group to enthuse about OU quality. From the start about a third of OU entrants had some previous experience of higher education. Most of them judged the OU to be more academically rigorous and intellectually stimulating than their previous institution as well as giving them better personal support. Over 2 million people have now studied with the OU and surveys show that one adult in four in the United Kingdom knows someone who has studied through the OU. Since most have a good story to tell the OU is well regarded by the general public.

The third stakeholder group to come on board were the employers. Today the OU enjoys very strong employer support with some 25,000 organizations giving financial support to their employees to study with the OU. While the relevance and quality of OU programmes are important factors it is also clear that the qualities of motivation and personal organization that distinguish OU students are also highly attractive in the workplace.

This does, however, cause the OU something of a challenge for its marketing strategy. Brand research shows that although the OU is well known, perceptions of its image are rather polarized. Those who have been students are devotedly enthusiastic but many others see OU study as the preserve of a special breed of self-starters with unusual determination and a capacity for self-denial. Today, when the OU seeks to serve 'second chance' students whose earlier education has been more rudimentary than that of the 1970s cohort, projecting an image that is both accurate and attractive is very important.

The issue of branding in higher education is topical. The commercial language of brands enables some universities to peddle an elite notion of higher education that they would hesitate to express in plain language. For centuries quality in higher education has been closely linked to exclusiveness of access. The OU's proudest boast is to have severed that insidious link by being open at entry but demanding at exit. Sadly, we can never assume that the battle to define quality by output has been finally won. OU strategy is to continue to stress its openness while also boasting unashamedly about its membership of the elite group of UK universities with the best national teaching quality rankings.

I conclude that the way we have developed the vision and strategy of the OU is entirely consistent with the aspirations of its founders. They wanted the OU to be as open as possible to ordinary people but they were also determined that when judged purely as a university it would be as good as the best. By attracting both 'second chance' and 'first choice' students we are achieving both aims.

Q. In your introduction to the 1998 OU Annual Review, you wrote of a new era dawning in the late 1990s and the need for the University to reflect on its mission and methods and prepare for the next millennium. Could you explain why and how these initiatives were undertaken and the outcomes?

A. The need for the renewal of mission and methods relates to changes in the 'four Cs' of context, customers, competition and challenges.

The context in which the OU operates is changing in notable ways. First, the focus of government policy for post–compulsory education is now on the further education sector with the declared aim of having more people study for less than a full degree. The OU is planning to introduce Foundation Degrees, which will be a more advanced and vocationally focused version of the US Associate Degree. Second, the devolution of political power and public funding within the United Kingdom combines with the trend of globalization to pull the OU two ways. On the one hand its students in Scotland will now be funded by Scotland, on the other it is operating some worldwide programmes wholly on fee income. Third, the development of the e-world poses exciting opportunities for the OU which, with nearly 100,000 students online in mid-2000, is now the largest university in cyberspace. Exploiting these opportunities will mean rising to the challenge of operating an effective electronic teaching and learning system at scale instead of being content with the information dumping that too often passes for e-learning. Fourth, having become used to the generous planning horizons associated with its many years in a sellers' market, the OU now has to demonstrate the nimbleness that a buyers' market demands.

The OU's customers are changing – by showing the assertiveness of customers instead of the docility of students. This phenomenon is familiar to all universities. At the OU its manifestation is less in the behaviour of current students, who remain impressively devoted to the institution, than in the decisions of potential students who go elsewhere if the OU does not offer exactly what they want. The result is to make course enrolments more volatile from year to year and to force the teaching system to operate to tighter deadlines. Industrial and government partners are also increasingly important customers and the OU is learning to work with such partners to deliver programmes that neither party could handle alone. A recent example is a national programme for training teachers to use IT in the schools. Developed jointly with a major equipment vendor it reached 40,000 teachers within four months of launch.

The OU's competition is also changing. For most of the 1990s the OU's strongest competitors were former polytechnics offering evening courses on campus. Today more and more institutions, including some new for-profit players, are offering courses at a distance. It is too early to see how all this will shake down but the OU does not intend to cede its world leadership in university distance learning.

This creates the challenge of creating a common understanding of the OU's unique advantages and gaining the staff's commitment to exploit them in very practical ways. There is no silver bullet, but the process of change is advancing rapidly along a broad front.

Q. You've said that the general thrust of public policy in the United Kingdom is now to imbue the whole higher education system with the same values as those upon which the OU was based. What opportunities does this provide for the OU to assume a new leadership role in the system and help reconfigure what you have described as 'the eternally challenging triangle' of cost, access and quality?

A. As Oscar Wilde famously remarked, 'There is only one thing worse than being talked about, and that is not being talked about.' For its first 20 years, despite being the UK's largest university, the OU existed on the margins of the system and was funded in a different way. This changed with the 1992 higher education reforms, which put the OU on all fours with the other universities. The OU's subsequent performance in operating with the widest access at the lowest cost – while also getting better quality ratings than nearly all other institutions – did not make it popular. For this reason, and because the OU is *sui generis* and therefore not part of any of the three or four informal sub-sets of UK universities, it is difficult for the OU to lead other than by example. However, the example is powerful and most other universities implicitly or explicitly draw on the OU in teaching their own students and as a benchmark for their own distance learning activities.

Q. As Vice-Chancellor, what roles have you played in helping to establish the goals and strategic directions for the University and in implementing change?

A. The overworked analogy of the conductor of an orchestra does seem appropriate here. The success of the OU is built on the coordinated contributions of thousands of able people and a successful Vice-Chancellor needs to call on a range of instruments.

Sometimes I have acted by example to create goals implicitly, as when I gave priority to e-mail over paper for internal communication on arrival in 1990, and when I took one of the OU's Web-based courses myself as a student in 1999.

At other times I have, by my own involvement, demonstrated the approach and style we should adopt in dealing with important external pressures. Examples were our enthusiastic engagement with the process that integrated the OU with the rest of the UK higher education system in 1993 and our decision at the same time to extend our 'parish' to the whole of Europe.

Then there are times when an initiative identified personally with the Vice-Chancellor helps to hasten change. The best example of this was the earmarking of £10 million for the INSTILL (Integrating New Systems and Technologies into Lifelong Learning) programme in 1995. This included the setting up of the Knowledge Media Institute, which brought together our liveliest talents to conduct leading-edge research and development on Internet use and to scale up these technologies for student use. Its success has exceeded my wildest expectations.

Throughout there is the constant commitment to raise continually the OU's reputation and image. I believe that a leader should spend more time creating meaning for people than making decisions for them. Hence my careful personal attention to preparing hundreds of speeches and newspaper columns (see www.open.ac.uk/vcs-speeches/), treating every one as an opportunity to interpret values, celebrate success, and set goals.

Most of all, I've simply encouraged those who were most ambitious for the OU and intervened on their behalf. As a result new programmes have been launched (eg, Languages, Law and soon, possibly, Medicine), the OU's international operations have been put on a sound footing, and operations across the institution have become more professional and purposeful.

Q. In the past, you have been relatively cautious in advocating expansion and migration into the Web, citing problems of copyright, preferences of faculty and students for print, convenience of text and limited access to computers. Have you changed this assessment, and if so in what ways and for what reasons?

A. My first principle here is that you don't experiment with live students. Given the scale at which the OU operates it is irresponsible to introduce new methods until you are sure that they are technologically robust and pedagogically superior. The electronic submission of assignments is a good example. The OU handles 1 million student assignments a year, so if even 1 per cent goes astray, that means

10,000 unhappy students. As a technology-based learning system the OU has seen too many false dawns of new technologies to believe there is a magic medium, or that any new development will completely invalidate what has gone before. Above all the attitude of the student body is crucial. In the early 1990s I was politely heckled at the annual student conference for suggesting a rapid migration to the online world. Only two years later the conference was chastising me for not moving fast enough.

This is an area where a leader, like Janus, has to face both ways. There is a duty to chivvy the internal community to get on with the job of taming new technology and applying it at scale. My colleagues would regard me as a techno-enthusiast. When speaking externally, however, I feel the responsibility to puncture some of the hype and to remind people that our aim must be effective teaching and learning, not technology for its own sake. I don't believe that I come across as a Luddite in these fora but I do push those who urge technology as the answer to tell us first what the question is.

Q. What particular theories, principles and experiences have helped shape your particular leadership style? And what leadership qualities do you look for and how are these developed in the OU's managers and staff?

A. I am fortunate to have had an extraordinary range of leadership opportunities and to have worked with some outstanding mentors. Aside from experience in school and in my early career I have spent 10 years at the vice-presidential level and 16 years in presidential positions in five very different universities in four jurisdictions. I find questions about leadership and management style difficult because I find that effectiveness requires one to adopt different styles to suit different situations. When I went to Athabasca University, for example, there were lots of ideas swirling around but very little sustained follow-through. So I concentrated, in a rather formal and legalistic way, on getting some deliverables delivered. When I moved to the OU it was quite the opposite. The OU was brilliant at the nitty-gritty of delivery but needed to be clearer about its place in the world. I decided to let others get on with the delivery and worked at making the OU raise its sights over the wall and engage with the outside world.

Among my senior colleagues I look for commitment to the values, energy, enthusiasm, loyalty and credibility across the institution. I try to create a team where people grow to like each other and enjoy working together. I find annual objective setting to be a valuable way of developing clarity of purpose and allowing me to supervise with a light touch. We have an extensive management development programme at all levels and have found 360° evaluations to be a good starting point. Since most leaders on the academic side reach management positions through election we stress effective induction, although we are working on a process to identify and bring on potential high-fliers provided it does not conflict with our strong belief in equal opportunity.

Q. What lessons have you learnt about leadership in expanding the OU's profile and activities overseas?

A. The first lesson is that the involvement of the head of the institution is even more important in overseas work than in domestic activities. This is not just out of respect to the overseas partners but in order to make one's own judgements about the opportunities and challenges that particular overseas ventures will bring. My own rather international career enables me to bring greater experience to the assessment of such situations than most OU colleagues and therefore to detect more readily where cultural differences cause difficulties.

The second lesson is that there have to be appropriate incentives for the individuals and units across the OU on whose work the success of the overseas programme depends. Whereas conventional universities can often ring-fence the involvement in a particular overseas venture to a single department and a few individuals, the OU's systems create interdependencies right across the institution. However, this is also what allows the OU to operate overseas at scale.

The third lesson, however, is that for the OU and its partners at least, overseas operations must be grounded in a strong academic relationship. In the late 1990s, with 30,000 people taking OU courses outside the UK, it was essential to put our overseas relationships on a business-like footing. The intentions were good, but we nearly overdid it and I am now placing the emphasis on creating a vibrant network of academic relationships between institutions and individuals around the world.

Q. How do you suggest that open universities and other distance teaching universities should react to the new global and technological forces of change?

A. I believe these forces of change oblige all institutions, and particularly those already operating at a distance, to spend time developing a clear vision of what they want to be and a candid appreciation of their strengths and weaknesses in relation to those aims. Clarity is always good, but the most challenging feature of the reappraisal required by the present context is that it obliges us to focus as much on what we mean by being a university as on the issues of distance education.

How do the university's ambitions differ, for example, from those of a for-profit institution? There are curricular questions. Does the university wish to offer a broad curriculum or concentrate on the so-called 'low hanging fruit' of business and IT? What is our vision of the relationship between the student and the institution? Is the student an individual customer with whom we should conduct an efficient commercial transaction, or are we trying to create an academic community? Are we aiming to transfer knowledge by imparting information and answers, or are we trying to create understanding by making the student ask and answer questions? Addressing such issues is not a trivial or quick task, but the university will emerge stronger from grappling with them.

Q. What skill sets do you see as necessary in CEOs and managers confronted with the need to establish or renew open learning systems, the rush of technological change and the challenge of overcoming organizational and individual resistance?

A. I do believe that prior knowledge of open learning systems is helpful, even if the new environment calls for systems that will be different from those of the 20th century. A wide variety of other experience is very useful. I am certain that I was better equipped for leading the OU after 20 years in a diversity of Canadian universities than I would have been through a career in another UK institution or in the OU itself. Working in very different settings trains you to keep your antennae constantly switched on. Being skilled at environmental scanning and persuasive at interpreting the radar screen to colleagues is what distinguishes the best leaders in this age of change.

In overcoming organizational and individual resistance to change it helps if you are visibly committed to the core values of the institution. Failing such commitment it is too easy for the institutional immune system to reject your renewal strategy. The OU, for example, is imbued with an egalitarian spirit. Since new teaching media may add expense for students it is easy for opponents of change to argue that 'unless everyone can have it, no one shall have it'. Understanding such attitudes and staying close to the student body is essential in setting an appropriate pace for technological change.

In a very large and successful university like the OU, which has institutionalized innovation to a remarkable degree, one source of resistance to change is the belief that since the existing systems work on a large scale it would be dangerous to tamper with them. Naturally this view tends to be held by colleagues who have occupied their posts for many years. I have found the most useful skills in addressing such resistance are perseverance and detailed knowledge of institutional processes. Most people who work in universities are intelligent and persistent discussion of better ways of doing things does produce results.

Finally, I make the obvious point that in leading and managing open and flexible learning the skills of openness and flexibility are valuable, not just as metaphors but because learning thrives on open discussion and technology-based teaching requires a flexible approach to new opportunities.

Chapter 15

Indira Gandhi National Open University and the Distance Education Council: institution and system building in India

Professor Abdul Khan *is Assistant Director General for Communication and Information, UNESCO. He was formerly Vice-Chancellor of India's Indira Gandhi National Open University (IGNOU) and Chairperson of the Distance Education Council (DEC), the apex body for the subcontinent's 9 state and 62 dual-mode universities. Professor Khan has also served in senior positions with the Commonwealth of Learning, created by the Commonwealth Heads of Government to encourage the development and sharing of open learning and distance education knowledge, materials and technologies. He discusses leadership issues in open and distance higher education in India.*

Q. How does IGNOU's mission to serve disadvantaged groups and communities translate into strategic planning and management initiatives?

A. IGNOU has played a critical role in establishing and building the credibility of open and distance learning in India. Its success as pioneer and system leader can be attributed to the careful attention we've given to translating our major objectives into key strategic planning and management initiatives. Our three main thrusts are:

1. Reaching disadvantaged groups.
2. Enhancing the use of appropriate technologies.
3. Promoting quality assurance.

The focus on democratization, on mass education provision with equity, necessitates our taking initiatives to identify or create adequate mechanisms to reach disadvantaged groups and communities. We convened a special taskforce to examine how to 'reach the unreached', people in remote and educationally backward regions (the Indian Government has delineated 148 'black hole' districts across the country), the disabled, women and girls and minorities. In the light of the recommendations of this taskforce, we're now making concerted efforts to expand the infrastructure and develop suitable courses and programmes for specifically targeted groups within the educationally and socio-economically backward members of our society. Backwardness in the Indian context has its origins not only in class hierarchies but also in caste and feudal structures. Eligibility to pursue learning is dictated by birth, not merit. Access to education has traditionally been provided only to higher castes, lower castes being considered unworthy of education. This caste divide ensured the backwardness of lower castes and preserved the rigid hierarchy of feudal society. However, with the advent and expansion of open and distance learning, this will change. Age-old barriers will crumble and gradually disappear.

Technology has a critical role to play in expanding access and we've successfully created a media mix of low-end and high-end technologies appropriate for remote and backward regions of the country. And we seek to combine innovative 'hand tooled' and carefully crafted courses with adequate delivery mechanisms to achieve economy of scale. We see three aspects of technology access needing our attention: physical access; capacity to access; and ability to create relevant content. Physical proximity to technologies or connectivity is of course important – you can't teach them if you can't reach them. Even where there's connectivity, disadvantaged groups and communities may not be able to use the technology because they lack the requisite competence and confidence to use these tools to further their learning experiences with or without the mediation of a learning institution. An inadequate response to the need for such technological and media literacy will only create another barrier to meaningful participation in learning. The third aspect of access is to ensure that the disadvantaged have opportunities to be agents of influence rather than receivers of information and knowledge. They should be enabled to change content delivered by technology, to make it more culturally and otherwise relevant.

IGNOU is widely recognized as a provider of quality educational programmes and products. It has the advantage of being able to adopt flexible course design and development strategies. It also has access to a countrywide resource pool of expertise – its courses and programmes have been enriched by the contributions of an estimated 10,000 experts. These features combine to give the university an edge in quality assurance and developing national standards. Our courses compare favourably with the best in the world. We've won accolades for the quality of our educational materials, the Commonwealth of Learning has recognized us as a Centre of Excellence and IGNOU's materials and one of our students have received COL Awards for Excellence. Within India, IGNOU's diploma and degree programmes are considered equivalent to similar programmes offered by conventional universities.

Q. How do you assure quality and measure and reward success at IGNOU?

A. Quality assurance has been one of my primary concerns. Today, IGNOU is counted among the top nine academic institutions in India, largely because of the quality of its self-instructional programmes and materials. However, we must ensure that the standards of our programmes and services continue to improve. Because of our large enrolment and the involvement of several external agencies, our student support services need attention. Towards this end, we've constituted another taskforce that is in effect a quality assurance mechanism, planning and monitoring the implementation of activities as per schedule. This taskforce and other IGNOU committees represent informal mechanisms for ensuring quality. Formal mechanisms such as regular performance appraisal systems have so far had no significant response. Hiring and firing is impossible within the Indian university system because the security of service is implacable and the contractual arrangements don't provide for performance-based reward or punishment. So institutional and individual success can only be measured by informal performance indicators. We are, however, in the process of finalizing work norms for staff in open and distance learning institutions across the country at a formal level under the auspices of DEC.

At the institutional level, our enrolment figures, the general public perception and our recognition as a Centre of Excellence are positive performance indicators. At the individual level, success can be measured in terms of contribution to the institution and personal achievement – the number of units written, audio/video cassettes developed or new programmes launched, upward mobility achieved, membership of various committees and councils and contributions to the corporate life of the institution. There are limited opportunities for rewarding success but it is possible to acknowledge quality and good performance by providing opportunities to participate in international conferences, conferring additional responsibilities and involving staff in activities that interest them.

Q. What roles do you play in setting and implementing the strategic directions and standards for the University?

A. One of my foremost concerns is building strategic alliances with public and private educational and technology providers. Such alliances are critical in bridging existing gaps in education provision and promoting:

- extension activities;
- research;
- maintenance of standards;
- utilization of appropriate ICTs.

Strategic alliances with nongovernmental organizations have found particular applicability in promoting the extension activities of the university, empowering disadvantaged groups and community-based approaches to development. The proven success of some NGOs (nongovernmental organizations) in developing locally-relevant and innovative programmes and delivery strategies make it worthwhile to combine IGNOU's strengths in distance learning with the rich field experiences of these agencies. Such alliances have demonstrated their effectiveness in, for example, disaster management, primary school teaching, training rural youth, science and technology for sustainable development, participatory planning, HIV/AIDS awareness, and training women to work in self-help groups. The development and delivery of our computer literacy programme for adolescent school dropouts is a particularly interesting example of a strategic alliance with NGOs. IGNOU provides low-cost, non-formal distance learning for these technology 'have-nots' and the NGOs provide the counselling and monitoring of individual students.

An IGNOU-UNESCO Chair, established through a memorandum of understanding between the university and UNESCO, constitutes an important strategic alliance in promoting research in teacher education through distance education. This Chair has been instrumental in networking and twinning with teacher education institutions and the 310 fraternal UNESCO Chairs across the world and improving the quality of programmes through research studies, policy papers, and database development on teaching/learning materials for distance teacher education.

Technology is crucial to India as an emerging knowledge-based society, for expanding the reach of extension activities, fostering networks of scholars and raising standards of provision. It also creates a digital divide between the haves and have-nots and this has to be combated through appropriate mechanisms. We've launched major initiatives in interactive radio and television. Interactive academic counselling has moved beyond its pilot phase of teleconferencing to the national TV network and 184 stations of the national radio network, offering unparalleled opportunities for interaction with disadvantaged and highly dispersed learners in remote, rural areas. To provide a further impetus to these initiatives in interactive radio and television, we're also improving our student support services, and upgrading our study and regional centres for multimedia access and interactivity, particularly in backward areas including rural and tribal belts.

IGNOU is now the nodal agency for India's first fully-fledged educational TV channel, *Gyan Darshan* (Knowledge Network) on the national *Doordarshan* (Television) network which makes us the only university in the world entrusted with the onerous task of coordinating and operating a national channel devoted exclusively to education. This channel can change the 'face' of education as we know it in our country. It will shift the emphasis from study centre learning to home- or workplace-based learning, which will help our learners immensely because they'll have easy access to programmes without need to spend time, effort and money reaching the centres. This dramatic thrust towards democratizing education needs to be carefully nurtured to realize its potential. And it needs a systematic, pragmatic approach to integrating the broadcast programmes with curriculum and course content in print/lecture mode to serve learners in both the distance learning and traditional institutions.

It's imperative to expand our use of ICT. Strategic alliances with technology providers have given our students access to the Internet, especially for computer courses. We've constituted another taskforce to explore ICT applications in human resource development, promote an ICT culture, new academic initiatives and educational networking, reach out to disadvantaged groups and review our existing infrastructure and investment requirements. Our primary concern is to make our systems more learner-centred. We've set up telelearning centres and initiated interactive radio counselling to improve interaction with our learners. ICT is also being harnessed for more effective performance by our finance and administration divisions.

Networking and collaboration with other institutions and agencies enables us to harness the finest intellectual and infrastructural resources in the country. We see resource-sharing, networking and collaboration as key strategies for India's educational providers in the coming years. We're already attracting major funding for HIV/AIDS awareness, *panchayat raj* (self-governance at the village level), construction worker training, and other community-focused programmes and our securing the commitment of national agencies in these projects is an indicator that we're moving in the right direction.

Q. What leadership role do you play in the Distance Education Council?

A. India has a vast distance education infrastructure of nine State Open Universities and 62 Distance Education Directorates/Correspondence Course Institutes. IGNOU constituted the Distance Education Council to promote open and distance learning and establish quality assurance mechanisms, standards and performance indicators appropriate to Indian contexts, by:

● Formulating norms and guidelines for offering programmes of study through distance mode.
● Developing and monitoring quality assurance systems in the State Open Universities and Correspondence Course Institutes.
● Developing quality assurance manuals in programme development and delivery.
● Developing self-assessment manuals for assessment and accreditation of State Open Universities.
● Capacity-building for quality assurance through staff training and development activities.
● Preparing norms and standards/guidelines for support to the State Open Universities and Correspondence Course Institutes.
● Providing technical assistance to the State Open Universities, adopting a credit system and common grading pattern for student evaluation.

The State Open Universities share IGNOU's programmes and courses, adopting, adapting or translating these for larger numbers of students, an arrangement that ensures that quality study materials are available to more people at affordable costs. There is inevitably some scepticism about one university dispensing largesse to other equally autonomous bodies and to address this, we've dispensed with the hierarchical structure that characterizes a patron–client relationship and adopted the more egalitarian approach of networking and partnership. We find this interaction among equals far more meaningful and productive.

There is significant representation on the DEC by the Ministry of Human Resource Development, University Grants Commission, the State Open Universities and Correspondence Course Institutes. The involvement of these key players in decision-making is particularly important in sustaining the development and implementation of suitable benchmarks, standards and performance indicators. We have organized several conferences and have constituted various committees to assess, promote and coordinate quality and consult on this issue with faculty and administrators in the open and distance learning institutions.

As chairperson of the DEC, I have been particularly concerned with promoting the work ethic in open and distance learning institutions, which I see as critical to maintaining standards. Open and distance learning requires institutions to operate differently from traditional institutions. It transforms the roles of teachers and administrators, necessitates concerted and continuous teamwork and calls for the development of new benchmarks of individual and collective performance. We've identified work norms and parameters for institutional assessment including mission and goals, support structures, personnel management, monitoring and quality assurance and research and development, and for programme design and development and delivery including institutional support, quality assurance and research and development. The subsequent development of performance indicators constitutes another major effort in ensuring quality in educational products and services.

The other functions of the DEC are:

- Promoting open and distance education.
- Providing assistance in establishing new State Open Universities.
- Providing grants for human resource development in State Open Universities and Correspondence Course Institutes.
- Providing financial support to the State Open Universities and Correspondence Course Institutes for improving student support services, infrastructure development and new technology.
- Providing support to Correspondence Course Institutes transforming course material into distance mode and upgrading programmes.
- Providing coordination, funding, training and support for downlink, wide area network and local area network development.
- Developing a database on India's open universities.
- Identifying a common pool of courses and programmes for sharing by distance education institutions.

Q. What lessons have you learnt about strategic planning and strategic management?

A. Education providers, especially in the higher education sector, are facing difficult times. The creation of infrastructure and development of programmes to meet the exponential demand for educational provision needs massive investment. This is well beyond the capacities of governments. Private funding and initiatives in open and distance learning now contribute substantially to sustaining postsecondary education. However, there is an inherent contradiction in the mandates of open and distance learning systems and the private sector agencies, and excessive reliance on private contributions can undermine efforts to reach disadvantaged groups and communities. Initiatives in educationally backward regions need heavy initial investment and provide little return. So for-profit organizations tend to ignore the concerns of such regions and communities. It is therefore imperative that these continue to be supported by government.

I've had to deliberate on the need for innovative entrepreneurial strategies to enhance our resource pool and I've been able to reconcile the need to promote business interests with the need to combat negative attitudes towards academic institutions 'engaging in commerce'. As a result, we've established IGNOU Consultancy Services, which are revenue-generating, but not operated on a for-profit but a cost-recovery basis. Consultancy Services are responsible for:

- Providing consultancy services for educational institutions, governmental, public sector and nongovernmental organizations and non-formal agencies, both national and international.
- Sharing IGNOU's technology expertise in distance education and training.
- Developing and delivering short-term specialized courses and customized training programmes to specific client needs.
- Marketing IGNOU's educational and training modules, materials and services.
- Marketing faculty's specialized capacities.

I've also found that it requires sustained effort to project the strengths of the institution when there are detractors questioning the credibility of the institution and the open and distance learning system as a whole and that the media have a critical role in creating a positive image of both individual members of staff and the institution as a whole. I've found this to be an approach to public information that has worked well in the Indian context. Two years ago, we were faced with considerable negative reporting about the university – especially in regard to the effectiveness of our material distribution mechanisms. Once our system was functioning satisfactorily, we decided to project our achievements through the media. Our efforts were successful and so we've now established a Public Information Unit to sustain a communication strategy of promoting our innovative approaches to taking education to the un-reached.

Of course, no strategies, however perfectly devised, can be effective unless there is commitment on the part of all concerned. In a large organization such as IGNOU, we need commitment from all of the external as well as the internal agencies involved. We depend upon external support for all of our course development and production and service delivery. Long-term planning can't yield successful results unless resource commitments by the agencies concerned are forthcoming and one of the greatest problems we face is 'ad hocism' in resource allocations. In order to avoid this, we try to ensure that resource allocations are made on the basis of proper planning and full justification. We also face the constant pressures of time-bound implementation. If external agencies such as the postal system or the counsellors at the study centres fail to deliver, the overall efficiency of the system is undermined. Another potential stumbling block is our reliance on the existing conventional institutions. However, while resistance to innovation is of course sometimes inevitable, we've succeeded in enlisting the support of a large segment of the Indian educational system. We need now to press home this advantage.

The greatest challenge is to inspire all of these agencies and individuals involved to deliver services of the requisite quality. Our organizational structures are hierarchical but the need to enlist the participation and support of colleagues is democratic. So there's a pull in opposite directions, which leads to a constant struggle to establish a viable work culture. Personal example doesn't always succeed. And as I say, hiring and firing is hardly possible. Achieving optimum efficiency therefore becomes an exercise in creative management. We need to make the best use of the capacities of every individual, building on their strengths and overcoming any weaknesses.

Another serious constraint on our plans to reach out into the community and help the disadvantaged and realize the potential of technology is the skewed development of technology infrastructure in India. We are still facing a huge gap in infrastructure provision in rural areas as compared to urban areas. This issue must be urgently addressed, especially through strategies to promote community rather than individual access.

Q. What principles of leadership and management guide you in your work?

A. I think it was Peter Drucker who once said that management is about doing things right while leadership is about doing the right things. I've always believed in consensus-building and teamwork – in building a culture of unity through recognition of individual strengths and efforts. Discipline in our professional lives, a strong work ethic, and a sense of institutional pride are some of the areas that I'm particularly interested in strengthening at IGNOU. These cannot be imposed from above. You have to find ways and means of securing the commitment of one's colleagues and inspiring people to perform, stretching the limits of their potential. This, I believe, is the most challenging aspect of leadership!

Q. But how can you encourage and support innovation and change throughout such a large institution, across all the regional and study centres and through the DEC?

A. Leadership can't be confined to the person at the helm of the institution or organization. There needs to be leadership at all levels, by deans, directors, faculty heads, section heads and so on. It's important to recognize the value of teamwork, consciously evolving a culture of congenial relationships on the basis of shared values and principles. It's not easy to do this in an environment long dominated by command and control structures including caste and class hierarchies. At IGNOU, we try to enlist wider participation by setting up taskforces such those as those I mentioned earlier. We endow these with the power and authority to take decisions and implement them and this approach has yielded good results. But I must admit that we still have a long way to go.

No one has a monopoly on good ideas. In order to change and streamline some of the problematic operational areas, we've organized intensive brainstorming sessions – some involving over a hundred faculty members. This has resulted in several excellent recommendations. And we encourage individual and team initiatives in both programme design and development, as shown in our recent participatory planning for innovative programmes in women's empowerment and skills development for leather and construction workers.

We've also diversified and extended our approaches to delivery. Now, we don't just have the regional and study centres but also partner institutions and distance learning facilitators. The latter scheme is specially designed to involve unemployed youth, retired personnel or housewives in providing student support services. These facilitators promote and publicize IGNOU and the open learning system in their area of operation, provide pre-admission guidance, co-conduct induction meetings with staff from the regional centres, provide general counselling to learners, maintain student records and provide regular feedback to regional centres. They also facilitate assignment submission and evaluation and learner participation teleconferencing sessions, provide monthly activity reports to the regional centres, maintain expenditure accounts and link with the regional centre/student affairs cell back at headquarters.

Q. What qualities of leadership do you look for in your managers and staff?

A. The basic quality any leader must have is professional competence and a high level of efficiency. In addition, he or she must be totally committed to the values and principles of the institution, to its work ethic and to promoting its objectives – in our case, the objectives of access, quality and equity – which ultimately impact on the community as a whole. To find all of these virtues in a single individual may not always be possible. But what is possible is to encourage participation, delegate responsibilities and authority, provide opportunities for independent decision-making, and associate colleagues with work at both national and international levels.

Q. What skill sets do you see as necessary in CEOs and managers involved in establishing or renewing open learning systems, particularly in developing countries?

A. There's a multiplicity of attributes required for managing change. First and foremost, the leader in open and distance learning must be open-minded and receptive to innovative ideas. In this field, we have no established traditional models to follow. We traverse uncharted territory. The leader must also have the imagination and ability to take risks. We live in democratic times and the leader also needs to inspire and motivate, to generate consensus and consent. A technology orientation is also a necessary qualification, the wisdom to discern which technologies are suitable in which contexts. Networking and negotiation skills are necessary to keep the institution ahead of the fierce competition. And finally, the leader must ensure that education moves away from being, as French philosopher Althusser (1971) puts it, 'an ideological state apparatus' and becomes 'a practice of freedom'. As Richard Shaull (1972: 13–14) says in his introduction to Paulo Freire's *The Pedagogy of the Oppressed*:

> Education either functions as an instrument which is used to facilitate the integration of the younger generation into the logic of the present system and bring about conformity to it, or it becomes the practice of freedom, by means of which men and women deal creatively with reality and discover how to participate in the transformation of the world.

Chapter 16

Athabasca University: change management in a non-traditional university setting

Professor Dominique Abrioux, President of Athabasca University (AU), discusses providing leadership and new directions for Canada's Open University.

Q. AU was founded in 1970, but when you were appointed as President in 1995, it was going through a difficult period. What steps did you take to provide a new sense of purpose and direction?

A. In 1994/1995, the Government of Alberta's need to eliminate the provincial debt gave rise to a 21 per cent reduction in the base operating grants of the four public provincial universities over the following three years and for reasons communicated in writing to the university's Governing Council, AU's grant was to be reduced by a further 10 per cent. The Government was dissatisfied with AU's low graduation rate, with its perceived desire to deviate from its distance education focus, and with its apparent over-involvement in international education at the expense of its provincial clientele.

Internally, Athabasca University was also in disarray. Support for, and confidence in, the senior management and executive ranks was at an all-time low, and this was only exacerbated by the difficult and stressful labour negotiations needed to adjust successfully to the dramatic reduction in provincial funding. Instead of working for the betterment of the institution, many staff were working for themselves and saw their future as quite apart from that of the institution. Rumours abounded about the imminent closure of AU or its annexation by the Alberta government to the University of Alberta, and the incumbent president's announcement of his pending resignation led some to construe this as evidence of the institution's pending closure, while others saw this as an opportunity for the institution to reassert itself and take control of its own destiny.

As an internal appointee with extensive experience as a faculty member and administrator, my learning curve was fortunately very slight. I was able to take office with firm convictions about the major dimensions of my leadership. On the one hand, I recognized the urgency of redressing the Government's low esteem and minimal appreciation of AU; on the other hand, I saw – and still do see – my job primarily as articulating in consultation with the University community an ambitious, clear and common vision, and developing the optimum institutional climate, such that each and every employee could contribute to the best of their ability to its realization.

I was convinced that once government better understood the different ways in which AU was fulfilling its mandate, its appreciation of our accomplishments would increase significantly. With that in mind, I personally assumed responsibility for the government relations dossier and within a year had renegotiated AU's mandate so that its diverse roles were understood, valued and entrenched in official government documents. The continuing need for a non-traditional institution to communicate effectively with government is apparent when one juxtaposes one of the reasons for the Government's extreme dissatisfaction with AU in 1994, a low graduation rate, with the fact that fewer than one in three of our students have, as a goal, the completion of an AU credential. A further 50 per cent transfer credits obtained from AU to their home institution, and 20 per cent are not interested in a credential from AU or from another Canadian university as they only want to take a few courses for the purposes of professional or personal development.

This change in mandate set the stage for improved governmental recognition for AU's system-wide contribution and served to reassure the University's staff that hitherto we would be judged by criteria applicable to our particular institution and mandate.

The importance of treating mandate statements as fluid documents and periodically revisiting them to ensure they accurately reflect institutional practice was evidenced by another official revision to Athabasca University's mandate in 1999. This time, I wanted to anticipate any concern that the government might have with the fact that AU was a provincially-funded institution, while half of our students resided outside the province. After persuading government that this resulted in a net benefit to our Alberta students and Alberta's economy, our mandate was formally changed to reflect a Canadian and international focus, an irony that escaped few given the institutional chastisement and reduced funding endured in 1994–97 for focusing insufficiently on Alberta!

Q. What principles and experiences have shaped your particular leadership style?

A. My second major thrust on assuming AU's presidency involved establishing and nurturing a positive institutional climate. I firmly believe that whereas leaders cannot of themselves change an organization, they certainly are directly responsible for establishing the environment within which change can occur.

My initial challenge was to develop a climate of trust and cohesiveness and a value-driven leadership model. At an early meeting with AU staff, I presented my vision for the organization and the values I would seek to embed throughout the university, especially amongst the senior administration: trust, respect, openness, accessibility, accountability, innovation and student-centeredness.

Value-driven leadership is premised on leading by example and seeing the values one wants espoused reflected across all organizational structures and decision-making processes. In addition to reviewing organizational structures and introducing a much flatter hierarchy, I had to ensure that my personal *modus operandi*, and that of the executive and senior management, exhibited the very principles that I wanted associated with the organization. This necessitated significant change amongst my senior colleagues, but as an internal appointee I had been able to make my intentions in this regard very clear to the Governing Council.

In addition to replacing or eliminating all but one of the senior executive and several of the senior manager positions, three important reorganizations took place, each reflecting the values that I wanted to nurture. First, the Human Resources department was eliminated and payroll, benefits, etc, were assigned to Finance, and the more human, personnel-related functions to the Office of the President (with a professional responsible for each of Labour Relations and Staff and Students Relations). Second, a new division, Student Services, was established with its own vice-president with executive responsibility not only for the normal functions of this office (registry, advising, counselling, regional centres) but also computing services, previously the responsibility of the Vice-President Finance and Admin-istration and which had long since ceased to be driven by student needs. Third, the faculty structure was eliminated and replaced by some 12 academic departments, each reporting directly to the Vice-President Academic.

Without micro-managing the organization, I employ a hands-on approach to management and expect others to do likewise. Students and staff alike have ready access to me through e-mail, telephone/voice-mail, and personal interaction. I tutor a small class to underline why we exist as an organization, and I sit at the negotiating table with all labour groups. I continue to advocate and, I hope, demonstrate the values that sustain a climate in which continuous change is recognized as a key criterion for success.

Q. As President of AU, what role do you play in strategic planning and strategic management?

A. As President, I've been involved in two institution-wide strategic planning activities. The first led to the Governing Council approving a Strategic University Plan (SUP) in 1996; the second concluded with Council approving a Strategic University Plan Update in 1999. And on an annual basis, I'm responsible for leading Council in weekend strategic planning retreats. The development of rolling sub-plans of the SUP, such as Systems Development Plans, Technology Integration Plans or Student Access Plans, are assigned to the appropriate vice-president.

Because it was critical that the floundering institution quickly embrace a vision and direction that re-established and maintained AU's reputation as Canada's premier distance educator, the development and approval of a strategic plan constituted a key initial responsibility. As incoming president with a staff keen for direction and decisiveness, I was accorded considerable latitude in establishing the strategic plan. Aptly aided by my newly appointed Vice-President Student Services, we resisted pressures to form a committee and seek diverse input at the outset – the previous practice at AU. We adopted a more prescriptive approach: writing the first draft ourselves, then distributing it widely for review and feedback before tabling it at our Academic Council and Governing Council for approval. This process proved successful and has now become standard procedure for the SUP and its rolling sub-plans.

Two different balances struck in the SUP have been key to its successful implementation. The juxtaposition of bold change and relative stability; and the balance between vision and reality. For example, the 1996 SUP sought to move the University from a primarily print-based and telephone-supported model, to an increasingly electronic one, a direction that many influential staff at that time did not support. This was nevertheless achieved, primarily because the SUP also clearly spelt out that this would not be done at the expense of AU's current client-base. No student would be disenfranchised: unless the course necessitated the exploitation of e-learning, this would remain an alternative for the student. The other delicate though essential balance in strategic planning, the need to anchor the visionary aspects in reality, was exemplified in the SUPs' strategic visionary sections being juxtaposed with the strategic implications for organizational development, institutional policy-making and fiscal policy-setting. Not only were clear directions and goals set out, but the obstacles to be overcome in attaining these – which provided the framework for annual operational planning by departments.

Q. The Chair of the AU Governing Council suggests that the university faces the challenge of retaining its leadership position when so many other providers are entering the field. What does the future hold for AU?

A. Interestingly, while competition in university distance education has never been fiercer, AU is performing better than ever. Five years after dancing with closure, we have 22,000 students, twice as many as in 1995, and we anticipate another doubling of enrolments by 2004. The graduation rate has also more than doubled. AU has been rated higher than any other postsecondary institution in Alberta in an independently conducted, standardized student satisfaction survey, and in each of the last three years, has been the most highly rated of the 23 provincial postsecondary institutions according to the government-published Key Perform-ance Funding Indicators. All of this has been achieved against a decrease in governmental funding (from Can\$17.5 million in 1993–94 to Can\$14.3 million in 1999–2000) and while imposing the lowest increases in tuition fees in the province.

While it's true that the distance education market is becoming more and more competitive, the market is also expanding tremendously. Increased competition also forces providers to improve the quality of their courses and support services, for to do anything else would represent only a short-term gain. I started my career at AU in 1978 and I spent my first 20 years justifying the validity and effectiveness of distance education. Now my task and that of my colleagues at AU is far less difficult: rather than constantly justify the very nature of what we're engaged in, we need only compete on equal terms, based on quality and price. Distance education represents our one and only core business. If we can't rise to this challenge, we ought not to be in the business.

This notwithstanding, I have a responsibility as President of AU to provide direction to ensure that AU will continue to be a major player as the marketplace variables change. Today, individualized (as opposed to cohort-based) distance education remains our trump card and will continue to differentiate us from most of our competitors. Individualization is not only the hallmark of the digital era, it is *the* reason why students enrol at AU. For the most part, they start their courses when they please, complete them at their own speed, and interact with tutors, other students and staff in their own time. AU's challenge is thus to maintain the flexibility of its individualized home-study approach while taking advantage of the increased interactivity that e-learning enables and that will soon be expected of all distance education models.

Domestically, moreover, the escalation of credentialing has provided new markets for distance educators, and AU intends to maximize these opportunities. This is particularly true insofar as two-year graduates of college diploma programmes are concerned, as they're increasingly required by their employers to obtain degrees. By specializing in the articulation of diplomas into degrees, and by developing new degrees to ensure that the curriculum remains relevant and maximum transfer credit can be justified, AU will continue to expand its market.

The internationalization of distance education undoubtedly provides the greatest opportunity for market gains and AU is strategically placed to benefit from this. The 1996 SUP defined North America as our principal market and all the required policies and infrastructures are now in place to expand into the USA and to significantly increase on the 500 students currently resident in that country. We'll achieve this by independent institutional advancement and through strategic alliances such as the one recently signed with the United States Open University (USOU). Elsewhere, international markets will be pierced through partnerships that depend on a local agency to provide marketing, advising, admission, registration and exam invigilation services, while AU provides course content and electronic tutorial support. In some instances, the unbundling of learning materials, tutorial support and course assessment will also provide expanded market opportunities. A case in point is AU's four-year partnership with TAC, a private Japanese company specializing in the preparation and provision of materials and tuition for bookkeeping and accounting. AU provides some 500 adult Japanese learners intending to sit for the American CPA (Certified Public Accountant) exams with learning materials and summative assessment for 10 regular AU courses, while TAC provides on-site learner support and tutoring.

International expansion is critical to AU's future, for several reasons. First, fixed costs will be amortised over much larger numbers of students, thereby making the institution more cost-efficient. Second, Canadian students will benefit from enriched learning experiences as international students become their peers. Third, and most significantly from a public policy perspective, by becoming a strong international player, AU will protect its regional turf and ensure that the local educational agenda is defined by Albertans.

Q. What lessons have been learnt about managing off-campus centres, networks and services?

A. AU has a modest network of regional centres – one in Edmonton and one in Calgary – but these have consistently attracted more AU students than other Canadian centres (about 2,500 each in 1999–2000) and the University has consequently chosen to provide on-site student support services (primarily advising, registration, computer lab and exam invigilation). The AU model does not anticipate in-person tutorials and learning centres do not in and of themselves provide a framework for pedagogical support to the learning processes.

The most important management lesson from the integration of these satellite storefronts into AU's human, administrative and technical systems, concerns the need, and its implication, for regional autonomy and accountability. Students and prospective students prefer to minimize their contact points with the University, and the 'single-window service' philosophy the University advocates in its centralized interactions with students must be available in regional centres. These centres must be empowered to implement institutional policies and procedures, and to make exceptions, without the approval of the central administration or department. Given the complexity of AU as an organization, the importance of effective internal communication processes, human and technical, in achieving this goal cannot be overstated. And the Intranet plays a vital role at AU in the provision, sharing and accessing of consistent and reliable institutional information that staff require to be empowered and perform effectively. Nowhere is this more evident than in providing 'single-window' student support services in AU's regional learning centres.

AU tutors, some 300 in total, are part-time and unionized, work out of their homes, and report to the academics responsible for the courses they support. In the past, tutors have provided telephone support to learners at pre-arranged times and graded assignments that students mail them. The University now equips all tutors with voice-mail, Internet access and e-mail accounts. Increasingly, communication between learners and tutors takes place asynchronously: learners compose and leave voice-mail or e-mail messages at times convenient to them, and submit their assignments as e-mail attachments or online.

The digital era has created an expectation for just-in-time service that any successful distance educator must rise to. At AU, this has meant developing, implementing, publishing and monitoring institutional service standards. Their application to the tutorial workforce has proved to be a major challenge, as there is a fundamental contradiction between 'part-time' and 'just-in-time'. The latter requires continuous availability; the former is premised on only sporadic availability. AU wants its tutors to bring complementary workplace experience to their tutoring function, so full-time tutoring is not a preferred option. Fortunately, the University won a formal challenge made by the tutors' union in which the union argued that the University was contravening the Employment Standards Act by not paying a minimum of three hours' pay (the minimum payment period set out in legislation for employees who report physically to work) every time they turned on their computers to check for e-mail messages. A satisfactory solution to just-in-time service by part-time tutors has been arrived at by differentiating the service requirements according to the amount tutored, assuring a turn-around of 24 to 48 business hours for everything but the correction of assignments and exams, while publishing the service standard guarantee as 48 hours so as not to confuse students. The only complete solution to this dilemma sees just-in-time services assured by a team of part-time service providers, working together behind a single window interface. This, however, gives rise to a different problem, the de-personalizing of services, because a learner's numerous interactions will no longer be with the same tutor.

Recognition of the off-setting advantages and disadvantages of these three key variables (part-time workers, just-in-time service, personalized attention) and of the need to be flexible and combine these in various ways to meet the needs of different learners and different courses, has proved to be the most significant recent management challenge in this area.

Q. AU also offers courses for First Nations students. How are these provided for?

A. For the most part, AU's delivery of courses and programmes to First Nations students is cohort-based and onsite. We take our courses to the student's location and work with the local educational authorities to provide the optimum environment for success. This often involves devolving many of the student support services to the local indigenous providers (who act as brokers by selecting different course offerings and programmes from different institutions), training them in AU's rules, regulations and procedures, giving them access to our Intranet pages, and empowering them to make the best decisions for supporting the particular needs of their community of learners.

These partnerships tend to be long-standing and AU also consults with our indigenous partners when developing its curriculum and delivery plans, and particularly programmes likely to attract aboriginal students. Similarly, these partners are consulted during our appointment of tutors, and, because of the particular skills and sensitivities required in these settings, the university is no longer required to follow seniority provisions in its tutorial collective agreement when making these appointments.

Q. How does AU assure quality and measure and reward success?

A. The academic quality of our learning materials and activities is assured through a rigorous review of courses and programmes during their conception, development and delivery. Our course teams draw on disciplinary and instructional expertise both internal and external to the university and once developed, programmes and courses are reviewed cyclically by external teams.

The nature and quality of support services are also key to success. With this in mind, AU has developed a set of service standards governing the acceptable length of time for responding to, and processing, telephone, mail, and e-mail requests for information or services from any department or employee. These standards are published on the AU Website and in brochures given to every student enrolling in a course. Moreover, the university lists in that same documentation the position and phone number of the contact person responsible for ensuring each identified service standard. A similar inventory of service standards is being developed for internal interactions, and will shortly be available on the Intranet.

Internally, student satisfaction with the quality of their total learning experience is measured through an annual survey and one-off focus groups conducted by AU's Institutional Studies office. Since 1999, the provincial government also conducts a student satisfaction survey, using a standardized measurement tool for all publicly funded postsecondary institutions. In the first and only published results to date, AU achieved the top rank.

Overall institutional progress and success are monitored through annual reporting to the Governing Council in accordance with Management Internal Key Performance Indicators (MIKPs). While incorporating many of the system-wide governmental key performance indicators, which are primarily a measure of past performance, AU's MIKPs are derived from the 'Balanced Scorecard' approach and seek also to measure the institution's preparedness for future success. To this end, performance measures have been developed for indicators such as quality of courses and learning, innovation, Web-presence, customer and student satisfaction, collaborations, staffing and workplace well-being.

At AU, we recognize that rewarding success engenders further success and to that end we use all the standard tools such as merit increments and employee recognition programmes (for teaching, research and service). However, in what is probably unprecedented in Canadian public education, the Governing Council also chose to award all staff with a significant 'productivity bonus' in 1999, and again in 2000, in recognition of the institution's overall success as measured in the governmental KPI and student satisfaction survey results, and the MIKPs.

In its day-to-day practices, moreover, the University adheres to the important principle of reinvesting any financial gains that result from the self-initiated re-engineering of processes or applications of technology in the units that introduced the innovation. For example, the tutorial budget is formula-driven on a per-course registration basis and represents by far the greatest amount of flexible dollars at an academic department's disposal. Those that are successful in reducing their unit costs through redesign or technological innovation retain the financial gains they're able to generate, even if central administration has contributed financially to the development of the innovation.

Q. *What qualities of leadership do you seek to develop in your managers and staff and see as necessary in CEOs and managers confronted with the need to establish or renew open learning systems?*

A. Adherence to my value-driven management system is a *sine qua non* for participating in my management team. Thinking outside the box, controlled risk-taking, willingness to recognize mistakes and the ability to redress them, are also very important for successful leadership and management. If leaders and managers admit their inevitable mistakes, so too will the staff at large, and an organizational climate which is accepting of this is better prepared to challenge its assumptions and thereby renew itself.

CEOs and managers also need to have a thorough understanding both of their own business and, increasingly, of the external competitive environment. Only by knowing, or quickly learning, the intricacies of the organization's core functions can they determine whether their vision and the changes required for its implementation are realizable. In this regard, a key factor in successful change management involves knowing the acceptable limits of change and just how, and how far, one can push and pull the organization with a view to its repositioning.

Chapter 17

University of Wisconsin-Extension: exercising leadership in complex organizations

Professor Donald E Hanna, *Professor of Educational Communications and former Chancellor of the University of Wisconsin-Extension, in the United States, discusses the organizational issues and political realities of introducing and sustaining change in a large and complex educational institution.*

Q. As Chancellor of the University of Wisconsin-Extension, what were your goals with respect to open and flexible learning when you took over and did these need modifying over time?

A. The University of Wisconsin-Extension is a separate institution within the University of Wisconsin System, and is responsible for ensuring that the System is responsive to meeting the diverse educational needs of citizens of the state and beyond. Its programmes are diverse in mission, scope, delivery, and content. They include:

- Non-formal, non-degree programmes in agriculture, family living, 4-H youth development (focusing on leadership skills and knowledge building for 5–18-year olds), and community development assistance delivered face-to-face at a local county level by full-time specialists and faculty members.
- Public radio and television delivered through local, state and national partnerships.
- Continuing education programmes in many academic and professional fields offered both independently and in concert with the continuing education units of each of the 14 other institutions within the University of Wisconsin System.
- Credit courses by correspondence (one of the first such programmes established in the United States).
- A range of instructional support programmes, including three conference centres and technology support for interactive audio, voice and data programmes.

UW-Extension is an eclectic collection of interests, partnerships and community coalitions that range from water quality to farm transitioning, and from 'virtual' school classrooms to new product innovations. Its organizational structure is unique in the US. It has an annual budget of US$160 million and with significant funding coming from both local governmental entities (counties) and the state, and outside the direct control of the flagship UW-Madison campus, it is also a very political entity, one that is closely tied to the politics of state and county government.

Lawrence Weinstein, a former UW Regent, wrote a book in 1992 around the theme that changing the UW-System was akin to 'moving a battleship at rest with one's bare hands'. My initial view of UW-Extension was similar, except that my metaphor was that it was a large, slow, tanker equipped with a hundred independently driven propellers, trying to coordinate its activities with others who couldn't figure out why the organization couldn't move more precisely and accurately in their direction.

I was recruited to the position of Chancellor by the President of the University of Wisconsin System with the primary purpose of updating its programmes in distance learning and re-establishing the institution's reputation for innovation in distance learning. With little investment throughout the 1980s in the interactive technologies being employed by other universities, faculty had not developed a significant experience base with these technologies, even though the institution had retained many excellent personnel who were pioneers during the 1960s and 1970s.

One of my primary tasks was to provide a more supportive environment for those faculty members with particular interest in supporting Wisconsin's economy and quality of life through technology and distance learning, and to build a more positive institutional and technological structure for distance learning and other technology-assisted programmes. I can tell you that there was significant opposition from those who believed that technology would replace faculty members, would reduce the local presence of faculty, and would otherwise change the mode of delivery that for the most part had bypassed the use of electronic technologies. However, the institution was also blessed with many committed and experienced professionals who were enthusiastic and creative in providing examples of what could be done as an organization, and over time, my goal was to provide opportunities for these faculty and staff to demonstrate in a variety of ways internally and externally the capabilities and benefits of distance learning and appropriate application of technology.

Q. What challenges did UW-Extension face in rebuilding its open and flexible learning infrastructure during the 1990s and how did you address these?

A. In 1993 upon my arrival at the university, I asked to see the interactive distance learning facilities of Extension. Based upon my knowledge of Extension's formidable history, its early and aggressive endeavours in independent learning led by world class individuals such as Charles ('Chuck') Wedemeyer, and its pioneering work with audioconferencing, I expected to find modern, up-to-date classrooms in a facility befitting the university's history and prestige. When I was taken to Radio Hall, the headquarters of Instructional Communications Systems (ICS), I encountered an overcrowded facility with small, dank, dark classrooms, housed within a century-old building that was once the university's heating plant. The building had no central air conditioning, no pathways for wiring, no appropriately-sized classrooms, and no plans for renovation or improvement. The programme's primary claim to fame had been its pioneering work in the 1960s in creating one of the world's first educational teleconferencing networks, with work that resulted in the design of the first audio bridge and the formation of a company that became a worldwide powerhouse in teleconferencing called DaRome (named after Daryl and Jerome, the two Extension engineers who developed the bridge).

The staff of ICS had been significantly downsized through reductions initiated in the mid-1980s with the elimination of its Center for Interactive Technologies, an advanced application experimental programme. My first major task was to reposition this unit and rebuild its capacity; a second major task was to locate and build a telecommunications facility appropriate for an institution about to enter the 21st century. A third task was to strengthen the ICS unit with programming bases on all of the UW campuses, with other technology support units, and to encourage academic department use of the facility, especially from the Madison campus.

Shortly after touring the Radio Hall facility, I met with a number of key institutional administrators and faculty to discuss the institution's programmes and its use of technology. At that time, very few of the faculty outside Madison had access to the Internet. Even more surprising was the perspective that technology in general and the Internet in particular were perceived by many as a threat to the organization. The gap was wide between those who were fearful of negative impacts on faculty roles and responsibilities for teaching, and those who saw technology as a long-term benefit for improving access.

Overcoming this level of organizational scepticism, and reducing anxiety and fear that technology would replace people and ultimately reduce the need for the institution, was a long-term challenge that required continuous dialogue, raising of faculty and staff awareness of and experience with technology, and gradual progress in acquiring and applying new technologies. Also important was gaining credibility through successful applications for external funds.

From a broader perspective, I confronted three direct challenges, but overall perhaps one major all-encompassing challenge, that of changing the culture of Extension from one comfortable with stability, continuity and inertia, to one of accepting and embracing the need to change, with a readiness to formulate new strategies and to adapt processes and structures to accommodate new and emerging areas of programme needs. I believed then, and still believe, that this reorientation and repositioning with respect to change is the fundamental issue for UW-Extension, and for all universities in the coming decade.

The first challenge was to advance those Extension programmes that would meet the educational needs of the future, rather than continue all-out attempts to save those that had been important in the past. I pursued several strategies to accomplish this goal and encouraged our leadership team in these directions as well, all with the ultimate goal of introducing avenues for new ideas, proposals and programme offerings. These strategies included:

- Consistently advocating and shaping a vision of an institution open to change.
- Reaching out to form new partnerships and strategic alliances.
- Reallocating funding to pursue new opportunities.
- Using technology as a vehicle for organizational change.
- Establishing horizontal communications across the organization as critical paths for information flow.
- Rewarding individual and team efforts to improve skills, unit performance and cross-programme communication, cooperation and collaboration.
- Recruiting of personnel from outside the organization.

The second challenge was to rebuild support for the technological infrastructure of Extension, and to re-establish its leadership for innovation and change in the field of distance learning and creative use of electronic technologies. This challenge had three dimensions.

The first dimension of meeting this challenge was to rebuild the technology infrastructure that had been de-emphasized during the 1980s despite the fact that this was a time of rapid development of new distance education interactive technologies all across the globe. Facilities were woefully outdated, and programmes and technology support units were substantially separated from each other and from the programmes they were intended to support. With early support from the UW System President and the Board of Regents, plans were developed to build a state-of-the-art distance education centre and to submit a proposal for the funding of this centre. The result was that funding was secured in 1995 for what became the Pyle Center, an advanced communication and technology support framework from which the institution could advance its own practice and provide national leadership.

The second dimension of building leadership capacity for innovation was to provide broad-based training and development opportunities for faculty and other staff who wished to experiment with new instructional technologies. Funds were reallocated to enable departments and units to support more comprehensively the training and development of staff in creative ways.

The third dimension was to develop a climate of communication, interaction and cross-programme and division activities. A number of institution-wide fora, seminars and discussions were held around the themes of technology and change, and internal programmes and innovative faculty members were featured. The challenge of becoming an institution seeking change and innovation was largely one of attitude and culture, and it was vital to introduce new dimensions of thinking and practice and challenges from the external environment, to build internal awareness of these as opportunities, and to forge partnerships with other organizations actively engaged in meeting new demands and needs.

The final challenge I had to confront was maintaining funding for the institution in the eye of a significant funding attack on the University System by the Governor and State legislature, an aggressive action that seemed to be targeted toward Extension. During my first two years, I took several risks, with the support of the University System's President, toward consolidation of programmes and more efficient use of existing resources, all within an environment of significantly reduced funding for the University as a whole. Some of these steps and proposals were extremely politically controversial outside the University, even with the support of the President. In January 1997, I resigned my position because it had become clear to me that I no longer enjoyed sufficient political support to withstand external political pressures or to make the decisions necessary to continue to lead the institution. This was one of the most difficult personal decisions of my life.

Q. You're a strong advocate of partnerships as a strategy for organizational change. What successes and failures have you had in this regard?

A. Well, I do believe strongly that change in organizations generally is aided and shaped by the external environment, especially one as dynamic as the one that universities are currently facing across the globe. Jack Welch, former CEO of General Electric, puts it this way: 'When the rate of change outside the organization exceeds the rate of change inside the organization, the end is in sight'. An organization that always looks inward for direction and ideas is one destined to remain buried in the support of the past.

One of the ways that organizations stay current is to interact with other organizations directly and intimately toward purposes that are important to both organizations. During my time at Washington State University, I focused upon helping to build national and regional coalitions of institutions working together toward a common goal. The ideas gained from these interactions were extremely helpful in educating our leadership about both the opportunities of moving toward open and flexible learning, and some of the operational details of how to do so most effectively. The formation of the National Universities Degree Consortium for the purpose of joint development of programmes and support for nationally delivered degrees is one example. A second is linking with community colleges in Washington to jointly offer bachelors degrees at a distance across the state of Washington.

At the University of Wisconsin, we developed partnerships with state government and with the private, non-profit and foundation sectors to deliver new programmes in leadership and strategic development for non-profit organizations, with the private sector to advance the use of telecommunications in communities throughout Wisconsin, and with leading technology organizations to advance the use of the Internet and the Web to improve instruction and increase accessibility to our programmes. In all of these activities, the values, knowledge and expertise brought in by other organizations and introduced to UW-Extension were perhaps the most valuable organizational outcomes for UW-Extension. Concepts of entrepreneurial action, learning by experimentation, and creating new organizational processes were literally avenues for introducing new ideas and change into the organization. Of course, these benefits came at a price of efficiency, control and focus, and thus the strategy was not without its internal critics.

With respect to failure, I found that several partnerships where I had predicted that similarity of mission, goals and programmes would facilitate successful collaboration simply did not materialize, much to my disappointment. Whether these failures were due to the inevitability of local competition for prestige, resources or other forms of external or political recognition, or simply as a result of individual personality incongruence is still a major question for me.

Q. What principles or experiences have shaped your particular leadership style?

A. First, I believe that organizations have goals and purposes that transcend individuals and leaders, and it is essential that leaders believe in these purposes and the ideals that undergird them. Without ideals and purposes, actions are meaningless. For me, embracing these ideals and seeking to achieve them is the first and most fundamental act of leadership, and being willing to make sacrifices on behalf of them is the well from which passion is drawn, from which perseverance is sustained, and through which courage is formed. Bringing this orientation to leadership positions provides perspective on both the opportunities and challenges faced by the organization, and provides a platform from which principled and engaged leadership can emerge and develop. When strategies are formed on the basis of political rather than programmatic considerations, something is lost within any organization, and within a university what is lost is not only personal integrity, but the fundamental reason why universities exist: to pursue truth and knowledge wherever this pursuit may lead, and to disseminate this knowledge widely to improve the lives of people.

I also believe strongly in the values of teamwork and team-based leadership. Such an environment is dependent upon open communication, the development of a strong sense of trust and personal loyalty to each other, not for the sake of protecting political agendas, but for the sake of advancing shared visions and programme goals.

Finally, I have had the good fortune to have had several outstanding leaders as mentors and as models to follow. Beginning at the University of Illinois, where I was surrounded by creative individuals who were also excellent leaders, and continuing at Washington State University, where I experienced the impact that vision and leadership could have on a university and a state, mentoring has been an important factor in shaping my perspectives and orientation toward leadership. Mentoring often occurs informally and is highly under-utilized as a formal organizational strategy for developing leadership. Every leader should also be a mentor to multiple people within the organization, and every faculty and staff member in a healthy organization should expect to be mentored by multiple people. If mentoring is absent within an organization, the organization's vitality and health are at risk.

Q. What hard lessons have you learnt about leading change in large and complex institutions like UW-Extension?

A. UW-Extension was perhaps the best learning environment I have had, and I learnt many lessons about organizations that I continue to apply and to teach and write about. Perhaps the biggest 'hard' lesson I have learnt is that even in 'humane' organizations, being true to personal values and preserving one's integrity can in certain circumstances exact a very high political price. It has been said that leadership involves a balance between principled action and political reality, and that the successful leader in complex organizations never allows events to come to a point where a choice must be made between the two. I am ever more sensitive to this challenge but also cognizant of the risks that must be taken in organizational leadership and the possibility that events outside one's arena of influence may coalesce to create that very undesirable choice.

With respect to open and flexible learning, leaders are often advancing programmes that are not in the mainstream of organizational thought or practice. As a result they are particularly susceptible to being out of step with their organization. Therefore they must both diligently guard against being in the position of having to choose between principle and politics, and at the same time, if they have passion for their organization and its goals, prepare themselves for just such a possibility.

Second, the creation of learning environments and learning organizations based upon team-based principles and strategic decision-making can be a daunting challenge. One of my mentors at Washington State once commented, and I've never forgotten this, that the right people can work together to make the worst organizational structure function effectively, and the wrong people can disrupt the best organization almost single-handedly. People with common vision and positive attitudes are critical to an organization on the move. Defining organizational purpose and enlisting those in leadership who are enthusiastic and positively oriented toward advancing this purpose is very important. Spending time assessing this attitude at the front end of change can be extremely productive as the organization moves forward. Recruiting such people to leadership early on is equally important, and great care should be exercised.

The third lesson I have learnt during my administrative career is the importance of 'fit' between the personal style and characteristics of the leader and the characteristics of the organization. William Bridges (2000), in his book *The Character of Organizations*, suggests that, like individuals, all organizations have a set of personality preferences. Using the Myers–Briggs Personality Indicator as a framework, Bridges analyses the degree of fit between individual leadership characteristics and preferences, and those characteristics of organizations. Some organizations are open to change and others are not. Some leaders are interested in promoting change and others are committed to preserving the status quo. A leader must carefully analyse and assess the characteristics and behaviour of the organization to determine the best approach for introducing change, and be open to modifying his or her own personal style to better fit the organization.

Q. What do you see as the main issues for traditional and dual-mode universities arising from globalization, deregulation (increased competition) and technological change?

A. Universities are facing a very different world as technologies remove protective geographical boundaries around fixed physical campuses. In the United States, these historical geographic boundaries, often identified in the form of concentric circles drawn around campuses, have been buttressed by state policies that have served to protect the market territory of private non-profit universities from intrusion by public universities with state support, and also to protect public universities from programmatic competition from each other.

Increasingly, the public seems to be saying that those individuals who benefit from higher education should pay more of the cost of their education, which is forcing universities to become more competitive in their strategy, focus more on serving those who can afford to pay, and to experiment with new technologies that enable them to reach broader audiences. Increased expectations that universities respond aggressively to a new market of adults needing access to higher education to compete in the workforce further advances this trend, as does a concomitant change in the public's assessment of individual versus societal benefit from higher education. In Wisconsin, where there has been low-cost tuition and a focus on serving the state from within, new policies for distance education have been established that allow tuition in these programmes to vary according to factors such as the programme's cost, the ability of the market to absorb a particular tuition level, and the priority of the programme.

Campuses are also able for the first time to use the argument that serving students from out of state and even across the globe at in-state tuition levels is appropriate because these students will in effect enable the programme to be offered at a reduced cost to Wisconsin residents. These new policies depend upon the assumption that use of technology actually lowers overall costs by spreading programme costs over more students, and it's very likely that this assumption will be found to be faulty in many instances. Nevertheless, the old foundations for policy are gone, and new ones based upon the public benefit from both increased competition and the use of technology are being advanced in their place. One can see that if these premises are widely accepted and advanced by all institutions locally, regionally, nationally and globally, the effect on leadership and strategy development will be profound as new 'rules of engagement' are developed. The challenges and opportunities will be enormous, and institutions will have to carefully assess their position in entirely new ways.

Q. What qualities and skill sets do you see as necessary in CEOs and senior managers establishing or renewing open and flexible learning systems and possibly confronting resistance to such change?

A. First, I believe it is essential that CEOs and senior managers in open and flexible learning have a vision and a passion for advancing their programmes. Without firm beliefs about the role and contribution these programmes make to enhancing people's lives, leaders are unlikely to gain the support these programmes require, especially in institutions whose primary purpose is not perceived to encompass making programmes accessible across distance and time.

A second quality that is highly underrated in managing and overcoming resistance to change is persistence and refusal to yield to apparent apathy or failure. The observation by W C Fields that 90 per cent of (success in) life is simply showing up, can be extended to leadership. Being there, day in and day out, is critical, and in universities where decisions are haphazard and often uncoordinated, being there consistently greatly enhances one's ability to shape desired outcomes.

Also, the ability to form strong leadership teams and to engender learning within and across the organization can greatly improve the organization's capacity for change, its self-confidence and morale, and its long-term viability. This also requires the opportunity and the judgement to select people who value team activities and action, who can engender and facilitate teamwork, and who are comfortable working in team-based environments. These skills are not widely developed in our educational system today, so organizations have a responsibility to help their members to acquire and to practise these skills. I would point to Washington State University's multicampus system and its extended degree programmes as an example of where all of these came together under the leadership of President Samuel Smith to enable the university to develop a comprehensive strategy for reaching out to new constituencies across the state of Washington. Penn State University, under the leadership of President Graham Spanier, Vice-President James Ryan and World Campus Executive Director Gary Miller is another example of where vision, passion, judgement, persistence, and teamwork have combined to produce a new institutional vision, strategy, and set of important programmes.

A final quality I believe is essential is to stand for something, and stick to it even when it is risky to do so. The leaders I have most admired, inside and outside universities, have been those who have taken unpopular positions and who have fought through adversity to gain respect for their positions. Because universities are risk-averse organizations, they are not fertile grounds for growing such leaders. Where do we find such leadership in our universities and how do we sustain it? What can people currently in leadership positions do to support those willing to take such risks? In a dynamic environment, the inclination and willingness to support risk-taking by others seems to me to be a major expectation for leadership in the future.

Chapter 18

Partnerships for change

Professor Dato' Gajaraj Dhanarajan discusses leadership issues arising from his previous role as inaugural Director of the Open Learning Institute of Hong Kong and his current role as President and CEO of the Commonwealth of Learning (COL), a Vancouver-based intergovernmental organization created by Commonwealth Heads of Government to encourage the development and sharing of open and distance education knowledge, resources and technologies to help developing nations improve access to quality education and training.

Q. What do you see as the main challenges and opportunities for distance education in developed and developing countries?

A. Global social, economic, scientific and technological developments present us with enormous challenges, opportunities and capacities to improve the lot of human kind. Those of us in education are at the centre of such changes. In the past, the speed of change allowed us time to reflect and deliberate. Today, the speed of change does not permit such luxury. We don't have five years to plan the next five years. Nor can we be confident of the value of our prior knowledge, the tenure of our jobs, the direction of the next wave of change, or the security of knowing our current skills to be economically and socially relevant. We need the capability to acquire new knowledge, to think fast and act faster, to know what to learn, to search for sources for learning, and to apply that learning to useful purposes. Many need these capacities. Few possess them.

As a teacher, I found it frustrating that our traditions of delivering education were so inhibiting, both in reach and methods. Perhaps this was what attracted me to the principles of open learning and the practice of distance education. It gave me hope that it was possible to reach those considered unreachable. Despite the hype about democratizing education and equity as a key principle of educational policy, the culture of academe hasn't changed in these regards. But it must if we truly believe what we say in our learned forums and writings about equality of opportunity for all peoples. It seems awful to me that a human endeavour that employs some 50 million individuals and costs the world close to US$1,000 billion (Hirt, 2000) still keeps education out of reach of more than a fifth of the world's population. Spending another US$1,000 billion will not change the situation much unless we use all available resources wisely and effectively. This is the challenge to all political leaders, educational policy makers and teachers: to bring education to the user – whether it's the girl in an Afghan village who's not permitted into school for cultural or religious reasons or the upwardly mobile young New Yorker whose work schedule doesn't allow attendance at night school to study for an MBA.

Q. As Associate Director (Academic) and later Director of the newly established Open Learning Institute of Hong Kong (now the Open University of Hong Kong), what were the leadership challenges you had to respond to?

A. June 1989 in Hong Kong was the month when the then Governor of Hong Kong signed the legislation enabling the establishment of the Open Learning Institute of Hong Kong (OLIHK). It was also the month that the People's Republic of China sent shock waves throughout Hong Kong by its bloody behaviour in Tiananmen Square. People were losing confidence in the Territory and fearful of the 1997 handover. Not a good month to launch a distance teaching establishment totally dependent upon fee-paying students and long-term commitment from its clients!

The OLI was mandated to provide opportunities for higher education through open learning, to be self-funding within three years, to be subject to external validation and to begin operations within three months of the signing of its Charter. It actually fulfilled all of these expectations. During those first three years, it underwent two successful institutional reviews by the UK Council for National Academic Awards and the Hong Kong Council for Academic Accreditation, obtained external validation for 17 undergraduate programmes, presented about 81 courses in English or Chinese, graduated its first 150 students, and became independent of the public purse. By the time I relinquished office in August 1995, the Institute had further graduated some 3,917 students, had reached a student enrolment of 20,085, was financially self-sufficient and had been through a further external audit which deemed the institution capable of self-accreditation, thus paving the way for the OLI to become the OUHK, which it did in 1997 (OUHK, 1999). It also subsequently received Awards of Excellence from The Commonwealth of Learning in 1998 and from the International Council for Open and Distance Education in 1999.

I believe many of the OLI's achievements were directly attributable to our planning strategies to make the organization educationally useful, economically viable, politically acceptable and academically respectable in Hong Kong and internationally. If these objectives hadn't been met, closure of the Institute could have been predicted. It was my responsibility to ensure that the Institute survived.

Our planning was no paper exercise full of platitudes, but an unambiguous statement of the nature, types and names of the courses we would offer, the enrolment numbers, the fees we would charge, the costs of designing and developing the courses, the hours of tuition and the income to be generated. We also made a risk assessment. It was in every sense a *business plan*, something that academe was not comfortable with at that time. Underpinning our planning were reminders that we were a service industry, that our clients were right to expect products of the highest standards supported by services of impeccable quality, that we had to provide education to internationally acceptable standards and award credits on the basis of transparent and rigorous exit standards, that we had to be sensitive to the needs of the end user, and that we had to be a financially sustainable non-profit enterprise in a highly competitive market – and that our fees had to be affordable. I was lucky in having colleagues who came from many parts of the world but shared this vision of open learning and running a public service on a business platform and who were not afraid of addressing these difficult practical and philosophical issues.

Someone once said that leaders are not born, but made. Well, the OLI made me a CEO; I grew through that experience. The staff, students and Board expected me to be honest, prudent, transparent and knowledgeable. I joined the OLI with a belief in the potential of distance education in that compact city-state where access, not distance, was the challenge. Hong Kong enabled me to test many things I thought possible: the importation of course materials for a local curriculum, the importance of learning support systems, flexibility in the pace of learning, a generous approach to prior learning, a division of academic labour, and an open admission system that was almost heretical in the Mandarin culture of Hong Kong academe.

With little political interference from government and lots of enthusiasm from a committed team, the OLI achieved greater success than many dreamt possible. As CEO, my job was to ensure that there was never a drying up of ideas to make the OLI a functioning reality and an asset for Hong Kong. This meant being informed, being involved, being accountable, seeking and using the best advice I could get, appointing staff with a commitment and dedication to the task and ultimately being responsible for the tasks entrusted to me, a personal obligation both contractually and morally. Commonsense, an eye for detail, passion and belief in the cause and a sense of the practical were also necessary assets.

Q. What are the origins and mission of The Commonwealth of Learning (COL)?

A. Since its inception, COL has been guided by the Briggs Report (Commonwealth Secretariat, 1987) and the Daniel Report (Commonwealth Secretariat, 1988), which spelt out its expected contribution to Commonwealth cooperation in education. COL can call upon its own critical mass of knowledge and experience. Its headquarters staff specialize in components of distance education. They maintain contact with national and international experts in their fields and are well informed on needs in Commonwealth countries and the policy options that can be realistically adopted for open and distance education. But we're a small agency. So we also mobilize Commonwealth cooperation and change agents. Between 1989 and 1999, COL used 400 consultants from 39 Commonwealth and four non-Commonwealth countries and the significant feature of this was that the exchange of expertise was 'South–South' as well as 'North–South'.

COL is expected to mobilize knowledge and expertise in a field of education and training that's both new and undergoing rapid technology change. Both factors raise daunting policy issues for governments, educators and trainers. Those who manage and provide education and training must understand the demands of distance education for funding, trained personnel and supporting resources and must have policies, funding arrangements and management systems that will enable effective distance education to occur. To help bring about such sensitivity, knowledge, skills and policies, COL adds value by:

- Creating and developing institutional capacity (by assisting with basic policy and management requirements).
- Seeking and channelling support for distance education projects and programmes.
- Providing information and consultancy.
- Engaging in staff training in the techniques and management of distance education and supporting the training efforts of others.
- Establishing communication links between like-minded colleagues working to common objectives, institutions and Commonwealth distance education associations.
- Undertaking and supporting evaluation and applied research (which are not prominent features in most Commonwealth countries' education systems).
- Facilitating access to the existing stock of teaching materials for adoption or adaptation, or as exemplars or guides.
- Commissioning and promoting the adaptation and development of teaching materials.
- Exploring recognition of prior academic credit (the restrictive policies of many countries and institutions for the recognition of qualifications or partially completed qualifications gained in another country are impediments to open learning within and between countries).
- Advising on the development of local study centres, tutoring, libraries, laboratories or workshops.

Our 10 years of work seems to confirm the pragmatism of the recommendations of the Briggs and Daniel working groups. Our past should be a guide to the value we can add to the Commonwealth's educational agenda. The reality and the technological richness of the new decade will enable us to do more. COL must explore how best to bring to the attention of Commonwealth governments the potential of the new environment for widening access to learning by the millions still denied this opportunity.

Q. How do COL and its partners encourage and support innovation and change in education and training?

A. When the world was not 'globalized', those of us with a global perspective did global work because it was the right thing to do. The new globalization is mostly about profit, market, trade in services, pricing skills at what the market can pay, etc. This makes the environment very difficult for small organizations with a global mission, such as COL. We don't have all the skills needed to fulfil our mission in-house, nor should we. We're expected to make optimum use of the skills, knowledge and experience of our Commonwealth colleagues. In utilizing that expertise, COL can't compete with the larger better-funded international and national development agencies. We encourage Commonwealth colleagues with modest financial incentives but offer in return collegiality, work at the cutting edge of educational development, and a sense of purpose and mission. This approach works despite the slave wages we pay. We have some of the best rather than the best-known distance educators working for us – as partners in capacity-building, catalysts for collaboration, and providers of knowledge in distance and open learning and technologies.

COL's vision is to be not only supportive of national and institutional agendas, but to add value to their planning and undertakings by working with them in:

- *Conceptualizing activities typically lacking in ready-made solutions.* This was of course the main reason for COL's creation – to work at development frontiers where the possibilities of distance learning, technologies and the specific circumstances of 54 countries come together and for COL staff and consultants and the people in the regions, countries and institutions to collaborate in conceptualizing the issues and solutions.
- *Arranging alliances and partnerships.* Fostering and cementing strategic alliances are of prime importance to COL. There are many distance education institutions in the Commonwealth and other countries and COL must seek to work cooperatively with these and complement, not compete with, their activities. It's not currently one of COL's functions to provide distance education programmes but there is increasing pressure for this and we shall seek to develop such programmes with and through existing providers. It is also imperative that COL develops close working relationships with national educational administrations and national, regional and international development assistance agencies. COL's first decade coincided with the global discovery of open and distance education as an effective alternative method of tackling massive educational and training challenges. Its second decade can be expected to see further confirmation of this and an expanded role for distance and open learning. Working closely with other agencies, we can help develop ideas to the point where these agencies can either share in, or take responsibility for, further funding, development and implementation of distance education initiatives. Also, new kinds of working relationships have to be fostered between the very different cultures of education, technology and telecommunications. This opens up new and problematic fields of interest. In this context, COL is unique among international agencies, with its core professional staff including experts in technology and telecommunications as well as education and training.
- *Building models of good practice.* COL has to resolve the inner contradictions of its mission and means. It must be responsive to the different expectations of

the 54 Commonwealth countries, but through the energies and talents of a small core of professional staff. COL's way of squaring this circle is to select projects, which in their development and operation, become exemplary – not as prescriptions but as practical demonstrations of factors to be taken into account in achieving workable solutions.

- *Brokering.* In Commonwealth settings, where the vast majority of members are developing countries, many are small, and all are hard pressed financially and lacking in an adequate supply of expert knowledge, COL can play an important brokering role, particularly in regard to accessing information and course materials, intellectual property, and negotiating purchase and usage agreements. These are challenging tasks, but COL needs to make continuous efforts in this role.
- *Commissioning.* The ability to commission is strategically important to COL. The advent of digital technologies makes it possible to create generic learning materials for global use and yet allow enough latitude for local adaptation. COL needs to embark on this in a significant way.
- *Networking.* Effective cooperation calls for a multiplicity of networking arrangements. COL's unique contribution until now has been its knowledge and expertise in open and distance education and the access it can provide to the knowledge of other practitioners. COL's future networking strategies could take several forms. It could build links with Commonwealth governments, education and training agencies and major development agencies. These links could lead directly to the development and delivery of training and learning projects. COL has also been instrumental in helping to set up a number of distance education professional associations in the Commonwealth. These links need further strengthening.
- *Advocacy.* A very definite signal of the importance that Commonwealth governments are giving to distance education is reflected in the range of projects COL is undertaking in association with government institutions and development assistance agencies. COL has a continuing role in giving definition and leadership to distance education and the means by which it might implemented.

Q. Much of COL's work involves partnering with education, industry, donor agencies, and so on. What issues need to be addressed in such collaboration?

A. We have to explore a working relationship with industry a lot more than we've done so far. Towards this goal, we've set up a small associated venture called COL International, which will work with industry and business. Our work with the others you mention has its ups and downs. Our experience very much resonates with the observations of the 1986 Advisory Group on Commonwealth Cooperation in Open Learning and Distance Education, which were that success depends on:

- complementarity – partnerships based on mutual respect, trust and benefit;
- mission clarity and articulation;

- institutional commitment;
- government and community support;
- organizational structure;
- leadership – the vision, time and interest that the leaders of partnering institutions bring into the venture.

Q. What strategies do you personally favour for determining the purpose, scope and values of open learning and planning and assessing performance?

A. There seems to be general acceptance that we're in the midst of a knowledge-based environment. Food production, conflict resolution, cultural preservation, conservation, environmental protection, governance, participation in civil society, health, business, manufacture all depend on access to knowledge, application of knowledge and exchange of knowledge. Yet, some two-thirds of the world's 6 billion people simply don't have a clue how to get there. For me, this is where open learning has its greatest application and challenge.

Putting that naïve side of myself aside, focusing on the lucky few million who are already in the business of using knowledge, the average technologist, unless refreshed, is said to become obsolete within two years. The same will apply to those who practise teaching, healthcare, social welfare, childcare, law, accountancy or even crime prevention, and the need to refresh their knowledge and skill on a regular basis will become a continuous obligation. As designers of learning for a learning society, educators face tremendous challenges in addressing the needs of the coming century.

The opportunities are limitless, but need not be limited to the public sector. A relationship with business, industry and other private sector entities is another definite direction. Efforts in the area of continuous professional education need to be enhanced, since occupational relevance of courses is generally attractive to private funding. Such initiatives are already being experimented with in many parts of the world. These allow for learning contracts between teaching institutions and industry in which the learners receive credits for courses designed jointly by academic institutions and employers, certification for job training, assessment of prior experiential learning and many more options.

To meet the needs of the new learners and the future learning environment will require innovative organizations. Ways will have to be found to deliver courses at new locations, link networks of training sites, develop certification protocols, develop strategies for course development, provide clearing houses for course-related information and set in place systems that allow institutions to respond rapidly and meaningfully to needs, accreditation, credit banks and transfers. Institutions will also have to explore new ways of enabling students to continue their studies as they move from location to location, be willing to use materials not developed by themselves, develop courses jointly with others and radically change the methods by which they assess learning outcomes. The way these are mostly measured today is dull, irrelevant, rigid, continues to test memory rather than application, and non-challenging of the intellect.

Q. What do you see as the emerging issues and challenges for open and distance teaching institutions in the new millennium?

A. If trends in North America are anything to go by, most institutions of higher learning will have to make provision for a multimode way of teaching. This will be more due to market forces, competition and government pressure than any love of distance education by our academic colleagues. Globally, there will be other pressures. Demographic and socio-economic trends are such that there'll be:

● A diversity of participants in education and training – from those seeking basic literacy to those wishing to enter the 'University of the Third Age'.
● A diversity of goals – learners studying for a variety of reasons.
● A diversity of contexts – for many wishing to study, learning will have to be at the time and place of their choice.
● Use of technology. Technology now brings together, under one umbrella, the essence of print, audio and video signals, computer-assisted instruction, conferencing and group learning. The future challenge is to create pedagogies that use these modes of delivery to improve learning and the educational environment by providing:
  – increased and flexible access to information (isolated learners, preoccupied with other demands of living, require a variety of channels to access information on both academic and administrative matters);
  – increased and flexible interaction between mentors and peers (freedom from timetabled environments);
  – increased student time on-task (pacing learning through devices that set tasks and deadlines for judicious absorption of information, skills or knowledge and completion of learning);
  – opportunities to vary the pace of learning;
  – learning that is relevant to daily lives (a curriculum that is appropriate and sensitively transformed into learning experience);
  – greater response to individual circumstances (mass education does not necessarily have to dehumanize the learning process);
  – regular and sensitive encouragement to continue learning (counselling for success).

As the forces surrounding the educational environment impel educational institutions to move away from being elitist, exclusively high-cost, campus-based and faculty-centred to one where the focus is the learner, access is mass, cost is low and the world is the campus, some fundamental shifts in the methods of teaching and learning will have to take place. The experience of distance educators will be an invaluable guide for future practice.

Q. What skill sets do you see as necessary in leaders and managers confronted with the need to establish or renew open learning systems and, in some cases, organizational and individual resistance?

A. I rely on four traits to help me in my work. They are not all skills; a lot has to do with attitude as well, with respect for the people we serve and work with. I'm not sure these points will apply to other leaders in their individual circumstances, but they're almost universal values, so one can't go wrong giving them some consideration:

- *Knowledge.* In distance education, as in other professional practice, those who lead must have knowledge of the field. Titles, privileges, grand offices and entourages of assistants may symbolize office but do not evidence leadership. Judgements are based on knowledge; choice is exercised on the basis of know-how.
- *Passion and persuasion.* If you're truly passionate about your cause, even sceptics pause to think and reconsider. Open learning has gained momentum and strengthened over these past 30 years because its pioneers were passionate about its value and persuasive in their arguments.
- *Vision.* It helps to know where a CEO wishes to take the institution. As Theodore Sorenson (1987) said, 'Our vision must appeal to our hopes and our needs.' Visions of the future are not always fulfilled, much less easily or instantly. CEOs must think beyond next week and next year. Their eyes must be on the horizon but their feet must be firmly on the ground if they're to build institutions that endure.
- *Team player.* An effective CEO is not a solo performer with a supporting cast but part of a team of talented individuals, many smarter than the CEO. Introducing distance education into an educational environment is a major effort demanding teamwork. One person, even a terrifically charismatic leader, is never strong enough to make all this happen.

Chapter 19

Leading change in the expanded K-12 classroom

Dr Brian Talbott founded the STEP•Star Network, one of the most successful US Star Schools programmes. He now serves on the Universal Service Administrative Company Board, which oversees the telecommunication E-rate for schools and libraries, and is the National Executive Director of the Association of Educational Service Agencies.

Q. As Superintendent of Educational Service District 101 (ESD 101) in Spokane, Washington, you initiated one of the first and most successful satellite-based K-12 programmes in North America. What made you believe in such a system?

A. I came to ESD 101 with a strong conviction that distance education could become the great equalizer. My experience from 1965 to 1975 as teacher, vice principal, principal and superintendent taught me that students had many different needs and came from unique cultural, social and economic backgrounds. Nothing brought this into perspective more than my six years in the Granger School District, an agricultural community in Eastern Washington. Here the minority students were the majority. We were continually trying to expand and broaden the courses available for our students while faced with limited finances and a lack of qualified teachers.

Later, as superintendent of ESD 105 in Yakima, Washington in the late 1970s, I saw how resources could be leveraged by forming consortia among school districts in such areas as special education, traffic safety, transport, media services, financial services and data processing. I realized that Educational Service Agencies were best positioned to do this leveraging on behalf of the entities they served and by so doing, could significantly improve the quality of education. At ESD 105 I also served on the Board and later as the Chair of the KYVE Public Broadcasting Station. Seeing the power of television, I started asking questions about how we could use this medium as an educational tool within the school setting.

I became superintendent of ESD 101 in Spokane, Washington in 1981, a region of over 14,000 square miles with 54 private schools and 59 public school districts ranging from 6 to over 30,000 students. At my interview, ESD Board member Carl Putnam, one of the brightest, most forward thinking and committed individuals I've ever met, asked me what I proposed to do to expand course offerings for the rural schools. He felt strongly that if we didn't do this, the rural schools would be unable to compete with the larger school districts and that this would contribute to the demise of small rural communities. I suggested that we could use distance learning to level the playing field and the entire Board encouraged me to explore this option. Their support never wavered during the 16 years I was superintendent and general manager of the STEP•Star Network. Without this commitment over the long haul from the Board, ESD 101 would never have been as successful as it was. The STEP•Star Network is a tribute to the Board doing what was right for the students and allowing management the freedom to hire outstanding personnel to deliver education to students anywhere, any time, in our region and across the nation. They had the vision, the perseverance and the strength to accomplish this when hundreds failed to even see the opportunity.

Q. You launched the STEP•Star Network in 1986. How did you plan for this?

A. The decision to start this network was based on a needs assessment that clearly showed the necessity of improving educational quality and equalizing educational opportunity throughout the region. The only approach we could all agree on was satellite-based distributed video with two-way audio. Our assessment showed that initially, this wouldn't be as cost-effective as the traditional classroom but that as more districts and students participated the costs could be lower than the regular classroom. The assessment also showed the need for teacher support. We planned at the start that our programming would supplement, not replace, existing staff, concentrating on foreign languages, advanced maths, advanced placement English classes and unique niche elementary courses like 'Young Astronauts', supplemental elementary units in art, science and mathematics and in-service programmes for teachers. In order to ensure that STEP•Star would remain eligible for all levels of funding, ESD 101 decided to establish its Educational Technology Division. The STEP•Star Network became part of this division allowing continued eligibility for federal, state and local funding.

Q. What challenges did you face in setting up the STEP•Star Network, and how did you address these?

A. The critical components were establishing strong public/private partnerships, hiring qualified personnel, meeting the cost of distance learning, sustaining opportunities for student interaction and involvement, and accommodating various state and international regulations.

We recognized the need for strong public/private partnerships. The private sector knew the television industry and we knew education. By working together we could achieve a form of 'edu-tainment'. Our students were the *Sesame Street* generation and extremely receptive to learning through distance education. The first year we tried working jointly with a university, but the telecommunication department's priority was training people for entertainment and news TV and our educational direction didn't fit with their goals. Further, the university faculty interpreted our mission as being in conflict with the traditional classroom model they supported. So, in 1991 we moved on to a new public/private partnership.

We bid the project nationally. RXL Communications of Seattle, Washington was awarded the first five-year contract and with hard work on both sides we were able to bring the two staffs together. In 1996, the contract was re-bid and the successful bidder was Educational Telecommunications Services (ETS). Under this contract, ESD 101 was responsible for selecting and upgrading equipment on an as-needed basis and was responsible for the instructional portion of the network. ESD 101 subcontracted production to ETS, and ETS hired and managed the production personnel and assisted ESD 101 in acquiring equipment and installing a portable and fixed downlink, two studios and a master control room. The key to our success was making this operation as seamless as possible. This meant both staffs had to work together as a team even though they were hired, managed and paid directly by ETS or by ESD 101. In reality it was seamless to the outsider, but was really an independent company operating within a public entity. Our goal of reaching out to the students and providing quality in-service training for educational personnel through synchronous or asynchronous programmes could never have been accomplished without this concerted effort to merge the public and private cultures. It isn't easy to marry two cultures as different as business and education but there's no doubt, in my view, that this was the correct approach and what made the STEP•Star Network so successful.

Hiring the right personnel for our new venture was another challenge. We needed production, technical and administrative staff who shared the vision and commitment of the Board, public/private partners and participating districts, teachers who were comfortable with satellite-based teaching, and classroom facilitators, graders and teacher assistants. Depending on state laws and regulations, the facilitators, who ensured online materials were available and equipment operational at the start of sessions, could be certified teachers, teacher aides, parents, community volunteers, administrators or student leaders. Some of our best facilitators were community volunteers and teachers who believed in open learning, some of the poorest facilitators were weak teachers or those reluctant to support open learning. We recruited a strong, well-qualified team, some of whom are still with the project. This team then went on to deliver live interactive instructional programmes to a large diverse clientele ranging from students in rural–remote sites near the Arctic Circle to students in some of the nation's largest urban and suburban districts.

Another significant challenge was gaining major financial commitments from federal and state governments, the corporate sector and local communities. Without Star Schools support from the US Congress and the commitment of the Office of Educational Research and Improvement of the US Department of Education, the STEP•Star Network and the other Star Schools projects wouldn't be where they are today. The STEP•Star Network has spent over US$50 million over the past 14 years. By leveraging federal, state and local dollars with eligible E-rate dollars from the Universal Services Program, over 500,000 students across the

United States have received affordable and cost–effective distance learning courses. Among our business partners was Apple Computer who supported the project from its inception and helped us design the technical support system for online delivery of classroom materials, tests and grading. This early commitment also ensured a sophisticated back–end technology development support team responsible for the interface between the teacher and the student.

Another challenge was figuring out how to provide for student interaction and involvement. With schools participating from Alaska and Hawaii to Virginia, we had numerous scheduling conflicts due to the six time zones. We also couldn't match the schedules of our own local districts. Some students had to study the courses asynchronously and had to have additional scheduled times to talk with their teachers and graders. We designed a system that allowed students access to teachers and graders throughout the day, which meant that staff had to be available from 7 am to 10 pm to accommodate the students, parents and time zone differences. The distance education teachers designed an outreach programme that provided opportunities for them to meet with their students at the studio or in cluster groups around the country. There was also heavy reliance on toll–free phone numbers and the Internet.

State and international rules, regulations and restrictions also presented some barriers. We agreed to have our teachers certified in the various states, but some of the requirements were ridiculous. For example, one state required our distance education teachers to take their first aid course because ours wasn't approved in their state! In another state, only certain textbooks could be used so we had to either change texts throughout the country or get our texts through their approval process. Over time, as distance education became more accepted, many of these regulations were removed and the states refocused their attention on course quality, the most important consideration.

On the international scene, we had Canadian schools wanting to take our distance learning courses, but regulations prohibited them from participating even though they could receive our satellite signal. On the other hand, Mexico took our classes at one of their universities, using our materials and support system. We also had the problem of time zone differences in sharing our courses in the Pacific, something we resolved by forming a strong reciprocal partnership with the Honolulu–based Pacific Resources for Education & Learning that serves the United States in the Pacific region and by exchanging distance learning classes with them.

Another challenge we anticipated and thereby avoided was the crucial need for sustainability and continuity. ESD 101 had key people who kept moving the project to the next level. The Board even planned for the transition between myself and Dr Terry Munther who became superintendent and general manager of the STEP•Star Network. Had the administration and Board not planned for these and future changes this programme would not be the premier K-12 educational distance learning programme that it is today. Through hard work and commitment we overcame these challenges and distance education became a reality for ESD 101.

Q. What strategies did you use to enrol the support of parents, students, teachers, school superintendents and school boards across the various states?

A. The easiest groups to convince were the students and their parents. In many instances the teachers were also quick to give their support, especially for courses that weren't already part of the curriculum. Another incentive was the access to in-service training and professional development so they could move on the salary schedule. Early on the school boards and the superintendents were concerned about the costs, but these were partially alleviated by providing subsidized receive equipment to the participating sites. In the beginning the hardest group to persuade were the principals, because the financial support often came out of their budgets and they needed to figure out how to appropriately staff the distance learning classroom. However, with the increased use of technology and the need to expand courses the principals came to realize the value of open learning. To gain support from all of these groups, we spent a lot of time working one-to-one with interested districts. We also marketed our network at educational trade shows like the Association of Educational Service Agencies, American Association of School Administrators, National School Boards Association and at various teacher and principal state-wide meetings.

In the early 1990s we added cable television to our satellite delivery system. This expanded access not only to public and private school students but also to home schoolers. We also partnered with the Spokane Community Colleges and local universities to provide high school equivalency diplomas, adult literacy, college and/or clock hour credit programmes for adult learners. Offering various levels of credit enabled us to further eliminate many of the initial barriers and gain community support.

At one time the STEP•Star Network was cutting edge. Now what we do is more the norm and the old barriers are disappearing. Our challenge is to move the effort to the next level and be as inclusive as possible, especially with the expansion of the Internet and video streaming. We're looking at an increased number of K-12 online classes delivered via the Internet. One of the newest companies to enter this market is WebED (www.WebED.com) whose approach is to partner with education and jointly develop content. Their platform also allows professional development to be taken over the Internet. As such partnerships between the public and private sectors grow, students will have more choice in their learning and teachers more choice in their training.

Q. What were the main challenges in building the STEP•Star Schools into an ongoing programme, and how were these dealt with?

A. When you try to change an institution as large as K-12 education you'll encounter what I call the doubters and the watchers. When we started, I guess only 20 per cent of the educators were excited and felt we could pull this off; 50 per cent observed to see if it would work and another 30 per cent said it wouldn't. Half of this last group ignored us and the other half constructed roadblocks. I remember repeatedly seeing this pattern at numerous faculty meetings. We found the key was to work hard with the 20 per cent who were excited about the prospect of distance education. We learnt they could influence the observers and change attitudes in others and soon we had 70 per cent seeing distance learning as an opportunity to enhance their school's curriculum and receive on-site in-service training for credit. The latter gave us a growing cadre of supporters in rural areas who no longer had to travel long distances for training after a long hard school day.

When I look back, what was so difficult 14 years ago has now become common-place. When you're close to something you believe in you need to step back and recognize change takes time. In 1986 we started with 13 small rural districts. They were really pioneers in a new adventure and had the belief that they could change and improve education for their communities through distance education. The growth was very slow initially, but by 1999, STEP•Star was providing courses to over 200,000 students.

Q. What has shaped your particular style of leadership?

A. I remember a phone call I received about a month into the school year, from a rural superintendent I respected. The superintendent told me he had two students who needed to enrol in our first-year Japanese class. My initial response was, 'It's too late.' The superintendent then said, 'You're a risk taker, you need to take these two students.' I asked why. He told me the two students were always late or truant and were about to be kicked out of school. I also discovered their grades were poor and their dress, appearance and everything about their behaviour pointed to a term I have since erased from my vocabulary: a couple of losers. I thought, how could these students ever pass a class recognized by many colleges as one of the best high school Japanese language programmes in the country? Anyway, with some more cajoling from the superintendent I finally agreed to let the two boys join the class. I didn't tell the Japanese teacher anything about the students other than that I needed to admit them and that they'd work hard to catch up. Deep down I felt that in a couple of weeks they'd be gone. Not so! The boys went to work and did extremely well and in fact, graduated from high school. Yes, they had an exceptional teacher, but that wasn't all. First, with only contact through one-way video and two-way audio, neither the other students nor the teacher knew how they dressed or what they'd done in the past, so no judgements were made. Secondly, it was a fresh start for the students through distance education in their own school. Further, they were part of the TV generation that skipped school and stayed home watching television. The entertainment tool now became the educational tool and for these students the transition was easy.

I saw this scenario repeated numerous times throughout my career. As a result, part of my current leadership style is to support alternatives and choices for students in the public and private education systems. No one approach will fit all students. Some students learn extremely well through distance education while others need different approaches to learning.

I also believe a strong leader must have a passion for what he or she is doing. To be effective, a leader must also be visible and supportive and give people the freedom to carry out the mission and strategic plan with passion. Today you have to be a consensus-builder and then a decision-maker. If consensus can't be reached the leader must make the decision in a timely fashion.

I subscribe to the notion that somewhere, somebody has already done or is trying to do what you want to do. As a good leader you must seek out this information and try not to reinvent the wheel.

Q. What do you now see as the challenges for education and what can we learn from your experience of applying technology in K-12 schools?

A. The biggest challenge facing both K-12 and higher education is how ready the teachers and students are to utilize technology to enhance learning, and how prepared governments and various providers are to cross the digital divide between the haves and have-nots.

The second major challenge is to get cost-effective access to satellites, cable, fibre and equipment fast enough to keep up with demand. There have been numerous unsuccessful initiatives to partner with satellite delivery systems. Educational entities cannot afford the high cost of entertainment satellite time. Hopefully one of the existing companies or a new satellite company will step forward and assist educators to meet the continuing educational needs in a cost-effective manner. There is a tremendous opportunity for private business to partner with the educational community. If we're to have a well-trained, caring citizenry ready to take their place in the workplace we must reach out with technology to meet the growing demand for skilled labour. This is also a great chance for business to step forward and support the educational reform movement. There's no doubt in my mind that it's only through the effective use of technology that we can provide educational opportunities that will lead us through the 21st century.

Q. What qualities of leadership do you see as necessary and try to develop in those you work with?

A. I tend to be very practical and not get hung up on theory. I think a person has to be a visionary, adaptable, flexible and changeable. I grew up in an age where we had hand-cranked adding machines, black and white TV was in its infancy, and space travel was science fiction. Compare that to today's students who can't conceive a time without cellular phones, computers, the Internet and space travel. What will it be like 10 or 20 years from now? We don't know what the future holds, but one thing we can be sure of is change. We must envision flexibility and adaptability and use our leadership skills to embrace change.

Further, we must recognize that as educators and leaders we no longer have information boundaries. We have technological tools that allow us to teach the skills needed to utilize knowledge effectively. We must chart the course for incorporating technology into the educational lives of our students. Democracy is based on access to enlightened decision-making and our ability to utilize technology is the tool for sustaining our democratic principles.

Q. What skill sets do you see as necessary in the CEOs and managers of the open learning of the future?

A. They'll need a strong footing in the appropriate 20th century skill sets and the capacity to integrate these into a whole new set of 21st century competencies. They'll need to be visionaries who can utilize systems thinking and environmental scanning. And they'll have to be capable of convincing people to change. As Hampden-Turner and Arc observe:

> The most stubborn habits which resist change with the greatest tenacity are those which worked well for a space of time and led to the practitioner being rewarded for those behaviours. If you suddenly tell such persons that their recipe for success is no longer viable, their personal experience belies your diagnosis. The road to convincing them is hard. It is the stuff of classic tragedy. (Gharajedaghi, 1999: 3)

To overcome such resistance leaders will utilize data-driven decision-making. They'll recognize that collaboration and integration are critical in the new information society and the technological age has no boundaries. They'll have to manage the technological deliverables against benchmarks supported by strong accountability systems. And they'll need to commit early to solid technology infrastructures that align with the vision and economic realities of the organization or institution.

One of the best resources I know for managing success in the K–12 digital environment is *Technology in American Schools: Seven Dimensions for Gauging Progress* (http://www.mff.org/edtech/projects). These 'seven dimensions', as defined by Cheryl Lemke, past Executive Director of the Milken Exchange on Education Technology, and her team are:

1. Learners – are learners using the technology in ways that deepen their understanding of the content in the academic standards and, at the same time, advance their knowledge of the world around them?
2. Learning Environments – is the learning environment designed to achieve high academic performance by students through the alignment of standards, research-proven learning practices and contemporary technologies?
3. Professional Competency – is the educator fluent with technology and does he or she effectively use technology to the learning advantage of his or her students?
4. System Capacity – is the education system re-engineering itself to systematically meet the needs of learners in this knowledge-based, global society?
5. Community Connections – is the school community relationship one of trust and respect, and is this translating into mutually beneficial, sustainable partnerships in the area of learning technology?

6. Technology Capacity – are there adequate technologies, networks, electronic resources and support to meet the education system's learning goals?
7. Accountability – is there agreement on what success with technology looks like and are there measures in place to track progress and report results?

This framework, when combined with common sense, patience and the skills I've outlined, will certainly help tomorrow's leaders succeed. We're at the threshold of the most exciting time in the history of humankind. How our leaders respond to this challenge will determine whether or not our children can learn in new and exciting ways and whether or not we can truly have schools without walls.

Chapter 20

Leadership in institution building: the National Open School of India

Professor Marmar Mukhopadhyay, of the National Institute of Educational Planning and Administration, who was the Chairman of India's National Open School (NOS) between 1993 and 1996, describes his leadership role in an institution developed to serve educational dropouts and provide alternative foundation, secondary and vocational education.

Q. What attracted you to serve with NOS?

A. When I joined my village school, Udang, at sixth standard in 1954, there were 40 students in my class. By 1959, only 12 of us sat for the Board Examination, plus five of our seniors who had stagnated at different standards; only four succeeded. I knew those who dropped out – we grew up together – and by extension, I knew all those who dropped out of the Indian school system. Such a large, untapped potential and alarming underachievement! I felt that NOS was designed for people like my classmates and friends who were either unsuccessful in the traditional educational system or had to leave due to a variety of socio–economic compulsions.

I was invited in 1992 by the Appointments Committee of the Cabinet of the Indian Government to Chair NOS for a three-year term – 1993 to 1996. This committee was chaired by the Prime Minister of India, which indicates the importance attached to this institution and position. At that time I was also selected for the prestigious Ravi Mathai Chair at the Indian Institute of Management, Ahmedabad. This position was more attractive in terms of status and salary. I shared my dilemma with Sri S V Giri, then Education Secretary to the Government of India. His advice to me was, 'With your value systems and your concern for the rural poor, I feel you will enjoy working and shaping the National Open School more, and serving the cause of "your friends".' So I decided to take the less immediately attractive but more challenging position with NOS.

Q. How did you develop a new vision for NOS?

A. My thinking about NOS and vision building began as soon as the search committee sounded me out. I saw the need and potential to develop it as a national institution of open learning that could act as a laboratory or resource centre for quality open schooling. I also believed we could build an open learning movement at the school level in the states through which learners might learn through their mother tongue, and that we could become the largest open school in the world and a leader in the field. Such a vision might be construed as a personal ambition rather than an institutional vision. However, except for the international dimension, this vision was actually a synthesis of statements and recommendations by various committees and commissions.

Systems theory teaches us the critical importance of the environment in which systems are set. I was fortunate at that time that the University Grants Commission was headed by the legendary distance educator, Professor Ram Reddy, that the Education Secretary, Sri S V Giri, was a strong supporter of open schooling, and that the Education Division of the Planning Commission was headed by Dr Chitra Naik, an educator of great stature committed to the education of the deprived and the poor. The positioning of these three dynamic people at the three most strategic places in government provided the external environment for optimizing internal capabilities.

Q. What were your first steps to translate this vision into reality?

A. As soon as I took over at NOS in 1993, I reviewed all of the reports by the various committees and commissions referring to NOS. I also examined all of the internal documentation and operations relating to the setting up of NOS in 1989 as an autonomous organization in pursuance of the 1986 National Policy on Education by the Ministry of Human Resource Development, Government of India. The findings were rather unnerving because there were clearly mismatches between the expectations and the realities. The expectations were that NOS would function as a leader in open learning. In practice, it was bogged down in the delivery of courses and conducting examinations like any other school. The courses were comparable to those in conventional institutions and the instructional material rich in content. However, the production quality was poor. The tutors were bright young men and women who consistently performed well, despite being poorly paid. But the heads of department were weak. The organization itself was weakly structured. The Open School had been experimented with since 1979 as a project of the Central Board of Secondary Education (CBSE) and was later amalgamated with the NOS. NOS comprised three departments: academic, examinations and administration, but it was still perceived by the staff as primarily an examining body. There was a total absence of research and development activities and it was almost impossible to monitor the quality of the education and the examinations. As a consequence, despite being comparable in academic standards, NOS qualifications were not recognized for admission by many conventional universities.

I thus faced the need for structural and process interventions, resistance in the organization, and a requirement to take risks. I felt there was sufficient solid ground to build upon and we drew up a plan that envisaged NOS facilitating the establishment of 20 state open schools offering programmes through regional languages and becoming a National Institute of Open Learning with a strong research and development base to provide professional support to the state open schools. We began our journey by 'redrawing the map' in the minds of NOS staff. Slowly but steadily, the academic staff embraced the new vision, and NOS administration followed suit. The NOS examinations department, however, proved far more intransigent.

Q. What strategies did you employ to implement this plan?

A. Fortunately, there were several vacant academic staff positions. In making these appointments, we gave emphasis to qualifications and qualities equivalent to universities and were able to recruit more staff of high calibre. Another major shift in staffing was the recruitment of engineers, agricultural scientists, paramedical scientists and home scientists to strengthen our work in vocational education.

To build up our research and development activities and augment the academic staff, we designed major projects in Human Resource Development, Assessing and Enhancing Learning Skills, Policy and Planning, Regional Languages, Question Banking and Examination Reforms, Life Enrichment Programmes, and an Open Schooling Magazine. We secured funding from the Government of India for these projects, each with its own professional staff and director. This gave us about 30 additional academic staff.

Another major exercise was selecting and accrediting the study centres. Several unscrupulous agencies with commercial agendas had managed to become study centres alongside institutions that were genuinely committed to the poor and educational dropouts and that had good buildings, laboratories, libraries, workshops and well qualified teachers. There were also private schools running a parallel fee-for-service 'open school stream' for regular day pupils who found difficulty with science and mathematics. The main functions of NOS-contracted part-time staff at these centres are to provide Personal Contact Programmes, distribute learning materials and offer counselling services. We established criteria to determine the quality of the physical and human resources and those centres that appeared to fulfil our criteria on paper were inspected to verify the written information. The inspecting team was particularly assiduous in assessing the teachers' disposition towards open learning. This review process brought about a major change in the level and quality of the centres. Today, there are more than 1,000 of these centres, all across India.

NOS used to function only from Delhi. The importance of regional centres for coordination and monitoring of quality had long been recognized and we proceeded to set up regional centres in Calcutta for the eastern region, Pune for the western region, Hyderabad for the southern region, Agra for the northern region, and Guwahati for the north-eastern region. Each centre had its own director – typically a retired educational administrator – 5 to 10 staff, standby course material for any crisis in delivery, computers, audiovisual equipment, fax, Internet, etc. This structural reform strengthened substantially the quality of regional support.

Enrolment in NOS was growing but there was still a perception that its programmes and qualifications were inferior to those of conventional schools. We therefore undertook a major exercise involving the University Grants Commission to gain recognition from the universities, Indian Institutes of Technology (IITs) and Boards of Secondary Education. This effort yielded significant results, with NOS certificates recognized by all Boards of Secondary Education, the IITs and more than 150 of the 200 universities. This led to a further increase in enrolments.

With the increase in enrolments and the need for qualitative improvement in the self-learning materials (the curriculum had already been revised), I challenged the academics to develop new look, quality materials that were pedagogically sound and attractive to the learners, something they responded to within six months. Until this time, our programmes had been delivered primarily through print and face-to-face. We now developed audio and video programmes, installed a Digital Multimedia Centre, and experimented with voicemail.

To upgrade the quality of the Personal Contact Programmes, we devised modularized training programmes on tutoring, cooperative learning, problem-solving, counselling, etc, for the part-time staff in the accredited institutions and study centres and delivered these through print, supported by face-to-face and interactive television teaching.

To orient our students into the philosophy and strategies of open learning, we gave each enrolee a specially developed free book, available in English and Hindi. We also initiated a glossy, quarterly magazine featuring social issues such as AIDS, gender equity, etc, biographies of inspirational individuals such as Jawaharlal Nehru, Swami Vivekananda and Rabindranath Tagore, subject-based enrichment articles and tips for examinations, which was supplied free to every student for one year.

We developed a large number of vocational courses in agriculture, technology, paramedical studies, home science and information technology, and introduced a system wherein students could combine academic and vocational studies towards their examination. This upgrading of the status of vocational courses radically changed students' choices in favour of vocational courses.

Finally, we addressed the issue of providing programmes in regional languages. Until that time, NOS had offered programmes only in English, which helped dropouts from English medium fee-charging schools, and Hindi, which supported poor dropouts among Hindi speaking people, particularly in Delhi and its surrounding areas. Within two years, thanks to the fine efforts of our young staff, our entire secondary programme was translated into Malayalam, Tamil, Kannad, Telugu, Bengali, Manipuri, Gujarati, Marathi and Urdu and converted into other languages including Assamese, Oriya, Nepali and Punjabi.

We planned that NOS would concurrently work with the State Governments to set up state open schools, then hand over the regional language programmes and withdraw to provide only English and Hindi programmes. Each state open school project needed careful consideration of the organizational design, staffing structure, staff induction and career paths, selection, establishment and accreditation of study centres and quality assurance, and required state subsidies for the education of girls, the economically and socially deprived and physically and mentally challenged. We were able to launch programmes in Bengali, Urdu and Kannad and establish state open schools in Haryana, Madhya Pradesh, Karnataka and West Bengal. Andhra Open School was already offering education up to eighth standard and NOS offered secondary education material in Telugu. Subsequent to my departure, state open schools were set up in Kerala, Punjab and Gujarat and there was a renewed interest in such systems.

Q. What steps did you take to win over people's hearts and minds?

A. Besides vision building, developing process capability was the major challenge. I invested much of my time, energy and professional skills in building confidence and professional competence in the staff. The academic staff in NOS comprise: the core full-time academic staff who are largely responsible for curriculum design and material development; the subject experts and courseware authors drawn from various universities and schools; and the counsellors and tutors in the study centres and teachers in the conventional schools.

With respect to building confidence in the internal staff of NOS, I started to involve them with senior external experts, give them national and international exposure, require them to produce reports and write professional literature outside courseware authoring, and take over as project directors in order to broaden their horizons and give them a break from their normal duties. It took more than 18 months to pull them out of their cocoons.

With the courseware authors, we held meetings about the new perspective and philosophy of open schooling, the directions we wanted NOS to take and the need for quality in content and material. These were well received by the academics who came from the formal system and were largely critical of the standards of the open learning system. For the study centre personnel and teachers, we conducted workshops on management issues and student support.

Our endeavours were largely successful with the internal staff, but less so with the study centre coordinators and tutors, possibly because they were involved in conventional teaching throughout the week and found it difficult to switch over in the evenings and at the weekends to the new instructional strategies for NOS. It is always harder to inculcate new values and practices in part-time, distant staff.

Utilizing my acquaintance with university systems and scholars, we involved national experts in various NOS activities. When I invited a Vice-Chancellor and two senior professors to join an NOS committee, one of my young colleagues asked, 'Sir, will such eminent people come to NOS?', to which I replied, 'Yes. They will. If they won't come for NOS, they will to help a friend in NOS.' Involving senior academics from the various states of India demonstrated that quality cannot be compromised, exposed my colleagues to academic stalwarts in their respective fields and broadened their vision. This breadth of contact with the intellectual community of the universities was significant in developing and carrying through the new NOS vision.

Such involvement also helped to inform opinion leaders from the conventional system. For example, the eminent economist, Professor Tapas Mazumdar, wrote several articles on open schooling and its potentialities that made uninformed critics rethink the whole issue. This strategy also helped us in getting NOS qualifications recognized, since the very people who assessed quality for equivalence and recognition by the universities were serving on the various committees of NOS.

Q. What resistance did you encounter in this transformation of NOS?

A. The main problem arose as a consequence of examinations having formerly been the dominant activity of NOS. The Controller of Examinations enjoyed the extraordinary powers vested in his office, reinforced by powers of financial privilege. For example, there was a practice of flying squads visiting examination centres to check on copying and other malpractices. The Controller was empowered to draft anybody from the organization without prior approval of the concerned head of the department and reward them with a token honorarium – something I only learnt about when my personal secretary was drafted without my consent!

The shifting of emphasis to the academics created an identity crisis in the Examinations Department and there was tremendous resistance, not only within the Department, but also from those outside it who derived financial benefit from its activities. At one stage, the Examinations Department even declined to conduct examinations in regional languages. Clearly, this was a situation that had to be challenged.

Other resistance came from within the Executive Committee of NOS. Certain members had very little understanding of open learning systems and the interests of NOS. They looked upon the new vision as a personal agenda to enhance the careers of certain people within the organization.

There was also external resistance. Recasting the rules of accreditation impacted negatively upon many commercial entrepreneurs who joined forces against us, particularly when we were compelled to take action to assure quality. For the very first time, several examination centres were dropped for mass copying and mismanagement. As is typical in the Indian socio-political scene, our opponents ran to the politicians, including the ministers, accusing the Chairman of all sorts of misdemeanours. Fortunately, the Honourable Minister stood by the decision of the NOS.

As a student of management of change, I knew I faced two options – to use power-coercive strategies that are here and now with poor sustainability, or normative re-educative strategies which are sustainable but drawn out. As someone on a three-year contract, this presented me with a dilemma. In the end, I chose the normative re-educative process wherever this was most suitable – where minds were open – and used power-coercion wherever I considered any investment in the re-educative process as futile. For example, despite relegating administration to a secondary position behind the academic functions, I found that the head of Administration was talking of the new vision and I decided to work through the issues with him and his staff. But the Examinations Department brushed aside all new ideas and presented me with little choice but to use my authority to get things changed.

Q. What principles shaped your leadership and management style?

A. As a professional in educational management, I know that it is difficult to pinpoint principles of management that shape an individual's management style. Human beings are essentially value configurations and their core values are developed in early childhood. In the years of pre-adolescence and adolescence, these values are strengthened or weakened through contact with the alternative value systems of peers, teachers, the community, and so on. In my own case, having been born and raised in a rural society that is largely homogenous in its value systems, characterized by cooperation, helping others, sharing resources despite poverty, and mutual love and trust, the values inculcated in my home and childhood days were reinforced by the wider community.

At NOS, my leadership style was guided by the situation and by my accountability to the students. I made serious efforts to base decisions on facts; for example, redefining the vision of NOS in the light of the recommendations of various commissions and the internal capability of the staff. My second principle was to share the vision, albeit not always successfully. My third basic principle was to involve all of the organization, create a sense of purpose among the staff, give them latitude and recognize their efforts and achievements. To illustrate this latter point, between 1979 and 1992, only the NOS Chairman or heads of department went abroad for study visits or conferences. Between 1993 and 1995, seven junior academic staff were funded to attend professional conferences in New Zealand, Australia and other countries and present papers. These staff brought great credit to NOS and the approbation from overseas experts really enthused and encouraged them.

Q. How successful do you judge NOS to have been?

A. Referring back to our vision, NOS was able to set itself on a journey toward quality and spearhead the open schooling movement in India by promoting programmes in regional languages, professionalizing open schooling and developing a network of state open schools. Another major achievement was the recognition and acceptance of NOS by the universities and the employers on the one hand, and the learners on the other. Enrolments have increased phenomenally. However, compared to the estimated numbers of out-of-school youth, the present coverage is far too small. But then, how can an institution enrol 3 million people and offer education in 16 different languages?

The NOS has also scored on the international front. The International Commission on Education for the Twenty-first Century report to UNESCO, *Learning: The treasure within* (Delors *et al*, 1996) featured NOS. The Commonwealth of Learning invited NOS to edit an international publication on open schooling.

The UK Open University uses NOS as a case study in its international postgraduate programmes in open learning. NOS was involved in drafting the UNESCO policy document on open and distance education. As Chairman, I was elected to the Vice-Presidency (Asia) of the International Council for Distance Education (ICDE). And NOS has successfully hosted several international conferences and study visits on open schooling. In short, NOS has emerged as one of the world's prominent distance education institutions and a leader in open schooling.

But there have been lost opportunities. During 1993–96, we made a significant effort to develop courses in regional languages to accelerate the development of a state open school network. Unfortunately, this policy was reversed on my departure, and as a result, the open school movement slowed down.

Q. What lessons have you learnt from leading NOS that might help others following in your footsteps?

A. Running such a massive institution with such a radical philosophy was certainly a rich learning experience. Let me list a few major lessons I learnt about such institution building:

- Articulate a vision that will not limit the growth of the institution and that, rather than using apologetic terms like 'second chance' education, make bold statements about, eg 'alternative education of high quality'.
- Give careful thought to organizational design that can accommodate the future.
- Ensure that the pay, status and conditions for your staff enable you to recruit and retain the very best people as managers, course developers, teachers and tutors.
- Ensure that the state takes responsibility for providing funding for at least eight years of schooling and is equitable in supporting those who attend regular schools and those who take to open schooling. Open schooling can be self-sufficient, but should be funded through a mix of students' fees and government grants to subsidize the education of girls, learners from economically and socially deprived communities, and the physically and mentally challenged.
- Make sure that the open learning system is twice as good as the formal system because open learning systems are always suspected of being of poor quality. Involve outstanding scholars in curriculum development and take meticulous care over every aspect of the pedagogy and materials.
- Be constantly vigilant and monitor quality at every delivery point and make sure that learners are never exploited. The outreach and reputation of an open school depend upon the study centres and the study centre network must spread to every part of the country and the centres and their staff must be selected with care.
- Deliver your programmes through multi-channel learning systems using the available interactive technology to ensure outreach and participative learning.
- Offer a choice of courses and modules, timeframes, learning modes, credit accumulation, etc, but once the choice is made, ensure that quality is non-negotiable.

- Foresee and assess organizational dynamics as innovations are introduced and make strategic plans for strengthening the proactive forces and dissipating the resisting forces. As Lewin (1997) shows in his Field-Force Analysis Theory, innovations disturb the dynamic equilibrium of an organization and simultaneously activate proactive and resisting forces.

On the latter point, my interactions with institutions in the western world, particularly in the United Kingdom and United States, and my studies of the management of change in education in India reveal that the former have a greater capability for introducing and sustaining innovation and change regardless of the quality of the CEO. Indian organizations are far less formalized, and hence far more person-dependent. Their growth and development – and decay – depends largely upon the CEOs who tend to employ bureaucratic methods that suit those leaders who are weak in their ability to influence people.

For many senior academics, a contract as a CEO of an open school is a break from routine and a stepping-stone to a more attractive position, rather than a target in itself. Therefore, the first and the foremost requirement in selecting such a CEO is to ensure that he or she has a genuine commitment, indeed, emotional attachment, to the educationally disadvantaged and the open learning system. The CEO also needs skills in envisioning and developing a shared vision, strategic planning, human resource management, mentoring, interpersonal relationships, and linking with external agencies, national and international. Academic credibility is another necessary condition.

The chairmanship of NOS is a three-year contractual position and the incumbent has no role whatsoever in choosing his or her successor. Such a lack of continuity is a serious threat to NOS. Every chairman tries to prove his or her mettle in three years by adopting short-term strategies for faster results rather than planning for long-term institution-building. As a result, there are major pendulum swings in policies and programmes every few years. This must be a matter of serious concern.

Chapter 21

Treading a fine line: consultancy in open and distance learning

Bernadette Robinson, Special Professor of Comparative Education in the School of Continuing Education at University of Nottingham, UK, draws upon her extensive international experience in consultancy in open and distance education to discuss consultancy and leadership issues in developing countries.

Q. How is open and distance learning being used in developing countries?

A. 'Developing countries' covers a huge diversity in terms of development and infrastructure so caution is needed in generalizing about them. But one thing they have in common is an effort over the last 20 years to achieve universal primary education, secondary school growth, enough trained teachers and an expanded higher education. Open and distance education has been used as one way of achieving these goals as well as for non-formal and continuing education. It is increasingly incorporated into national education strategy as a means of reaching remote learners or larger numbers more rapidly at lower unit costs, although in some countries it remains marginalized or under-funded. It has achieved varying degrees of success and cost-effectiveness in developing countries (see Perraton, 2000).

In countries such as China, distance education has been part of a large-scale government strategy in pursuit of development goals. In other countries it has been introduced through donor-funded projects or initiated in partnership with institutions in developed countries, to help mid-career or postgraduate students study such subjects as development economics, teaching English as a foreign language, or management studies. It has been used to meet new educational needs in countries experiencing rapid economic or political transition, as in eastern Europe, central Asia and South Africa. In some cases, it has been used to contain social demand for education rather than expand the conventional system, for example, in Malawi where it has provided a lower quality, minimally funded secondary school alternative.

Some of the most interesting (and successful) applications have occurred in very challenging environments, as a consequence of thorough needs analysis, choice of relevant content, skilled and creative design, effective use of the limited resources and media available and a focus on the learner and the learning experience.

Q. What skills do you need as a consultant, working in these contexts?

A. From my own experience, I'd say technical expertise, appropriate 'hands-on' experience (not just 'book knowledge'), good interpersonal and analytical skills, energy, integrity, a sense of humour, an ability to work under pressure (and with little sleep), patience, cultural sensitivity, organizational skills, a capacity to motivate, to cope with the unexpected and juggle priorities, skills in rapidly digesting large amounts of information and evaluation sources, in using interpreters, diagnosing problems and negotiating solutions, avoiding or mediating conflict and producing readable and relevant reports quickly. I'm giving this as an ideal list of skills and qualities – I'm not claiming them personally!

Most of my consultancy work is heavily time-constrained, usually lasting two to four weeks, so the work's fairly pressured and I find I need three eyes: one to keep on the 'big picture' (the macro level of organizational context or system), one on the problems in hand (the purpose of the consultancy) and one on managing the consultancy process itself.

Why use consultants? There are several potential benefits. They can provide an independent view, offer new perspectives or technical input, cross-fertilize from other experience or confirm more systematically what an organization already suspects or knows. Because consultants are usually not part of the organization's culture or context, they are able to observe patterns of behaviour, decision-making and strategy that might not be apparent to organizational leaders and to reflect this back in a constructive way (though they need to be aware of their own 'cultural lens'). I find my role changes according to the context and particular requirements. I variously act as an analyst, resource person, guide or link to other people or information or development resources, a sounding board, an adviser or trainer, a facilitator, a planner, an evaluator, a go-between, a research partner, a system consultant in managing change and sometimes an advocate on behalf of a project or institution. All of this depends on having good in-country partners – they're the real experts on their own contexts.

Consultancy work is never dull and rarely without difficulties. Sometimes I work with multiple clients who present a combination of different agendas and expectations, often conflicting. Time is always a problem (especially when the terms of reference are unrealistic or poorly defined or delivered too late for adequate preparation). Sometimes the host organization doesn't prepare well so time is wasted in-country. The reverse can be true too. . . so much packed into a plan that it's impossible to carry it out. Clients can have quite unrealistic expectations, looking for instant solutions to long-standing, complex and apparently intransigent problems that no amount of consultancy input will solve.

I try to tread a fine line between being too directive and too non-directive, between proposing the safe-but-pedestrian solutions and more creative-but-riskier options, between setting targets and standards too high or too low, and between under- and over-estimating capacity, time or resource requirements. In cross-cultural settings, I've noticed that style can be misinterpreted. For example, a facilitative and non-directive style, seen as appropriate and skilled in a 'democratic' culture, may be interpreted as indecisive or weak in a more authoritarian one. The challenge for consultants is to adapt their style to the context while still getting the work done, and without compromising their professional integrity.

There's a prayer which I'm sure must have been created specially for consultants: 'Lord, give me the patience to accept the things I can't change, the energy and courage to change the things I can, and the wisdom to know the difference.'

Q. Are there particular strategic planning or management processes you favour in this work?

A. Consultancy work is really about problem solving and the problems are always different so the processes are, to a large extent, contingent upon circumstances. And whatever the consultancy focus, it soon raises broader organizational issues.

Essentially, I focus on the tasks of listening, understanding, analysing, confirming and consulting with others, developing scenarios or options as a basis for discussion and planning, and clarifying, gaining consensus on and recording, the action plans or key decisions still to be made. One strategy I try to adopt is moving my role from 'leader' or 'expert' to 'co-leader' or 'co-facilitator', and then to 'resource person' or 'mentor' in support of my in-country partners. Where there is prior experience and knowledge, it's possible to start at the 'co-leader' stage. But this is difficult to do when parachuting into a situation for a short single visit where there's the risk of making dislocated and de-contextualized input. Another important strategy is working in partnership with internal consultants or counterparts – key people in the sustainability of change and development.

Q. How does leadership affect the success of open and distance learning projects?

A. The choice of leader can make or break an open and distance education project. I have worked on at least one major national project where leadership (or rather the lack of it) was the main reason for the failure of an otherwise well-resourced, well-supported and well-timed project. In the same country at the same time, two less well-resourced projects succeeded because of strong and vigorous leadership. Sometimes in high-profile national projects the choice of leader is politically influenced and that doesn't always produce the best leader for the job.

Outstanding leadership is sometimes found in unexpected places. In large-scale projects, especially for non-formal education, I'm often impressed by the leadership demonstrated by individuals in the local community, the district officials, leaders of women's groups and local organizations, and so on. Their initiative and influence in mobilizing support and additional resources, commitment to their communities, energy and willingness to go the extra mile, confidence in dealing with people, problems and decisions and, often, their social connections are crucial to the success of the projects. Effective leadership at the centre is essential but by itself, not enough to sustain the momentum, especially in remote locations: strong local leadership has sometimes saved projects when central leadership was weak.

Q. Do you perceive any significant cultural differences in leadership styles between developed and developing countries?

A. Differences in leadership (and management) cluster round the four value dimensions first identified by Hofstede in 1980 (power distance; uncertainty avoidance; individualism; and masculinity). These can manifest themselves in differences in decision-making processes, leadership styles, levels of bureaucracy, the extent to which relationships are hierarchical and status conscious, the amount of delegation and decentralization permissible, and approaches to planning, quality control and evaluation.

If we take leadership styles in developing countries, there is often a preference for a personalized relationship over a contractual one and a tendency to depend more on the leader for guidance, support and advancement. There can be greater power distance (the level of acceptance of the unequal distribution of power in institutions and societies) in the boss–subordinate relationship. Power and respect are attributed more on the basis of status and social connection than technical expertise. This can affect speaking rights and discussion quality in meetings. Since hierarchies operate more strongly, leaders and managers in developing countries tend to make more use of directives, with the expectation of compliance. My counterparts in some countries are often amused when I suggest or request, saying, 'You are too polite: they won't do it if you ask that way!' In the collectivist cultures of some Asian, African and Latin American countries, maintaining relationships is often seen as more important than task accomplishment, so sometimes the former takes priority to the detriment of deadlines. In some cultures, sharing information may be seen as giving away personal power and helps explain the apparent reluctance to share information and work in teams. In former socialist countries accustomed to working in a command economy, planning can be the end-point or goal, and decision-making unfamiliar to local managers and undertaken reluctantly, thus affecting the effectiveness of decentralization in a distance education system.

Such features help explain the higher degree of bureaucracy and authoritarianism in some developing and socialist countries (and in a command economy). Bureaucracies usually operate according to well-established rules or operating procedures and well-defined roles and control mechanisms. In some countries the level of bureaucracy is excessive and impedes action; Brazil, for example, established a 'Ministry of De-bureaucratization' in the 1980s in an attempt to reduce its paralysing bureaucracy. Many developing countries operate in uncertain environments that do not fit well with the rational planning models found in Western management theory.

In terms of teaching and learning, there are deep-rooted cultural differences. These have taken on new significance with the growth of international programmes and the transfer of materials and courses between countries. Many of the models and recommendations of 'good practice' are Western in origin and rest on assumptions that may be inappropriate in other contexts. For example, learners and teachers in China have different understandings of their respective roles, value some kinds of learning (such as memorizing) differently, have their own conventions of academic discourse (evident in essay writing and discussion) and a distinctive pattern of cognitive skills as a result of learning a logographic script (Robinson, 1999). However, differences in teaching and learning are not just between developed and developing countries – they can also be found between European countries.

Planning and implementing open and distance learning has to start with the realities of the context of use. Routine transfer of models and practices does not work. At the same time, for open and distance education to succeed, a number of core activities and functions need to work effectively. So ways have to be found of achieving these in a manner appropriate to the context and culture. Some aspects will transfer without difficulty, some will need adaptation, some will need to be wholly re-conceptualized, and some will need to be invented. Understanding the context and culture is an important key to planning and implementing educational change, whether in developed or developing countries.

Q. What has shaped your leadership style in providing consultancy?

A. The strongest influence has come from my training and work as a psychologist. This has been an enormous help in providing theoretical perspectives and frameworks from different areas of psychology (social, cognitive and organizational), though I take a strongly practical approach to consultancy work. I had the good fortune early in my university career to work with a creative group of psychologists at Nottingham University who were interested in the dynamics of interpersonal and group behaviour. We ran experiential courses combining the approaches of humanist psychologists such as Carl Rogers with others developed at the Tavistock Institute in London for understanding group dynamics in institutional settings. I think this helped me to be facilitative and client-centred in my consultancy work and learner-centred in my teaching and training. One useful lesson I learnt was that groups in organizations often behave irrationally. This fits with Michael Fullan's conclusion, out of his influential research on managing educational change, that 'brute sanity' (aiming to achieve change through the force of rational argument alone) does not work and can end up reinforcing entrenched positions rather than changing them. However, in short-term consultancy, with pressure from different clients to deliver clear-cut results within short time-scales, it's sometimes difficult to attend to the process aspects adequately.

I also rely on systems thinking, especially when dealing with large, complex projects with multiple goals. I've found that systems analysis, even when working across cultures or in different languages, provides a useful communication tool in helping me and my counterparts clarify problems and practices, model solutions and re-conceptualize approaches, procedures, or structures. Though systems thinking may sound a bit abstract, its application is quite concrete and provides a way of involving others in building the evidence, analysing and testing out organizational realities and myths. What actually happens in a system is often not what those involved say or believe happens.

I incorporate a case study approach in my work whenever I can, since this can provide a rich understanding of an organization, project or activity in a context-ualized way. Such an approach requires competence in the inquiry methods of social science (interviews, questionnaires, focus groups, observation, analysis of documents and multiple methods for collecting and cross-checking evidence and inferences). I find that a case study approach provides a systematic framework for action and is useful when working cross-culturally. One limitation is the time factor. Good case studies take time to do whereas consultancy work is heavily time-constrained. Despite this, I've found it useful for evaluations, feasibility studies, project planning, and organizational analyses and change scenarios.

I can't conclude without referring to another significant influence on my consultancy work – working at the UK Open University. I joined the OU in about 1974 and was plunged into the excitement of distance education, then a relatively new and somewhat dubious life form. From then on, I gained wide 'hands-on' experience in different aspects of open and distance education, working in the School of Education and a regional centre, carrying out research and consultancy work on behalf of the university. I joined OUCICS (the Open University's Centre for International Cooperation and Services) when it was formed in 1978. This small group of lively staff became very active internationally in open and distance learning. We consulted for projects, institutions and governments in developed and developing countries and provided international training courses when the field was relatively new and little written about. My baptism of fire was a consultancy in India in 1979, when I led workshops on designing materials for teacher education at the universities of Mysore, Chandigarh and Kashmir. Since then I've worked in over 35 countries on a wide variety of different projects (around 130 or more) ranging from non-formal education for nomadic women in the Gobi Desert to postgraduate level online distance education in industrialized countries. An immensely valuable element of my experience over this period has been the creative and committed people I've worked with. I'm most grateful for what they have taught me (including songs I can sing but not translate) and I see my style of working as a product of many teachers in many countries.

Q. Are there particular opportunities or barriers that present themselves in developing countries?

A. Sometimes, even as an outsider, I can be a 'gate-opener'. I've taken opportunities to facilitate information exchange between groups working in isolation from each other or for the co-production of materials or joint provision of training. Occasionally this has progressed into national policy formulation for open and distance education. Sometimes I've been able to find funding for additional initiatives, training or professional development. In some circumstances I've been able to develop collaborative action research projects with in-country partners.

Recently, I had the (rare) opportunity to integrate distance education into national planning for primary teacher improvement in Vietnam (a major project funded by the World Bank, the UK government's Department for International Development and the Government of Vietnam).

Some barriers can be overcome, others have to be lived with or circumnavigated. Some result from tradition or circumstances, others from limitations in the physical infrastructure or inadequate funding (so often a major barrier in achieving good quality). The absence of an enabling policy framework is sometimes an obstacle. Open and distance education may appear in the education law in a country or be mentioned in major policy documents, but there is sometimes little more by way of plans or strategy. Even when these exist, there can be large gaps between the expressed policies and available finances.

Bureaucracy can present challenges. Sometimes development projects face a double dose of this, within the country itself and with the international donor agency. Each can have its own rules, requirements, forms of accountability, financial management and procurement systems, timescales and financial years. Aligning two sets of such requirements can be very time-consuming for project leaders and managers.

Q. What do you see as the main challenges to open and distance learning in developing countries?

A. I see three main challenges:

1. The achievement of quality.
2. The use of distance education to greater effect for those in most need.
3. The judicious and selective use of new technology.

I'm concerned that so much faith and resources are put into new technology, while ignoring past lessons about the failure of technology-led projects and important questions of quality, access and sustainability. The technological imperative is very strong in many developing countries. But what priority should ICT take when learners and teachers lack the basic minimum of facilities or learning materials, let alone the online connection (if it's available, working and affordable), the consumables to support downloading and printing, and the availability of technical support and power supply?

More information, evidence and guidance are needed to inform policy makers about the relative benefits and effective strategies for introducing ICT into low-resource contexts, and more attention needs to be paid to sustainability, which is an issue even in industrialized countries. For example, in the UK, the cost of ICT support (training, loading software, trouble-shooting, hardware and systems maintenance) is greater than the cost of the hardware. At the same time, the average life of a personal computer is two to three years, and while computing power doubles every 18 months the new software requires the extra power almost as soon as it becomes available, so the ongoing cost of upgrading also has to be added. Storing and archiving data costs can be considerable – for example, online journal use can cost more than hard copy versions – and yet these are often ignored or underestimated by planners. The benefits of access are obvious; the costs may be less so. Donor support cannot solve long-term sustainability problems.

Cost and access are currently major obstacles to adopting ICT in some countries and disadvantaged regions. This may change over the longer term if infrastructure and economic conditions improve. But, for example, Internet access in Mongolia or Vietnam costs more per month than the average monthly earnings and a computer costs more than most people's annual income. Large parts of both countries function with inadequate power supply. In the west of Mongolia last year, some provinces were without electricity for several months because of economic problems – I used the last of my laptop battery to type by candlelight wearing my gloves to keep warm. At the same time, schools and educational institutes were short of basic learning materials and heating though there was a lively local radio station running on a shoestring and producing topical and relevant programmes on education, information and entertainment for a few hours each day, thanks to the use of the provincial governor's generator.

I don't want to paint too negative a picture here. I'm enthusiastically involved in some interesting ICT initiatives. But I would like to see more realism about the potential and practicalities of using ICT in developing countries and in relation to other options. A key question is how to get the maximum benefit from scarce resources for learning.

The use of ICT needs to be well informed, selective, based on tried and tested strategies, evaluated and costed and realistically appraised in particular contexts and for particular educational purposes and compared with other practicable and valuable alternatives. At the same time there is still huge scope and need to use and improve other forms of open and distance learning.

Q. What knowledge and skills do you see as necessary in leaders and managers establishing or renewing open and distance learning systems, particularly in developing countries?

A. Many leaders and policy makers need to develop a better understanding of open and distance education, how it works, its management and staffing needs, its costs and how to manage standards and quality. Better understanding can lead to improved planning and stronger commitment to making it work well – but this also requires adequate resources.

To avoid being swept away in the rush to new technology, more focus should be put on educational purpose and quality of learning. Many countries are trying to improve the quality of learning from primary school to postgraduate education. This often requires a major culture shift, not a quick technical fix, and will need time and new knowledge and skills to support this development.

One valuable contribution leaders can make to the development of open and distance learning systems is to build a better information base for policy makers and decision makers. It is still surprisingly difficult to get even basic information about an institution's or programme's performance in open and distance learning.

This leaves large margins of uncertainty about the quality, efficiency, effectiveness and costs of the applications and outcomes. Such data are needed to substantiate achievements and claims, seek resource allocations and indicate priorities for improvement or new strategic directions. Leading change is not altogether a rational business, but without evidence to show and to underpin debate, it is all the more difficult.

Chapter 22

The International Extension College: leadership beyond the mainstream

Barbara Spronk, Executive Director of the International Extension College (IEC), in the UK, whose mission is to promote development and improvement in the quality of life in less-developed countries through the expansion of educational opportunities, discusses leadership in providing training, consultancy, information and technical support for the design, development and implementation of distance education programmes from non-formal to tertiary level.

Q. What gave rise to the International Extension College and how and by whom was it established?

A. The idea of the International Extension College grew out of the experience and success of the National Extension College (NEC) in Cambridge. Dr Michael Young (now Lord Young of Dartington) had been instrumental in launching NEC in 1963 as a pilot project for a 'University of the Air', which eventually became the Open University. From its earliest days NEC received requests for information and advice, and sometimes even for the right to use and adapt its courses, from new institutions, particularly in Africa. These requests led NEC to seek comparative information on distance teaching from outside the UK. It found that its own development benefited greatly from such contacts and that many other 'correspondence' and multimedia institutions recognized the need to tap each other's resources and to share experience. Thus the founders of NEC, Michael Young in particular, were led to believe that an institution should be set up to facilitate the international exchange of resources and experience and in this way to support the development of new and expanded distance teaching colleges.

The establishment of the IEC in 1971 was made possible by grants from a number of foundations and trusts. Its intended functions were:

● To help establish non-profit distance teaching colleges in countries where none of any size existed.

- To provide consultancy services to existing correspondence and multimedia education institutes in the evaluation, expansion and strengthening of their programmes.
- To build up an international resource centre, by collecting and making available information, documents, teaching materials and experience in this mode of teaching from all over the world.
- To carry out research and prepare and circulate publications likely to promote the sound development of distance teaching.

Q. In what ways has IEC had to evolve and change in response to changing needs?

A. The need for distance education in the developing world has changed, but has by no means diminished. A report on IEC's first year of operations opened with these words:

> There are not enough educational resources in the world to go round. Nor are they evenly distributed. As a result – as an Egyptian colleague put it to us last year – 'with traditional methods we have only managed to educate half the world'. (IEC, 1972: 5)

We could use the same words today.

However, there are more distance education providers now than there were in 1971, including a dozen universities that are the world's largest. There are also many more organizations advocating and supporting that provision, including international bodies such as the Commonwealth of Learning, and there are many more technologies to facilitate interaction among learners and teachers. To respond effectively to these changes, IEC has to keep reinventing itself. For example, there is no longer a pressing need to help establish distance teaching colleges, and in place of that, IEC has taken on a greater role in educating and training staff who work in distance teaching. IEC's mission, however, has not changed. In 1981, the report on IEC's first decade stated:

> We are more convinced than ever of the importance of distance teaching. . . as a means of making education, which is everyone's birthright, available more quickly to the majority of the world's people. (IEC, 1981: 7)

Twenty years on these words still apply.

Q. As Executive Director, what has been your role in establishing the vision, goals and strategic directions of IEC?

A. Taking up the post of Executive Director of IEC in 1996, I joined an organization with a quarter-century of success to its credit. My role therefore was not to establish a vision, goals and strategic directions from scratch. It was, and still is, to work with colleagues to affirm and refine IEC's vision in a way that both reflects current realities and enables IEC to work effectively within them. Not that I had the luxury of time to do this. There was only a little more than a month before my first Board meeting to do an environmental scan and analysis of our strengths, weaknesses, opportunities and threats, and prepare proposals for Trustees' consideration. I spent that month listening and learning, activities that come relatively easily to a social anthropologist trained in the methods of participant observation.

I have continued to listen, learn, propose and respond, always without the luxury of time. In a small NGO like IEC, with no sustained core funding, one lives by one's wits, always conscious of the need, literally, to earn one's salary through activities that bring in revenue. Time for planning, vital though it is, has to be found within the time and funding made available by other activities, and there never seems to be enough of either.

Q. You have worked with many governments, NGOs, educational establishments and in-country specialists in developing countries. What do you see as the critical leadership issues in these contexts?

A. In developing country contexts the obvious issue is poverty, specifically income poverty. Education leaders and managers face the continuing challenge of stretching scarce resources to cover seemingly endless demands. Distance approaches offer what seems to be an obvious solution: to take your existing intellectual resources − subject experts and trained teachers − and enable thousands to benefit from them instead of hundreds. If only it were that straightforward. It's not.

Education systems in these countries − almost without exception former colonies of some imperial power − tend to be copies of those imposed on them by their former masters, albeit under-resourced copies, complete with elitist curricula, approaches and attitudes more appropriate to staffing colonial admin-istrations than to expanding the economies and strengthening democratic structures in new nation states.

Fortunately income poverty does not equate with intellectual poverty. One of the privileges of working in distance education and development is collaborating with education leaders of enormous creativity and commitment who have been attracted to distance education because it seems to offer innovative answers to pressing problems. They also recognize the risks, however. Distance education looks suspiciously second-rate: how can a mode of teaching that does not bring students face-to-face with teachers, and worse, reaches out to encompass everyone, not just the brightest or most privileged, possibly produce the results comparable to those of conventional approaches? The greatest challenge facing leaders and managers in distance education is to convince major stakeholders that it is exit standards, not entrance standards, that matter; that effective learning is the main issue; and that such learning is not dependent on face-to-face contact on a regular basis. Not only is this an uphill struggle, it is also complex and multifaceted. Subject matter experts need to be convinced, then trained, to produce materials that facilitate learning rather than impress academic colleagues. Tutors need to be convinced, then trained, to run tutorials and comment on student work in ways that facilitate learning of content rather than simply transmit it. Managers and administrators need to be convinced that upfront investment, teamwork, a systems approach, and staff training and development are the *sine qua non* of distance education. They also need to be persuaded to resist the seductions of new technologies by asking hard questions about their appropriateness to teaching tasks, accessibility to learners and teachers, and cost-effectiveness.

Q. What strategic planning and management processes do you find useful in supporting change in developing countries?

A. My background as an anthropologist makes me suspicious of the pat formulas offered in much of the management literature. Management for me is a process of finding solutions that work. Solutions that work are those that arise from one's own context and fit that context. Experiences from elsewhere can inform and inspire these homegrown solutions, but they must not dictate.

I find quality assurance to be the most useful process in assisting educational leaders to support change. Everyone wants the highest quality provision possible, so one is immediately on common ground with one's partners or clients in discussing it. The first task is always to ask the client what they mean by quality. This forces a consideration of context, since 'quality' does not exist in isolation. Both internal and external contexts are brought into play, since it becomes quickly apparent that different stakeholders, including different functional areas within the organization, have different perspectives on quality. It also becomes obvious that priorities vary according to who is assessing quality and for what purposes. Discussions of quality, therefore, bring one forcibly back to first principles, and enable one to bring in every aspect of organizational life that is important to running a successful distance education enterprise: policy and planning, specifying standards, identifying critical functions, documenting procedures, continuous monitoring, staff training and development, cost-benefit analysis, and most importantly, staff involvement in and ownership of the quality assurance process.

Q. What theories, principles and experiences have shaped your particular leadership and management style for this work?

A. My ideas about management were shaped quite early. Both my parents were managers. My mother was also a trainer of mid-level managers in her organization, and I was introduced to notions such as the '9, 9' manager in discussions around the family dinner table. Blake and Mouton (1964) integrated the ideas of task and relationship orientations into a grid based on the concept that leaders vary from 1 to 9 in their concern both for getting things done and for people. They advocated what they called the '9, 9' orientation, which is goal-centred but seeks results through the participation, involvement and commitment of all those who can contribute. This 'team management' approach has stayed with me.

In political anthropology I became aware of the different types or levels of political organization that characterize human societies and was particularly struck by the existence of egalitarian societies in which there is no one overall leader.

For the sake of survival, leadership in any given task – foraging, hunting, tanning hides, preparing food, conducting ritual – is granted to those acknowledged to possess the greatest fund of knowledge, skills and experience. This mode of organization characterized human societies for most of human (pre)history. For me this constituted evidence that autocracy and struggles for power and control are not inherent in the human condition, but rather are functions of structure and circumstance. I have continued to draw affirmation and inspiration from that evidence.

At Athabasca University, my anthropological background led me into work with the local tribal councils of First Nations peoples with and for whom Athabasca was designing educational programmes. These peoples, originally hunters and gatherers of the plains and woodlands, have been affected – indeed infected – by the political culture of those who occupied and alienated their ancestral lands. Nonetheless there is still an egalitarian underlay to their dealings with each other, and with those outsiders privileged to work closely with them. I learnt a great deal from this work, in particular the need to expand our paradigms to include theirs, rather than reduce either to the other. Our business courses, for example, could 'serve both Wall Street and the (Indian) Reserve', in the words of the late Maggie Hodgson, director of a very successful, Native-run, substance abuse rehabilitation programme. This is an ideal we never achieved, but the strength yet gentleness of spirit of Maggie and others like her are still very much alive for me.

I have also been greatly influenced by the participatory approaches to education and organizing for education that formed the core of the 'Canada–Asia Partnership' project at the University of Calgary. In this, I worked with colleagues from Canada, Thailand and the Philippines to develop and deliver an intensive residential course for a multinational audience. We were a diverse group of facilitators, encompassing anthropology and distance education, drama and arts education, communications and even social epidemiology. The tenets of our work – sharing power and responsibility for learning; valuing indigenous as well as academic knowledge; using an integrated arts approach and problem-based, discovery learning as core methods for generating learning theory and practice; and recognizing that conflict is inherent to these processes and can be a creative tension – continue to inform my approach to teaching, learning and leadership.

Q. Do you find significant cultural differences in leadership, management and educational practice between developed and developing countries and if so, how do these impact on planning and implementing change?

A. One of the most frustrating things about the work we do as consultants (not inaccurately labelled 'hit and run' work) is the lack of time we have to delve deep enough beneath surface realities to get to the infrastructure of beliefs, values and norms that form the basis for and dynamic of the behaviour we see. What we typically encounter are educational leaders who have been educated in the West, probably in institutions more prestigious than the ones from which we graduated. These leaders know far more about the world from which we come than we do about theirs. They speak our language; we usually do not speak theirs. They interpret their world for us. If we are very lucky, we have access to other interpreters as well, who provide alternative or additional glosses on what we are seeing and hearing. Sometimes we are privileged to work with a particular group over a long enough period to learn how to behave effectively and appropriately. For example, in working with First Nations peoples for a number of years I learnt to become comfortable with silence and to stop rushing in to fill every space in conversation. Most of the time, however, we are proceeding on the basis of assumption and outright guesswork, rather than of deep knowledge and understanding of the 'home' cultures of those with whom we are working.

This can have disastrous consequences. Early in my work in Thailand, I was woefully unaware of the importance to those in positions of authority of 'saving face'. Thais tend overtly to accede to those in authority over them. Everyone knows, however – or is supposed to know – that this overt behaviour bears little relationship to subordinates' covert or consequent behaviour. The important thing is to keep everyone smiling and the wheels of social convention and discourse nicely lubricated. In my first meeting with the new rector of the university with whom we were working, he indicated how important it would be to make this project visible on campus, in Bangkok. All I could think was, 'This isn't in the plan: all project activities are to take place at a distance, in the towns and villages of the impoverished Northeast, and I don't relish the prospect of having to convince the funding agency that we now need to include Bangkok as well.' What I did not realize was that Thai rectors are elected to their posts, and that if they want to be re-elected they need to be seen doing things to benefit the faculty and students in Bangkok. If only I had simply nodded and said 'Yes, what a good idea, we'll definitely have to do that.' The local project director and I could have then come up with something Bangkok-based that would have satisfied the rector without alarming the funding agency, such as a splashy inauguration ceremony on campus at which the rector could preside. Instead I dug in my heels, explaining that the project plan could not be changed at this late date and that I had the funding agency to answer to. The rector kept smiling, but my overt and public challenge to his authority caused him loss of face, and cost the project two years of his finding ways to subvert and delay the project during his term. (Fortunately for the project he was not re-elected.) This is an extreme example of how significant cultural differences can impact on planning and implementing change, or at least on accomplishing one's objectives as a consultant to that process. It was a costly lesson to learn, but perhaps it is the hardest lessons that are the most likely to stay with us.

Q. The work of IEC encompasses non-formal modes of education and informal or what you call 'enculturation' and 'socialization' programmes. What are the main barriers to such initiatives and from your experience, how can these be circumvented?

A. The main issue one faces in working in non-formal education initiatives is their marginal status. Existing as they do on the margins of the formal system, they tend to be localized and small scale, and to lack the national structures and resources that characterize credentialed forms of education. By and large they are not taken as seriously as formal initiatives. Governments and donor agencies tend to consider them second-rate, stopgap solutions until the formal system can gear up to do the job properly. Non-formal initiatives within any national constellation of education programmes tend also to elude easy definition or classification, and are the most difficult to manage in any systematic way.

In spite of these difficulties, we at IEC persevere in working with our partners who are implementing these initiatives. We help them find ways to apply distance education approaches that will expand the reach of their programmes, and to apply for the funding to do so. We do this because we must. IEC's mission is to expand educational opportunities in less-developed countries. This necessarily means working at the margins of existing systems, pushing at the boundaries, finding ways to bring educational resources to those not served by mainstream education. These include refugees, displaced people, people still living in war zones, nomadic people and other ethnic and/or political minorities, the physically handicapped, and those living in geographically remote areas. These people may surface in the public consciousness from time to time, but by and large they are not popular causes; they do not benefit from much positive press. The only way we manage to circumvent these barriers is to work on a partnership basis with other, like-minded agencies, including international and local NGOs and international agencies such as UNICEF and UNHCR. We also work to ensure that non-formal initiatives are included in distance education conference and publication agendas, and to publish as much in the field ourselves as we can find time and funding for. The most recent example of this is *Basic Education at a Distance* (Yates and Bradley, 2000), our contribution to the COL series of annual reviews of distance education.

Q. How far do you feel IEC has come in realizing its aims and its clients' expectations? What plans are there for the future development of its services and how will these be pursued?

A. I discovered the answer to the first question during my first trip to Africa, shortly after joining IEC. The occasion was a meeting on non-formal education at a distance organized by COL, an event which brought together over two dozen African leaders in distance education. Almost to a person they had had some significant connection with IEC over the years, as students on the London short course or the MA in distance education, or as members of institutions in which IEC had played a formative and even founding role. This brought home to me in the most dramatic way possible the key role IEC has played in the development of distance education in Africa and beyond, a lesson reinforced by subsequent trips to Asia and the Caribbean.

To the extent that distance education has come a long way in these countries, IEC has come a long way. But it still feels as though our work has only just begun. We are constantly alert to new possibilities for extending the reach of our information, training and consultancy services. We continue to manage projects of our own, such as the post–literacy initiative we are carrying out with the Sudan Open Learning Organization. Increasingly however, we are doing so as partners in consortia led by large UK-based agencies such as British Council and Cambridge Education Consultants, contributing the distance education and materials development components to multimillion pound, national initiatives in countries like Bangladesh. We are continuing to expand our own information base and extend its reach through electronic means. As more and more of our students and other clientele gain access to the Internet, we are able to interact with them on a more regular basis using that medium. In addition to extending the delivery of our education offerings, we are expanding, enlarging and updating the content of those offerings. We're also moving some of our educational programmes on to a more commercial basis, ploughing any profits back into our core work, at the margins of educational provision, which remains our *raison d'être*. The needs are not diminishing, and neither are our efforts to meet them.

Q. What advice would you offer those responsible for leading and managing educational change in developing countries and those seeking to assist these leaders and managers?

A. I find it difficult to give generalized advice to people who are seeking solutions to specific problems in particular contexts. I would prefer to list those qualities I try to foster in my own approach to leadership. These are, in no particular order:

- A sure sense of self, knowing where one stands and what one stands for.
- The ability to create a positive climate for work and learning, by privileging description and analysis over judgement and evaluation, flexibility over strategy and manipulation, equality over superiority, and problem orientation over control.
- A continual awareness of the need to act on the side of and in support of those who lack the power and resources to change their life circumstances for the better.
- An astute sense and knowledge of how things work, especially of how political processes operate in shaping the situations in which one operates.

There is nothing new or original in this list. Chinese philosopher Lao Tzu phrased these principles some 2,500 years ago. I offer his words as the conclusion to and summation of my own (Heider, 1986: 135):

> The greatest martial arts are the gentlest. They allow an attacker the opportunity to fall down. . .The greatest administrators do not achieve production through constraints and limitations. They provide opportunities. Good leadership consists of motivating people to their highest levels by offering them opportunities, not obligations. That is how things happen naturally. Life is an opportunity and not an obligation.

Chapter 23

Jones International University: converging marketplace entrepreneurship and education

Glenn R Jones, US cable pioneer, author, founder and CEO of Jones International University™: The University of the Web™ and JonesKnowledge.com™ and creator of more than 20 Internet companies, who is known as 'the poet of technology', discusses leadership and fusing education with technology and private and public enterprise.

Q. Why have you invested so heavily in enterprises such as JonesKnowledge.com, e-education and Jones International University?

A. The seeds for this were sown many years ago. When I was a young US Navy officer serving on a ship carrying troops in and out of Korea, I spent time talking with sailors and soldiers about why they thought it was important to make the sacrifice of exposing themselves to military hostility. Many spoke generally about democracy, freedom and family, but I was struck by how few really focused on the foundations of democracy, the right of self-determination for the individual or specific mandates of our constitution and what they meant.

Many years later, when I visited the Vietnam Veteran's Memorial in Washington DC for the first time, I was again forcefully reminded of the sacrifices many have made in the name of freedom. War is such a terrible, brutal, devastating way of solving problems. Still, wars persist. And still, memorials are erected to memorialize those who give their lives, often without a satisfactory understanding of the philosophical and political processes that must be engaged to maintain basic human rights and opportunities. And, critically, I realized that many of their peers and children were likely still to be missing out on some of these fundamental lessons. I concluded that those of us who were concerned about this reality, who were still alive and who had the means to address the problem, had an obligation to react.

Further reflection led me to believe that if there was to be resolution at all, it must be entwined with education. Accessible education for everyone, no matter who they are, where they are or what their condition in life might be.

It was also apparent from statistics available in the late 1980s that governments alone could not fund this level of global lifelong education. The world's capital markets had to be engaged. For Wall Street and other like markets to become involved, the educational activity had to be economically self-sustaining, indeed profitable, and have a very attractive potential financial future.

Accordingly, in 1987 I became very involved for the personal obligation I felt, and my companies became involved because they shared the belief that education can be an immense and profitable market. Because of their legacies in the telecommunications and technology businesses, these companies embraced the notion that they could ultimately deliver quality education at a much lower price to perhaps millions of people, pay taxes, and make money.

In terms of a market, in the late 1980s the concept of lifelong learning was creeping into the consciousness of both adults and employers. The latter were dealing with the accelerating necessity to train and re-train their employees, while those in the workforce had begun to confront the reality of changing technologies, production techniques, and management processes that required new learning. People were living longer and healthier all at once, and this meant that many wanted to go back to school to finish degrees after retirement or prepare for second and third careers.

This made for a total environment ripe for new education offerings and delivery techniques. We were very early with our first Mind Extension University offerings via TV, but I think that the rush into the online education market by traditional institutions, employers and private companies during the last half of the 1990s has proved that this was indeed the right direction.

Q. What major challenges have you faced entering the educational marketplace?

A. When Mind Extension University was launched in 1987, we were not exactly welcomed with open arms by the education establishment. Many faculty organizations and education associations in the United States denigrated education via TV, both formally and informally. Distance education was regarded by many in this country as something for poor folks who couldn't afford to send their kids off to college, or for sparsely populated rural areas. And we were unabashedly saying we intended to make a profit at this.

Fortunately, we also had some allies from the education communities. Early on, such institutions as Regis University, Colorado State University, George Washington University, Penn State, the California State University at Dominguez Hills, Washington State University and others became our partners for telecourse learning. These were institutions where key faculty and administrators had recognized the growing need for learning at a distance in order to serve their student bodies more effectively and also sustain their enrolments. It was through the vision and willingness of our education partners such as these that Mind Extension University – now Jones Knowledge.com – was able to establish a toehold and eventually evolve into the multifaceted education organization that it is today, with affiliated companies including *e*-education, Knowledge Store and *e*-Global Library.

During our first few years, we also provided telecourses for K-12 classrooms. While some administrators were very willing to work with us, in other cases there was an ingrained inflexibility in the academic scheduling and pedagogy we couldn't make work with our technology. Now, it looks as though both the pedagogy outlook in K-12 and our technologies are finally converging. We're finding both high school and community colleges much more receptive to the offerings of courses online than they were previously when we were limited to TV. This is undoubtedly because of the presence of computers and online systems in classrooms, and especially because this technology is much more interactive than TV was a decade ago.

Q. You recently wrote a book on how entrepreneurial and non-profit organizations can create 21st century success. Can you summarize this for us?

A. Free Market Fusion (Jones, 1999) explains my philosophy on how the private sector – specifically entrepreneurs – and the public sector, including non-profits and governance organizations, can work together to realize accomplishments that neither might attain on their own and ideally, in ways that at the very least pay the operation's expenses and, preferably, make a profit.

For the Free Market Fusion process to occur, there must be a coming together of two or more entities, one or more of which is characterized as a for-profit enterprise and one or more of which is an institutional, non-profit, quasi-governmental, or government entity. Although this may result in the formation of new enterprises, typically at the outset existing organizations are the creators. Also, typically there is a background of significant common need, concern, or opportunity relative to the entities involved that generates support for resolution. At its ideal, the collaborative process inherent in Free Market Fusion can engender the tremendous release of energies that comes from looking at the world, not as a miasma of intractable problems, but as an arena of challenges awaiting exploration, initiative, resolution and reward. As in the physical fusion process, a new solution is accompanied by a burst of energy as new possibilities and opportunities open up to everyone involved in the process, both those creating the solution and those benefiting from it.

The fundamental concepts for Free Market Fusion came from my involvement with education-related projects beginning in the 1980s. Jones Knowledge.com and Jones International University are current manifestations of what began as private–public cooperative ventures. When we decided to pursue electronically delivered education, our intent was to help existing institutions do what they had already identified as an important part of their mission. Of course, along the way we also had to become involved in preaching the gospel of distance learning to both institutions and the public.

For education entities looking to apply free market principles today, I would recommend that they look to the circle of local businesses that may already be part of their supplier circle and invite senior executives to join a special group to tackle whatever venture is being considered. They may bring other expertise to the task as well, such as strategic planning and knowledge of technology life-cycles. Assembling a mix of knowledgeable entrepreneurship, educational professionalism and technology innovation is a good beginning step. If that mix is right, the rest of the path will emerge soon enough.

Q. What are the leadership qualities needed for such 'free market fusion' and new educational enterprises?

A. I would offer two important qualities. Neither can produce innovation and new ideas on its own. But combine the two, and I think you have a person who can work magic as a leader.

First, basic training and understanding in business fundamentals is absolutely essential. Many of the world's greatest ideas have sunk in a mire of incompetence, meaning that those with the great ideas didn't have the expertise to follow through with them, or passed them on to those who couldn't. For examples of how this maxim is not being properly applied today, we have only to turn to the plethora of e-commerce Web sites appearing on the Internet. Many are designed with marketing in mind, or order taking, or leading edge Web design, but very few demonstrate a true integration of all these elements that are necessary for true customer service and successful enterprise development. Second, they must be willing and imaginative risk-takers. Risk-takers must be willing to lay it on the line for a concept they believe will be successful. By risk-taker, I don't mean just being an outspoken iconoclast in the midst of a group of traditionalists or conservative practitioners of the middle-of-the-road management school. Risk-takers must have confidence to promote their ideas and beliefs because they know the fundamentals of their industry and have a firm grasp of the latest competitive intelligence on the arena where they want to launch a new venture. By thinking imaginatively, I mean being able to look at the obvious and then identify a path or spin on an idea that may be unconventional yet feasible.

Q. How should educational leaders approach risk in today's global dynamics and uncertainties?

A. How can an individual or an institution not take risks and hope to survive in the new global environment? I believe the key issue behind this question is not 'how', but 'why'. Leaders of education institutions are in a unique situation in our society, because they are in the business of helping mould society's participants, aka their students.

In the 'old' world of academia, the risks involved upsetting the faculty senate or the board of regents and receiving a vote of no confidence, at least at the college president or individual dean's levels. More than one college head was cashiered in the 1990s for daring to suggest suspension of the tenure system or for pushing to offer popular courses via Internet delivery. In the 21st century, the risks for education leaders are going to be very bottom-line in nature. Were student enrolments up or down in the past 18 months? How 'real world' are new course and degree offerings? How does the institution rate with employers (evidenced by corporate giving to the school, in addition to surveys)? Were the school leaders willing to recruit deans and department heads who agreed to put new faculty on contracts rather than tenure? How about requiring Web design and course delivery experience or credits as prerequisite skills for any faculty applicant?

While these concepts may seem anathema to some in academia, I should add that the changes are gradually becoming part of the campus fabric because they are part of the growing body of expectations from top students. These students make their school choices based on academic reputation, scholarships and financial aid, and access to those who are leaders and innovators in thought, word and deed. Many students won't attend institutions where faculty treats classroom time as a worrisome task of secondary importance to their own research and writing. Perhaps the true bottom line questions are just how much do the classroom lecturers truly love to teach, and can the leadership of the institution both recruit and hold on to the good ones? Becoming acclimatized to risk is an essential process for all education leaders to accept as a challenge; the risk environment is one that can become part of the daily routine, but moving through it without fear takes practice. If there is one solid bit of advice I might offer leadership selection committees for the coming decades, it would be to look for candidates who have had failures in their past, rather than just considering those with solid career success ladders. Those who have experienced failure will often be battle-hardened risk-takers with strategic and innovative skills.

Q. Jones International University was the first fully accredited online university. What were the challenges here and how were these overcome?

A. Since then, our accreditation has been extended to include an MBA programme and we will apply for other programme accreditations in the near future. The largest overall obstacle was the fact that we had to 'break the mould' in terms of how the accreditation bodies have traditionally reviewed and assessed education appropriateness. There were no classrooms to count or library stacks to view. Every thing exists electronically, managed and administered from a corporate office building in suburban Denver, Colorado.

In this regard, we need to give an enormous credit to the North Central Association of Colleges and Schools (NCACS). In no way did they lessen or relax the accreditation standards they require of traditional institutions, but they were very willing to consider an online university that replaced bricks and mortar with digital delivery. They provided us with a very thorough and, I must say, strenuous critique of our original self-study and application for accreditation. We answered their questions and requirements successfully by concentrating resources and enhancing our academic development to the greatest extent possible. They were obviously pleased with the result, and we gained accreditation on our first try.

One of the most interesting facets of how we fulfilled the accreditation requirements is the development of our *e*-Global library, a completely online library resource accessible by password to all of our students and faculty. We have developed a unique pathway to the majority of the resources required for each of the courses in the programmes that we offer online. In some cases, we have made arrangements with university libraries to provide lending privileges to our students by mail or through inter-library loan to have access to certain publications, research documents and books that are not available digitally.

There were protests from certain individuals and groups following our accreditation, most going to the NCACS and some quoted in *The Chronicle of Higher Education*. NCACS responded to those criticisms professionally and thoroughly. If anything, they had required more of us than they might have from a traditional institution seeking accreditation, so there were not any grounds for reconsideration. One of the reasons we wanted to go through the accreditation process was to establish a model that could ease the future burden of those who would follow.

Q. Are there particular strategic planning processes you find useful in your educational enterprises?

A. Sometimes entrepreneurs, particularly those who have been successful with a number of enterprises, are held up to scrutiny for moving so quickly from one project or enterprise to another. There are two overriding reasons they do this: first, because they have to move quickly in today's business environment to avoid becoming mired in unproductive enterprises; and, second, because many of them have developed an awareness to identify opportunities and possibilities beyond their immediate business focus or mission. Those who 'stay too long', so to speak, often do so because they simply don't know what else to do. They have what I call a 'negative scan awareness', meaning that they don't pay attention to the bigger environment around them.

My techniques for strategic planning go beyond classic strategic studies and the so-called strategic plan that many companies and education institutions produce. While this process is usually instructive for those involved, it also tends to be of short-term effectiveness. A classic strategic planning process often leaves out many of the tacticians within an enterprise who are responsible for making a business successful. The strategic planning group meets for several weeks, disappears to write a document, and then passes it down to those who have to make it work. While those who do the plan learn a lot, in the meantime the business environment is changing and market factors may have overtaken the process. The plan is presented in an all-day meeting, then gathers dust on a shelf for the next five years until a new management team repeats the process.

What we do as an alternative is to illuminate the 'north star', ie to develop a crisp picture of where we want to go and make it visible for everybody in the organization to see. After that, it is a combination of scanning and informal scenario planning. It can be done on an ongoing basis and provides maximum feedback and effectiveness. Scanning means teaching your managers an informal, but consistent discipline of paying attention to the interests and trends of their market-makers. In this case, market-makers mean students, students of all kinds and in many different situations. Then we get together as a group at least once a quarter and play the game of 'what if'. Details of the meetings are kept informally, and there is no formal outcome or final report. The result is the discussion of possibilities and the strategic conversation that takes place among the participants. Much of this discussion eventually surfaces in quarterly marketing and communication plans, in design features for new software, or the fine points in the design of a new course or degree programme offering. Part of the 'what if' scenarios never happen, but many of the elements do emerge or come on the horizon in unanticipated ways. The real advantage for those of us who do this is that when we see the situation arise, even from an unexpected source, we've thought and talked about much of it before and can attack the situation immediately and aggressively.

Q. What theories, principles and experiences have influenced your leadership and enterprise and what lessons would you pass on to those leading or aspiring to lead educational change?

A. It's most appropriate to begin with names here: Toffler, Socrates, Sun Tzu, von Clauswitz and Drucker.

Like most people, I have my share of personal mentors and role models from family, teachers, military commanders and business leaders. Most of them have demonstrated some of the basic lessons laid down by great teachers and leaders who have either written or been documented as to their principle belief systems. Fortunately, those beliefs are accessible to all of us in our pursuit of lifelong learning. And all of them have a common denominator: they embraced knowledge as the basis of power and success. Their examples and thoughts provide the following examples.

Alvin Toffler. He sees history as a succession of rolling waves of change and focuses on the discontinuities, or the innovations and breakpoints, therein. Toffler's 'wave-front' analysis opens the door to the identification of key patterns, such as the move from traditional agriculture and industry to a knowledge society, and allows us to plan and influence accordingly. This analysis, which I believe represents truly revolutionary thinking, leads to Toffler's conclusion that the intense change we are experiencing is not chaotic or random, but very much part of a discernible pattern. This perspective liberates one's intellect and will to react to change constructively.

Socrates. From the man who provided the foundations of the Socratic method of inquiry and debate, we inherited one of the most effective teaching models of all time. His questioning of authority, prevailing policy and public beliefs – using his method of debate – has become a cornerstone of free political systems. Unfortunately, he paid for his philosophy with his life.

Sun Tzu. 'If you know the enemy and know yourself, you need not fear the result of a hundred battles.' Sun Tzu introduced the concept of spying as a strategic implement. Today, that can be applied to competitive intelligence, which companies and executives regularly employ. Those who don't, have a high probability of failure.

Karl von Clauswitz. 'Knowledge must become capability.' This is a critical step in deploying a company. If you know your competitor's weaknesses, but do nothing to take the advantage while waiting for the competitor to fail, you will be left in a much-weakened position. In other words, when you see the adversary's weakness, attack. Always attack.

Peter Drucker. Truly a genius of management theory and a powerful observer. The lesson of Drucker is that he has been a student all his life. He demonstrates this by his thoughtful reflections on how the speed of technology is rewriting the management maxims he has espoused over three-quarters of a century. Now an octogenarian, Drucker still studies companies and the marketplace and has been one of the biggest proponents of the 'New Economy' theorists who are trying to warn old-line managers that the rules of the game have changed, whether you are in the education field or the communications industry.

Q. What skill sets do you see as necessary in tomorrow's CEOs and managers in education, faced with so much change and competition?

A. The skill sets, including fundamental education and learnings combined with an aptitude for risk-taking, have been covered in my earlier comments. Here are the key rules to be followed by those who have the skills, as adapted from my book, *Free Market Fusion* (1999):

- A supposed opportunity might only be break-even; be realistic when you are first scanning for opportunities.
- Gather your data and build your knowledge base while openly exploring the next steps of the process with your potential partners or financial backers. Be open about the process you expect to go through and solicit their ideas.
- Don't create sacred cows that bog down the process. Steps such as scenario building can be essential or completely dispensable.
- When moving with your partners into operations, the action phase, establish mutually agreeable performance guidelines, including timelines. Decide who is in charge; honour that agreement unless the operation is definitely on the verge of derailing.
- Throughout the process, consciously pay attention to the importance of imagination and fresh ideas. Be tolerant of them so that they are encouraged even if discarded later.
- Concentrate on solutions and desired results. Eventually, you must pay attention to conflicts, paradoxes and the like, but if you concentrate on solutions and results, conflicts might get resolved in the process.
- Recognize when it's over for you, or time to assume a new role.

Developing the habits of effective scanning, including good observation and ongoing research efforts while avoiding 'analysis paralysis', is part of the most important outcomes of any endeavour, regardless of how successful or unsuccessful a particular enterprise becomes. These are skills that will serve the manager and entrepreneur well in any capacity. In the end, the art of the hunch is very important, but is based upon and honed by the sum of experience and knowledge gained by the practitioner.

The final rule is to not let the process dictate the nature of the enterprise; discipline is important, but success often goes to those who recognize the next level or opening of opportunity, and chart an immediate course to reach it.

Chapter 24

Lessons for the future

Colin Latchem and Donald E Hanna

Ehrlich (2000) observes that a major contemporary human problem is that the rate of evolution in science and technology has been extraordinarily high compared to the pace of change in social attitudes and political institutions that might channel these new developments in more beneficial directions. Such an argument may be equally applied to work in the spheres of education and training where there is still a great need for expanded opportunity, organizational transformation and new and improved models for delivery. It has been the central thesis of this book that this can only happen where there is enlightened and transformational leadership.

Our interviews with some of the outstanding leaders in open and flexible learning from across the globe provide a rich mosaic of knowledge, experience, observations and conclusions that provide fresh ideas about leadership in this field. They offer the opportunity to link observations about leadership in practice with leadership theory in a way that is uniquely contextual to open and flexible learning. The observations are not prescriptive, but personal to the writers and their contexts. However, their insights suggest why we need transformational leadership in the field and what such leadership might involve when executed well. Further, readers may draw inspiration, courage and example from connecting personally with the strategies, struggles and successes of these leaders.

As concluding authors, we have conducted our own synthesis of values, concepts and strategies from these interviews and from our assessment of the literature of leadership affecting our field. We offer the following roughly hewn path for those who seek to lead in today's global, fast-paced, diverse and dynamic educational and training milieu.

Key leadership concepts

We begin by summarizing key leadership concepts, both consistent with theory and reinforced by the leaders contributing to this book.

Values and beliefs

Leaders in open and flexible learning:

- embody optimism and belief in the possibility of improvement;
- expect problems and challenges and view them as opportunities;
- are passionate about what the organization does and what they do;
- believe in 'serving' rather than 'managing' or 'leading';
- believe that learning is the key to human progress;
- are committed to the principle that access to learning opportunities for all people is a human right;
- believe in and have a predilection for change.

Characteristics and behaviours

Leaders in open and flexible learning:

- are persistent;
- continue to learn throughout their career;
- take risks;
- consider timing and exercise judgement in setting new directions;
- are patient;
- affirm the values of others;
- tolerate ambiguity;
- accept the controversiality of leadership;
- trust and respect colleagues and co-workers;
- select as members of their leadership team people with leadership characteristics;
- are reflective;
- consider both the human potential for change and the tolerance limits for change before promoting new directions;
- are flexible and able to combine opposites as needed – for example, vision and reality; change and stability; influence and humility;
- are willing to give up a leadership position and role when necessary;
- engage with opportunities and problems;
- take the lead in setting directions or pointing out the way not to go;
- drive change;
- set agendas;
- are persuasive;
- stand up to political interference for the good of the organization;
- communicate effectively;
- take advantage of and build on success;
- look for allies in every direction;
- reach out to 'outsiders' to support internal change;
- are team players;
- look for how others can contribute to meeting organizational goals;

- reframe organizational goals to reflect ongoing changes;
- pay careful attention to form and process as well as goals;
- hone their sense of humour as a leadership skill.

Leadership skills and abilities are, as the above suggests, complex and interrelated within an organizational context, the individual and a set of opportunities or challenges. The challenge to educators and trainers in open and flexible learning is to apply what we know about learning, cognition, content, technology and the new models of organization and delivery to enhance the human prospect. This calls for leaders who are agents of transformational change, who have a passion for maximizing access and quality in learning, who possess the capacity to see and work through 'the big picture', who see themselves as educators and social entrepreneurs, and who are capable of enabling other team members to acquire and exercise the leadership skills to put these new understandings to work in order to:

- Create new types of organization – for example, open schooling systems or virtual institutions.
- Transform mature organizations – for example, into dual-mode or flexible learning providers.
- Form new partnerships and strategic alliances.
- Change, innovate and improve programme and service development and delivery.

Strategies for leaders

The following suggested strategies for leaders in open and flexible learning are drawn from the literature of leadership and strategic change and our interviews with these leaders. While these are presented in linear form, they should be viewed as constantly interacting and active throughout any development process. These strategies may apply to leadership at the institutional, departmental or programme level.

Scan the environment

Involve your organization or team in analysing and making judgements about:

- national, state or local priorities for open and flexible education or training;
- community needs and obligations;
- new and existing markets for open and flexible education or training;
- advantages or opportunities that the organization no longer enjoys;
- current and potential competitors;
- technology trends;
- commercial opportunities and/or cost savings;

- unrecognized or underused internal and external opportunities and resources;
- opportunities for change, innovation and improvement;
- other trends/potential opportunities and threats.

Develop and execute a strategic plan.

Using this external/internal analysis, work with the key stakeholders to:

- create a vision statement for the organization's involvement in open and flexible education or training;
- define or reconfirm the mission in the light of this vision;
- define the strategic objectives and priorities;
- define the key target groups for the programmes and services;
- identify those groups and individuals who will be accountable for, and will implement, the innovation/change;
- determine the major risks and countermeasures;
- determine the costs and benefits;
- determine the workload and timeline factors.

Gain commitment

With the plan in place:

- 'walk and talk' the vision and goals;
- form a powerful coalition capable of leading the innovation/change;
- establish a sense of urgency and ensure that the managers, teams, lines of responsibility, support systems and resources are all in place for the task ahead.

Prepare for the change or innovation

Consult with and delegate responsibility to those responsible for:

- courses/programmes, delivery systems and support networks appropriate to the needs, characteristics, knowledge, skills and means of the targeted learners;
- intellectual property and copyright;
- staff development;
- ICT systems;
- costs, logistics and infrastructure;
- entry requirements/systems;
- administrative systems;
- assessment and examinations;
- accreditation, credit recognition and transfer;
- partnerships, alliances, etc;
- other elements likely to negatively or positively affect the processes and outcomes in the medium and long term.

Lead the process

Ensure that there is:

- consistency and support from senior and middle management;
- a clear understanding of what is to be accomplished, by whom, for whom, and to what timeline;
- sound costing and adequate funding;
- encouragement for risk-taking, a rethinking of staff workloads, investment in skills development, and commensurate reward and recognition;
- good management of the dynamics of the teaching, technology and administrative sub-cultures;
- a commitment to nurturing 'change activists' and potential leaders;
- support for the 15–20 per cent of staff who are 'early adopters';
- a commitment to quality assurance.

Achieve 'short-term' wins

Capitalize on successes by:

- aiming for visible performance or productivity gains from strategically important open and flexible programmes;
- providing 'risk' funding for these;
- ensuring that the key customers 'buy-in' to the new proposals and programmes;
- documenting and publicizing all successes and lessons learnt;
- sharing successful experiences with the 45–50 per cent of staff who are likely to change;
- changing any systems, structures or practices that seriously undermine the vision and staff endeavours.

Consolidate and encourage further innovation/change

Look for every opportunity to:

- reinvigorate the organization with new projects, themes and change agents;
- create internal and external networks for those involved in similar ventures to share ideas and experiences;
- use the increased credibility to change any outstanding systems, structures and policies that do not fit the vision;
- bring along some of the remaining 40 per cent of staff;
- hire, promote and further encourage and develop staff who will implement the new vision.

Institutionalize the new approaches

Help the organization to:

- standardize processes as they become proven and accepted;
- articulate the connections between these and the overall organizational success;
- plan for leadership succession.

And, if all else fails: create a new form of organization – for example, a commercial/entrepreneurial 'arm' or new strategic alliance.

A final note

Perspectives on leadership are coloured by many factors but, as our contributors remind us, most especially by assumptions deriving from the cultural lens through which we view the world. We have tried in this book to bring many different lenses to bear on the challenges and opportunities in leading education and training in the 21st century. We have sought to link theory and practice, combine vision and experience, and shape a future of passion for and commitment to the ideals and values of open and flexible learning. Our observations about leadership are also shaped by our perceptions of the complexity of the external environment and the demands for adaptation and renewal in our educational and training organizations. We hope we have provided a framework for current and aspiring leaders who must navigate this 'new world'. Good luck on your journey.

References

Abdullah, S (1998) 'Helping faculty to make the paradigm shift from on-campus teaching to distance education at the Institut Teknologi MARA, Malaysia', in *Staff Development in Open and Flexible Learning*, ed C Latchem and F Lockwood, pp 85–94, Routledge, London

Aitkin, D (1998) 'Inside story of a university life', *The Australian: Higher Education*, pp 32–3 (shortened version of a paper in *Journal of Higher Education Policy and Management*)

Alexander, S and McKenzie, J (1998) *An Evaluation of Information Technology Projects for Higher Education*, University of Technology, Sydney (http://www.iim.uts.edu.au/about/sa_pubs/cautexec.html)

Althusser, L (1971) 'Ideology and ideological state apparatuses', in *Lenin and Philosophy and Other Essays*, (tr) B Brewster, Verso, London

Anderson, D, Johnson, R and Milligan, B (1999) *Strategic Planning in Australian Universities*, Evaluations and Investigations Programme, Higher Education Division

Arenson, K W (1998) 'More colleges plunging into uncharted waters of on-line courses', *The New York Times*, Section A, p 16

Badaracco, J L and Ellsworth, R R (1989) *Leadership and the Quest for Integrity*, Harvard Business School Press, Boston, MA

Baldridge, J V, Deal, T E and Ingols, C (1983) *The Dynamics of Organizational Change in Education*, McCutchan Pub Corp, Berkeley, CA

Bates, A W (1995) *Technology: Open learning and distance education*, Routledge, London

Bates, A W (1999) 'Are open universities dead?', keynote address, the 13th Annual Conference of the Asian Association of Open Universities, Open and Distance Education Systems and Models Facing 21st Century's Information and Learning Societies, 14–17 October, Beijing, China

Bates, A W (2000) *Managing Technological Change: Strategies for college and university leaders*, Jossey-Bass, San Francisco, CA

Behling, O and McFillen, J (1996) 'A syncretical model of charismatic/transformational learning', *Group and Organizational Management*, **21** (2), pp 163–85

Bennis, W (1989) *On Becoming a Leader*, Addison-Wesley, Reading, MA

Bergquist, W H (1992) *The Four Cultures of the Academy: Insights and strategies for improving leadership in collegiate organizations*, Jossey-Bass, San Francisco, CA

Binney, C and Williams, C (1995) *Leaning into the Future: Changing the way people change organizations*, Nicholas Brealey, London

Blake, R and Mouton, J (1964) *The Managerial Grid*, Gulf, New York

Blanchard, K, Zigarmi, P and Zigarmi, D (1987) *Leadership and the One Minute Manager*, Fontana Paperbacks, London

Bloomberg, M (1999) National Press Club Telstra Address, Sydney Convention and Exhibition Centre, 24 June, Telstra Transcript

Blumenstyk, G (1999) 'A company pays top universities to use their names and their professors', *The Chronicle of Higher Education, Money & Management,* 18 June, p A39

Bogue, E G (1994) *Leadership by Design: Strengthening integrity in higher education,* Jossey-Bass, San Francisco, CA

Boshier, R W and Pratt, D (1997) 'A qualitative and postmodern perspective on open learning in Hong Kong', *Distance Education,* **18** (1), pp 110–35

Boshier, R, Wilson, M and Qayyum, A (1999) 'Lifelong education and the World Wide Web: American hegemony or diverse utopia?', *International Journal of Lifelong Education,* **18** (4), pp 275–85

Boyer, E L (1990) *Scholarship Reconsidered: Priorities of the professoriate,* The Carnegie Foundation for the Advancement of Teaching, Princetown

BP Audit Team (1995) *Use of Technology to Support Learning: Audit of University of Humberside,* University of Lincolnshire and Humberside (internal document)

Bridges, W (2000) *The Character of Organizations: Using Jungian type in organizational development,* Consulting Psychologists Press, Palo Alto, CA

Brown-Parker, J (1996) 'Nonformal leadership and management development: Making the practice reflect the theory', paper presented at the 1996 HERDSA Conference, Perth, University of Western Australia

Calder, J and McCollum, A (1998) *Open and Flexible Learning in Vocational Education and Training,* Kogan Page, London

Carnegie Council on Policy Studies in Higher Education (1980) *The Carnegie Council on Policy Studies in Higher Education: A summary of reports and recommendations,* Jossey-Bass, San Francisco, CA

CeHEP (1999) *CeHEP Prospectus,* Centre for Higher Education Practice, The Open University, Milton Keynes

Champy, J and Nohria, N (eds) (1996) *Fast Forward,* Harvard Business School Publishing, Boston, MA

Chandra, R (1997) 'Improving university teaching at The University of the South Pacific', keynote address, International Conference on Improving University Teaching and Learning: Asia–Pacific Experiences, Universitas Brawijaya, Malang, Indonesia

Chattell, A (1995) *Managing for the Future,* Macmillan, Basingstoke

Chipman, L (1999) 'Welcome to Lifetime Learning Inc', *The Australian: Higher Education,* 8 September, p 44 (an edited extract from a paper 'Visioning Our Future' delivered to the Central Queensland University Council)

Chung, F (1999) 'African educational responses to the challenges of globalisation', plenary address, Pan-Commonwealth Forum on Open Learning, 1–5 March, Brunei Darussalam, http://www.col.org/forum

Clark, J (1999) *Netscape Time: The making of the billion-dollar start-up that took on Microsoft,* St Martins Press, New York

Cohen, M D and March, J D (1994) *Leadership and Ambiguity: The American College President*, McGraw-Hill, New York

Cole, R E (ed) (1995) *The Death and Life of the American Quality Movement*, Oxford University Press, New York

Collins, J C and Porras, J L (1997) *Built to Last: Successful habits of visionary companies*, Harperbusiness, New York

Collis, B (1998) 'New didactics for university instruction: Why and how', *Computers & Education,* **31** (4), pp 373–95

Collis, B (1999a) 'Pedagogical perspectives on ICT use in higher education', in *The Use of Information and Communication Technology in Higher Education: An international orientation on trends and issues,* ed B Collis and M van der Wende, pp 41–70, study commissioned by the Dutch Ministry of Economic Affairs and the Ministry of Education, Culture and Science, Enschede: CHEPS (Center for Higher Education Policy Studies) (http://education2.edte.utwente.nl/ictho.nsf/framesform)

Collis, B (1999b) 'Telematics supported education for traditional universities in Europe', *Performance Improvement Quarterly,* **12** (2), pp 36–65

Collis, B and De Boer, W (1999a) 'Scaling up from the pioneers: The TeleTOP method at the University of Twente', *Interactive Learning Environments,* **7** (2/3), pp 93–112

Collis, B and De Boer, W (1999b) 'The TeleTOP Decision Support Tool', in *Design Approaches and Tools in Education and Training,* ed J van der Akker, R, Branch, K Gustafson, N, Nieveen, M and Tj Plomp, pp 235–48, Kluwer Academic Publishers, Dordrecht

Collis, B and Moonen, J (1994) 'Leadership for transition: Moving from the special project to systemwide integration with computers in education', in *Educational Technology: Leadership perspectives,* ed G Kearsley and W Lynch, pp 113–36, Educational Technology Press, Englewood Cliffs, NJ

Collis, B and Moonen, J (1999) *Report of a Study Trip,* internal document, Faculty of Educational Science and Technology, University of Twente (WWW document: http://users.edte.utwente.nl/collis/StudyTrip/sum-studytrip.doc)

Collis, B and Pals, N (2000) 'A model for predicting an individual's use of a telematics application', *International Journal for Educational Telecommunications,* **6** (1), pp 63–103

Collis, B, Peters, O and Pals, N (2000) 'A model for predicting the educational use of information and communication technologies', *Instructional Science* (in press)

Collis, B and van der Wende, M (eds) (1999) *The Use of Information and Communication Technology in Higher Education: An international orientation on trends and issues,* pp 41–70, study commissioned by the Dutch Ministry of Economic Affairs and the Ministry of Education, Culture and Science, Enschede: CHEPS (Center for Higher Education Policy Studies) (http://education2.edte.utwente.nl/ictho.nsf/framesform)

Commonwealth of Learning (2000) *Trainers' Toolkits*, Commonwealth of Learning, Vancouver and Asia Development Bank

Commonwealth Secretariat (1987) *Towards a Commonwealth of Learning: A proposal to create the University of the Commonwealth for Co-operation in Distance Education,* report of the Expert Group on Commonwealth Co-operation in Distance Education and Open Learning, chaired by the Rt Hon Lord Briggs of Lewes (The Briggs Report), The Commonwealth Secretariat, London

Commonwealth Secretariat (1988) *The Commonwealth of Learning: Institutional arrangements for Commonwealth co-operation in distance education,* report of the Working Group, chaired by Sir John Daniel (The Daniel Report), The Commonwealth Secretariat, London

Cunningham, S, Tapsall, S, Ryan, Y, Stedman, L, Bagdon, K and Flew, T (1997) *New Media and Borderless Education: A review of the convergence between global media networks and higher education provision,* Evaluations and Investigations Program, Higher Education Division, Department of Employment, Education, Training and Youth Affairs, Australian Government Publishing Service, Canberra

Cunningham, S, Ryan, Y, Stedman, L, Tapsall, S, Bagdon, K, Flew, T and Coaldrake, P (2000) *The Business of Borderless Education,* Evaluations and Investigations Program, Higher Education Division, Department of Education, Training and Youth Affairs, Australian Government Publishing Service, Canberra

Daniel, J S (1996) *Mega-universities and Knowledge Media: Technology strategies for higher education,* Kogan Page, London

Daniel, J (1999a) 'Entente cordiale', *Open Eye: The Magazine of the Open University Alumni Community,* 1 June, p 2

Daniel, J (1999b) 'Distance learning in the era of networks', *The ACU Bulletin of Current Documentation,* **138** (April), pp 7–9

Davies, J L (1995) 'The training of academic heads of departments' in *Directions in Staff Development,* ed A Brew, pp 118–32, The Society for Research into Higher Education and Open University Press, Buckingham

Davis, S M and Botkin, J W (1994) *The Monster under the Bed: How business is mastering the opportunity of knowledge for profit,* Simon & Schuster, New York

Dede, C (2000) 'Advanced technologies and distributed learning in higher education', in *Higher Education in an Era of Digital Competition: Choices and challenges,* ed D E Hanna and Associates, pp. 71–91, Atwood Publishers, Madison, WI

Delors, J, Al Mufti, I, Amagi, I, Carneiro, R, Chung, F, Geremek, B, Gorham, W, Aleksandra, Kornhauser, A, Manley, M, Quero, M P, Savané, M-A, Singh, K, Stavenhagen, R, Suhr, M W and Nanzhao, Z (1996) *Learning: The treasure within,* report to UNESCO of the International Commission on Education for the Twenty-first Century, Presided by Jacques Delors, TSO Books, London

Dhanarajan, G (1998) 'International and inter-institutional collaboration in distance education', in *Learning Together – Collaborating in Open Learning,* ed J M Barker, Proceedings of the International Conference hosted by the John Curtin International Institute, Curtin University of Technology, 20–22 April, Perth, Australia, pp 1–10

Dhanarajan, G, Ip, P K, Yuen, K S and Swales, C (1994) *Economics of Distance Education: Recent experience,* Open Learning Institute Press, Open Learning Institute of Hong Kong

Dighe, A and Reddi, U V (1996) 'Use of communication technologies in open learning, nonformal adult and community education', plenary address, Pan-Commonwealth Forum on Open Learning, 1–5 March, Brunei Darussalam (http://www.col.org/forum)

Dodds, T (1996) *The Use of Distance Learning in Nonformal Education*, The Commonwealth of Learning/International Extension College, Cambridge

Drucker, P F (1974) *Management: Tasks, responsibilities, practices*, Heinemann, Oxford

Drucker, P F (1985) *Innovation and Entrepreneurship: Practice and principles*, Harper & Row, New York

Drucker, P F (1993) *Innovation and Entrepreneurship*, HarperBusiness, New York

Drucker, P F (1996) 'The coming of the new organization' in *Fast Forward*, ed J Champy and N Nohria, pp 3–14, Harvard Business School Publishing, Boston, MA

Drucker, P F (1999) 'Beyond the information revolution', *The Atlantic Monthly*, October, pp 47–57

Duderstadt, J (2000) 'A choice of transformations for the 21st-century university', *Chronicle of Higher Education*, 4 February, p B6

Ehrlich, P R (2000) 'The tangled skeins of nature and nurture in human evolution', *The Chronicle of Higher Education, Section 2*, 22 September, pp B7–B11

Evans, T (1995) 'Globalisation, post-Fordism and open and distance education', *Distance Education*, **16** (2), pp 256–69

Evans, T (1999) 'From dual mode to flexible delivery: Paradoxical transitions in Australian open and distance education', *Performance Improvement Quarterly*, **12** (2) Special Issue: Distance Learning, pp 84–95

Evans, T, Nation, D, Rennart, W and Tregenza, K (1997) 'The end of the line or a new future for open and distance education?', in *Open, Flexible and Distance Learning: Education and training in the 21st century*, ed J Osborne, D Roberts and J Walker, pp 151–55, 13th Biennial Forum of Open and Distance Learning Association of Australia (in association with the Australian Association of Distance Education Schools), 29 September – 3 October, University of Tasmania

Farrell, G (ed) (1999) *The Development of Virtual Education: A global perspective*, The Commonwealth of Learning (http://www.col.org/virtualed)

Fisser, P (2000) *The New Meaning of Distance for Universities: Strategies, costs and implications*, internal document, Faculty of Educational Science and Technology, University of Twente (http://users.edte.utwente.nl/fisser/research.html)

Fitzgerald, M (1996) 'No mark for effort skews assessment', *Times Higher Education Supplement*, 5 April

Foreshaw, J (2001) 'UTS and i-Global aim high', *The Australian: IT*, 27 March, p 41

French, W L and Bell, C (1994) *Organization Development and Transformation: Managing effective change*, McGraw-Hill, Maidenhead

Fullan, M (1993) *Change Forces: Probing the depths of educational reform*, Falmer Press, London

Fullan, M (1999) *Change Forces: The sequel*, Falmer Press, London

Geer, D (1997) 'Going dual-mode: Exposing the paradigm shift', *Open Praxis*, **2**, pp 25–31

Gharajedaghi, J (1999) *Systems Thinking: Managing chaos and theory: A platform for designing business architecture*, Butterworth-Heinemann, Boston, MA

Gilbert, S W (1996) 'Making the most of a slow revolution', *Change*, March/April, pp 10–23

Gluyas, R (1999) 'Uni revolution', *The Weekend Australian: Weekend Business & Personal Investment*, 6–7 November, pp 37–8

Grant, J (1992) 'Women as managers: What they can offer organizations', in *Frontiers of Leadership*, ed M Syrett and C Hogg, Blackwell, Oxford

Hague, D (1991) *Beyond Universities: A new republic of the intellect*, Institute of Economic Affairs, London

Hall, J W, Thor, L M and Farrell, G M (1996) *The Educational Paradigm Shift: Implications for ICDE and the distance learning community. Report of the Task Force of International Council for Distance Education*, Standing Committee of Presidents' Meeting, Lillehammer, Norway, ICDE, Oslo

Hammer, M and Stanton, S A (1995) *The Reengineering Revolution: A handbook*, HarperBusiness, Sydney

Hanna, D E (1998) 'Higher education in an era of digital competition: Emerging organizational models', *Journal of Asynchronous Learning*, **2** (1) (http://www.aln.org/alnweb/journal/jaln_vol2issue1.htm#hanna)

Hanna, D E (2000) 'Emerging organizational models: The extended traditional university', in *Higher Education in an Era of Digital Competition: Choices and challenges*, ed D E Hanna and Associates, pp 93–116, Atwood Publishers, Madison, WI

Hannan, M T and Freeman, J (1989) *Organizational Ecology*, Harvard University Press, Cambridge, MA

Harry, K and Perraton, H (1999) 'Open and distance learning for the new society', in *Higher Education Through Open and Distance Learning*, ed K Harry, pp 1–12, Routledge, London

Hawkridge, D (1999) 'Distance learning: International comparisons', *Performance Improvement Quarterly*, **12** (2), pp 9–20

Healey, M (1995) *Prospero's Enchanted Isle*, University of Lincolnshire and Humberside

Hecksher, C (1994) 'Defining the post-bureaucratic type', in *The Post-Bureaucratic Organization: New perspectives on organizational change*, ed C Hecksher and A Donnellon, Sage Publications, Thousand Oaks, CA

HEFCE (1999a) *Use of TLTP Materials in UK Higher Education*, HEFCE 99/39, Higher Education Funding Council for England, London

HEFCE (1999b) *Teaching Quality Enhancement Fund*, 99/48; *Institutional Learning and Teaching Strategies: A guide to good practice*, 99/55, Higher Education Funding Council for England, London

Heider, J (1986) *The Tao of Leadership: Leadership strategies for a new age*, Bantam, New York

Hirt, N (2000) 'Will education go to market?', *The Unesco Courier*, February, pp 14–16

Hoare, D (1996) *Review of Management of Higher Education Institutions*, Department of Employment, Education, Training and Youth Affairs, Australian Government Publishing Service, Canberra

Hofstede, G H (1980) *Cultures' Consequences: International differences in work-related values*, Sage, Beverly Hills, CA

Horsfield, T (1999) 'A business led approach to open learning', report on Sectoral Developments and Issues, Pan-Commonwealth Forum on Open Learning, 1–5 March, Brunei Darussalam (http://www.col.org/forum)

IEC (1972) *One Year's Work: The International Extension College 1971–1972*, International Extension College, Cambridge

IEC (1981) *Ten-year Report, 1971–1981*, International Extension College, Cambridge

Illing, D (1999) 'No agenda for uniformity', *The Australian: Higher Education*, 4 August, p 34

Illing, D (2001) 'Online deal will cost unis millions', *The Australian: Higher Education*, 21 March, p 37

Jakupec, V (1998) 'Flexible learning in Australian universities: A comparative study', unpublished report, Faculty of Education, University of Technology Sydney

Jakupec, V and Nicoll, K (1994) 'Crises in distance education,' *Higher Education Review*, **26** (2), pp 17–32

James, J (1996) *Thinking in the Future Tense: Leadership skills for a new age*, Simon & Schuster, New York

Jevons, F and Northcott, P (1994) *Costs and Quality in Resource-based Education On- and Off-campus*, National Board of Employment Education and Training. Commissioned Report No 33, Australian Government Publishing Service, Canberra, ACT

Johnson, R (1996) 'To wish and to will: Reflections on policy formation and implementation in Australian distance education', in *Opening Education: Policies and practices from open and distance education*, ed T Evans and D Nation, pp 90–101, Routledge, London

Jones, G R (1999) *Free Market Fusion: How entrepreneurs and nonprofits create 21st century success*, Jones Digital Century Inc, Englewood, CO

Jung, I (1999) 'The development of virtual institutions in Korea', Appendix 9.1 to Robertshaw, M 'Virtual institutions in east and southeast Asia', in *The Development of Virtual Education: A global perspective*, ed G. Farrell, The Commonwealth of Learning (http://www.col.org/virtualed/index.htm)

Karelis, C (1999) *Educational Technology and Cost Control: Four models*, Fund for the Improvement of Postsecondary Education (http://www.ed.gov/offices/OPE/FIPSE/LAAP/reading.html)

Kimberly, J R (1988) 'Reframing and organizational change', in *Paradoxes and Transformation: Toward a theory of change in organization and management*, ed R E Quinn and K S Cameron, Ballinger Publishing Company, Cambridge, MA

Kimberly, J R and Rottman, D B (1987) 'Environment, structure, and performance: A biographical view', *Journal of Management Studies*, **24**, pp 595–622

King, B S (1999) 'Distance education in Australia' in *Higher Education Through Open and Distance Learning: World review of distance education and open learning*, ed K Harry, Routledge, London/The Commonwealth of Learning, Vancouver

Koul, B N (1998) 'Proactive staff development: The Indira Gandhi National Open University Experience', in *Staff Development in Open and Flexible Learning*, ed C Latchem and F Lockwood, pp 75–84, Routledge, London

Latchem, C and Lockwood, F (1998) 'Preface,' in *Staff Development in Open and Flexible Learning*, ed C Latchem and F Lockwood, Routledge, London

Latchem, C and Walker, D (2001) *Telecentres: Case studies and key issues*, The Commonwealth of Learning, Vancouver

Latchem, C, Abdullah, S and Ding, X (1999) 'Open and dual-mode universities in East and South Asia', *Performance Improvement Quarterly*, **12** (2), pp 96–121

Laurillard, D (1993) *Rethinking University Teaching: A framework for the effective use of educational technology*, Routledge, London

Le Grew, D and Calvert, J (1998) 'Leadership for open and flexible learning in higher education', in *Staff Development in Open and Flexible Learning*, ed C Latchem and F Lockwood, Routledge, London

Leibowitz, W R (2000) 'Law professors told to expect competition from virtual learning', *Chronicle of Higher Education*, p A45 (http://chronicle.com/free/v46/i20/20a04501.htm)

Lemke, C (nd) *Technology in American Schools: Seven dimensions for gauging progress*, Milken Family Foundation (www.mff.org/edtech/projects)

Lenzer, R and Johnson, S S (1997) 'Peter Drucker: Still the youngest of minds', *Forbes*, 10 March (http://www.forbes.com/forbes/97/0310/5905122a.htm)

Lenzinger, R (1995) 'The reluctant entrepreneur', *Forbes,* 1 September

Levine, A (1980) *Why Innovation Fails*, State University of New York Press, Albany, NY

Lewin, K (1997) *Resolving Social Conflict: Field theory in social science*, American Psychological Association, Washington, DC and Department of Education, Training and Youth Affairs, Australian Government Publishing Service, Canberra

Lewis, R (1993) 'Approaches to staff development in open learning: the role of a competence framework' in *Key Issues on Open Learning: A reader*, ed A Tait, pp 142–64, Longman, Harlow

Lewis, R (1995a) *New Learning Environment at the University of Humberside: Report on consultations held during 1994*, University of Lincolnshire and Humberside (internal paper)

Lewis, R (1995b) 'The creation of an open learning environment in HE', *Innovation and Learning in Education: The International Journal for the Reflective Practitioner*, **1** (2), pp 32–6

Lewis, R (1998) 'Staff development in conventional institutions moving towards open learning', in *Staff Development in Open and Flexible Learning*, ed C Latchem and F Lockwood, Routledge, London

Machel, G (1999) 'Our children must be armed with education', *The Australian*, 28 April, p 15

Machiavelli, N (tr) Gilbert, A H (1963) *The Prince*, Duke University Press, Durham, NC

Mason, R (1998) *Globalizing Education: Trends and applications*, Routledge, London

Mason, R (1999) 'The impact of telecommunications', in *Higher Education Through*

Open and Distance Learning, ed K Harry, pp 32–47, Routledge, London/Commonwealth of Learning, Vancouver

McGregor Burns, J (1978) *Leadership,* Harper & Row, New York

McIlroy, A and Walker, R (1996) 'Total quality management: Policy implications for distance education', in *Opening Education: Policies and practices from open and distance education,* ed T Evans and D Nation, pp 132–46, Routledge, London

Middlehurst, R (1995) 'Top training: Development for institutional managers', in *Directions in Staff Development,* ed A Brew, pp 98–117, The Society for Research into Higher Education and Open University Press, Buckingham

Minztberg, H (1994) *The Rise and Fall of Strategic Planning,* Prentice Hall, Hemel Hempstead

Moonen, J (1999) 'Costs, efficiency, and effectiveness of ICT in higher education', in *The Use of Information and Communication Technology in Higher Education: An international orientation on trends and issues,* ed B Collis and M van der Wende, pp 74–90, study commissioned by the Dutch Ministry of Economic Affairs and the Ministry of Education, Culture and Science, Enschede: CHEPS (Center for Higher Education Policy Studies) (http://education2.edteutwente.nl/ictho.nsf/framesform)

Moonen, J and Peters, E (1999) 'Wat is het rendement van het gebruik van ICT in het HO?' (What is the payoff of the use of ICT in higher education?), Chapter 3 in *ICT in Hoger Onderwijs Nederlands* (ICT in higher education in The Netherlands), ed W Veen, study commissioned by the Dutch Ministry of Economic Affairs and the Ministry of Education, Culture and Science, The University of Utrecht, Utrecht

Moran, L (1997) 'Flexible learning, technology and change: Divining the future from the past', in *Open, Flexible and Distance Learning: Education and training in the 21st century,* ed J Osborne, D Roberts and J Walker, pp 331–35, 13th Biennial Forum of Open and Distance Learning Association of Australia (in association with the Australian Association of Distance Education Schools), 29 September to 3 October, University of Tasmania

Moran, L and Myringer, B (1999) 'Flexible learning and university change', in *Higher Education Through Open and Distance Learning,* ed K Harry, pp 57–71, Routledge, London/The Commonwealth of Learning, Vancouver

Moreira, C F (1998) 'The distance learning dilemma', *The Star,* Education Section, 9 August, p 2

Morgan, R M and Hawkridge, D (1999) 'Guest editorial – global distance learning', *Performance Improvement Quarterly,* **12** (2), Special Issue: Distance Learning, pp 6–8

Mukherjee, N (1997) 'Lok Siksha Samsad' (Council for People's Education), *Open Praxis,* **2,** pp 13 and 21

Munitz, B (1997) 'New educational paradigm', videorecording of keynote address at the 18th ICDE World Conference, 2–6 June, The Pennsylvania State University

National Committee of Inquiry into Higher Education (NCIHE) (1997) *Higher Education in the Learning Society: Main Report* (The Dearing Report), TSO, London

National Council for Open and Distance Education (1996) *Quality Guidelines for Resource Based Learning* (http://cedir.uow.edu.au/NCODE)

Noble, D (1998) 'Digital diploma mills', *First Monday Online Journal* (http://www.firstmonday.dk/issues/issue3_1/noble/index.html)

ODLAA Times (1999) Open and Distance Learning Association of Australia, Canberra, August, **7** (3), p 6

Olcott, D and Schmidt, K (2000) 'Redefining faculty policies and practices for the Knowledge Age', in *Higher Education in an Era of Digital Competition: Choices and challenges*, ed D E Hanna and Associates, pp 259–85, Atwood Publishers, Madison, WI

OUHK (1999) *Learning for All: The first ten years of The Open University of Hong Kong*, The Open University of Hong Kong, China SAR

Patten, C (1998) *East and West: China, power and the future of Asia*, Times Books, New York

Paul, R H (1990) *Open Learning and Open Management*, Kogan Page, London/Nichols Publishing, New York

Paul, R (1998) 'Informing government and institutional leaders about the potentials and pitfalls of open learning', in *Staff Development in Open and Flexible Learning*, ed C Latchem and F Lockwood, Routledge, London

Perraton, H (1999) e-mail to Colin Latchem

Perraton, H (2000) *Open and Distance Learning in the Developing World*, Routledge, London

Poole, M (2000) 'Substance the key factor in new-style university', *The Australian: Higher Education*, 17 May, p 48

Puttnam, D (1996) 'Travel or technology', plenary address at the British Council/IDP Education Australia Colloquium, Universities in the Twenty First Century: Education in a Borderless World, 13–14 August, Singapore

Ramanujam, P R (1997) 'Distance education in the 21st century: Implications for developing countries', in CD-ROM Conference Papers of The New Learning Environment: A Global Perspective, the 18th ICDE World Conference, 2–6 June, Pennsylvania State University

Randell, C and Bitzer, E (1998) 'Staff development in support of effective student learning in South African distance education', in *Staff Development in Open and Flexible Learning*, ed C Latchem and F Lockwood, pp 137–47, Routledge, London

Richardson, J (2000) 'News and unis link in global venture', *The Australian: Higher Education*, 17 May, p 30

Robbins, H and Finley, M (1997) *Why Change Doesn't Work*, Orion Publishing Group, London

Roberts, J (1999) 'Project sponsors reduce IT risks', Gartner Group Report, *The Australian: Computers/Global Spotlight*, 24 August, p 2

Robinson, B (1999) 'Asian learners, Western models: some discontinuities and issues for distance educators', in *The Asian Distance Learner*, ed R Carr *et al*, pp 33–45, Open University Press, Hong Kong

Rowe, I (1999) 'Kemp critics stifle urgent reforms', *The Australian: Higher Education*, 3 November, p 29

Rowntree, D (1992) *Exploring Open and Distance Learning*, Kogan Page, London

Rumble, G (1987) 'Why distance education can be cheaper than conventional education', *Distance Education*, **8** (1), pp 72–94

Rumble G (1997) *The Costs and Economics of Open and Distance Learning*, Kogan Page, London

Rumble, G (1999a) 'Cost analysis of distance learning', *Performance Improvement Quarterly*, **12** (2), pp 122–37

Rumble, G (1999b) 'How will on-line education affect the costs and structures of distance education?', *Proceedings* of the 13th Annual Conference of the Asian Association of Open Universities, Open and Distance Education Systems and Models Facing 21st Century's Information and Learning Societies, 14–17 October, Beijing, Vol 2, HKSAR, China-USA, pp 680–95

Rumble, G and Oliveira, J-B (eds) (1992) *Vocational Education at a Distance: International Perspectives*, International Labor Office/Kogan Page, London

Sadler, P (1997) *Leadership: Styles – Role Models – Qualities – Behaviours*, Kogan Page/Coopers & Lybrand, London

Sayles, L R (1993) *The Working Leader*, The Free Press, New York

Schein, E H (1992) *Organizational Culture and Leadership*, Jossey-Bass, San Francisco, CA

Schoemaker, P J H (1992) 'How to link strategic vision to core responsibilities', *Sloan Management Review*, Fall, pp 67–81

Schon, D A (1987) *Educating the Reflective Practitioner: Toward a new design for teaching and learning in the profession*, Jossey-Bass, San Francisco, CA

Schulz, L, Szekeres, J and Ciccarelli, A (1999) 'Igniting the bureaucracy for customer service', paper presented at the 23rd Association of Tertiary Education Management Conference, September, Wellington, New Zealand (http://www.atem.org.au/conference/index.htm)

Seymour, D (1996) *High Performing Colleges: The Malcolm Baldrige National Quality Award as a framework for improving higher education*, Prescott, Maryville, MO

Shaull, R (1972) 'Introduction', in *Pedagogy of the Oppressed,* F Paulo, Penguin, Harmondsworth

Siaciwena, R (1999) 'Open schooling: Issues and challenges', report on Sectoral Developments and Issues, Pan-Commonwealth Forum on Open Learning, 1–5 March, Brunei Darussalam (http://www.col.org/forum)

Sorenson, T (1987) 'Leadership in Transition', address at the Future Focus Conference organized by the Ontario Liberal Party, Geneva Park, Ontario, 24 January

Spronk, B (1999) 'Nonformal education at a distance: A framework for discussion', report on Sectoral Developments and Issues, Pan-Commonwealth Forum on Open Learning, 1–5 March, Brunei Darussalam (http://www.col.org/forum)

Stinchcombe, A L (1965) 'Social structure and organizations', in *Handbook of Organizations*, ed J G March, pp 142–94, Rand McNally, Chicago

Tapsall, S and Ryan, Y (1999) 'Virtual educational institutions in Australia: Between the idea and the reality', in *The Development of Virtual Education: A global perspective*, ed G Farrell, The Commonwealth of Learning, Vancouver (http://www.col.org/virtualed)

Tinkler, D, Smith, T, Ellyard, P and Cohen, D (1994) *Effectiveness and Potential of State-of-the-art Technologies in the Delivery of Higher Education*, Occasional Papers Series, Higher Education Division, Department of Employment, Education and Training, Canberra, ACT

Toffler, A (1985) *The Adaptive Corporation*, McGraw-Hill, New York

The Training Agency (nd) *Ensuring Quality in Open Learning*, The Training Agency, London

Turoff, M (1997) 'Costs for the development of a virtual university', *Journal of Asynchronous Learning*, **1**(1) (http://www.aln.org/alnweb/journal/jaln_Vol1issue1.htm)

UK Funding Councils (1993) *The Funding Councils' Libraries Review Group Report*, UK Funding Councils (The Follett Report), TSO, London

Umar, Dato' Haji Abdul Aziz (1999) plenary address, Pan-Commonwealth Forum on Open Learning, 1–5 March, Brunei Darussalam (http://www.col.org/forum)

Uren, D (1999) 'Avoid corporate rot with more women at the top', *The Australian: Opinion*, 7 October, p 13

Viljoen, J (1994) *Strategic Management*, Longman Business & Professional, Melbourne

Weinstein, L A (1993) *Moving a Battleship with your Bare Hands: Governing a university system*, 1st edn, Magna Publications, Madison, WI

White, D (1999) 'A studied approach to "virtual" learning', *Daily Telegraph,* Business File, 9 December, p A9

Wice, N (1997) 'Vive le difference! The Net is a two-way street of world-culture' (http:home.zdnet.com/yil/content/mat/970/wice9707.html)

Yates, C (2000) 'Outcomes: What have we learned?', in *Basic Education at a Distance*, ed C Yates and J Bradley, Routledge, London

Yates, C and Bradley, J (eds) (2000) *Basic Education at a Distance*, Routledge, London

Yetton, P and Associates (1997) *Managing the Introduction of Technology in the Delivery and Administration of Higher Education,* Fujitsu Centre, Graduate School of Management, University of New South Wales, Sydney, Evaluations and Investigations Programme, Higher Education Division, Department of Employment, Education, Training and Youth Affairs, Commonwealth of Australia

Zaleznik, A (1996) 'Managers and leaders: Are they different?', in *Fast Forward,* ed J Champy and N Nohria, pp 229–46, Harvard Business School Publishing, Boston, MA

Author index

Subject index

Open and Distance Learning Series

Series Editor: Fred Lockwood